Nikolai
RIMSKY-KORSAKOV

SYMPHONY No. 2
'Antar'
(Suite Symphonique)
Op. 9

1875 version
revised 1903

Study Score
Partitur

SERENISSIMA MUSIC, INC.

INSTRUMENTATION

3 Flutes (3 doubles Piccolo)
2 Oboes (2 doubles English Horn)
2 Clarinets in A (1 also in B-flat)
2 Bassoons

4 Horns in E and F
2 Trumpets in E and F
3 Trombones
Tuba

Timpani
Percussion
(Triangle, Tambourine, Tam-Tam, Cymbals, Bass Drum)
Harp

Violin I
Violin II
Viola
Violoncello
Bass

Duration: ca. 26 minutes

ISBN: 1-932419-60-8

This score is a digitally enhanced unabridged reprint of the
score published ca.1946 by Muzgiz, Moscow.
The score has been reduced to fit the present format.

Printed in the USA
First Printing: January, 2010

SYMPHONY No. 2

Antar – Suite Symphonique

Second version (1875), with 1903 revisions

I

Nikolai Rimsky-Korsakov, Op. 9

SERENISSIMA MUSIC, INC.

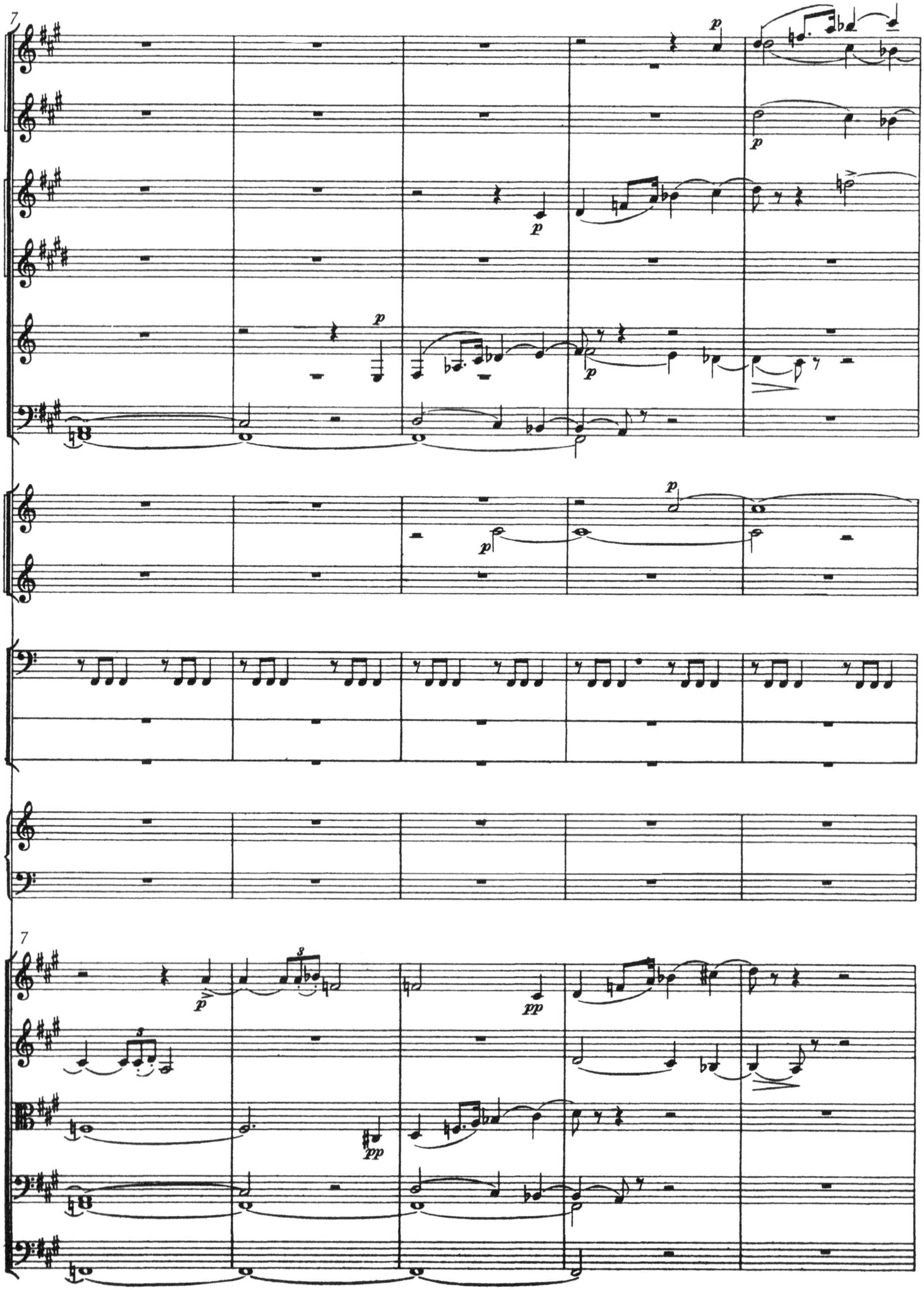

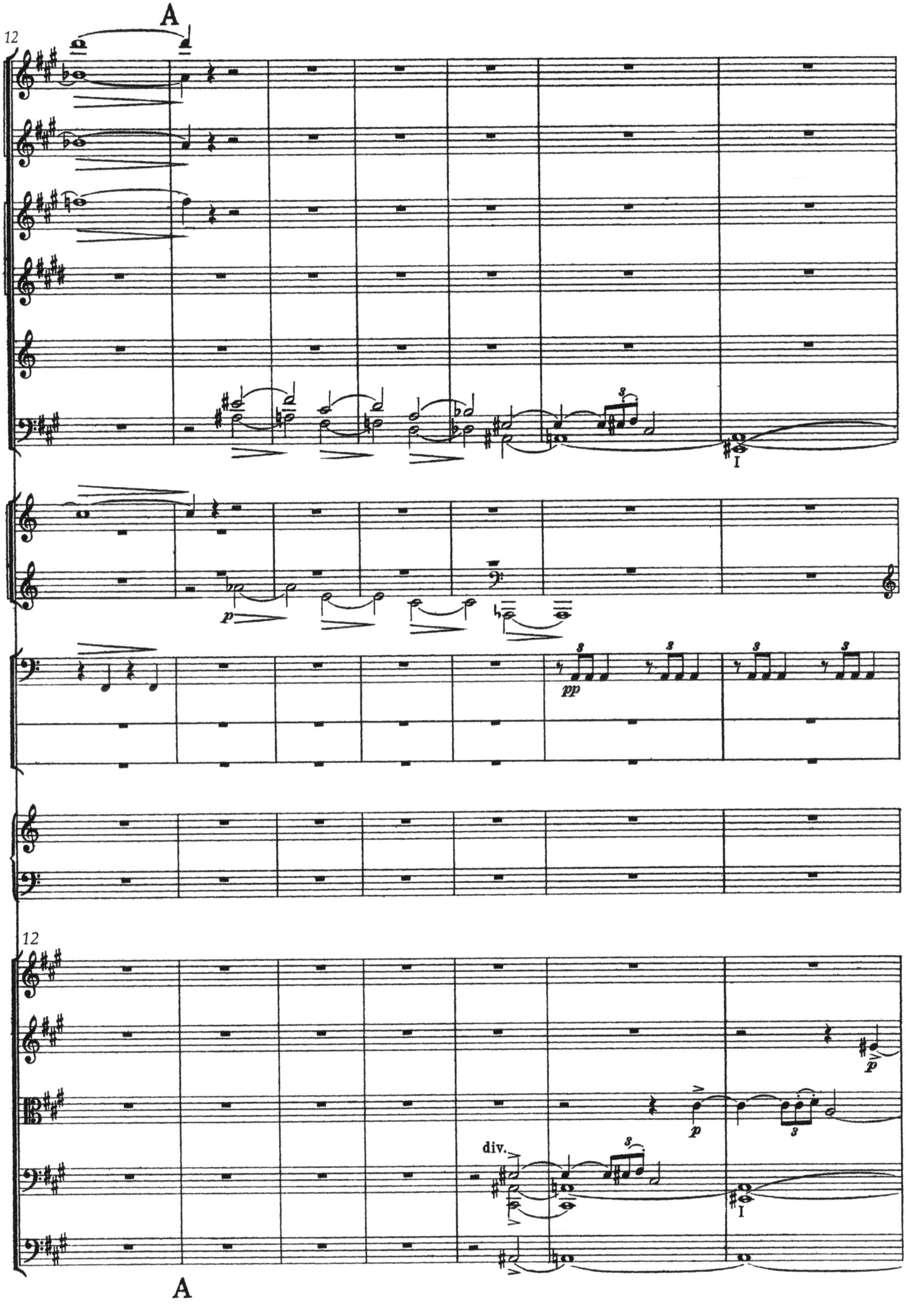
12
A
I
p
pp
div.
A

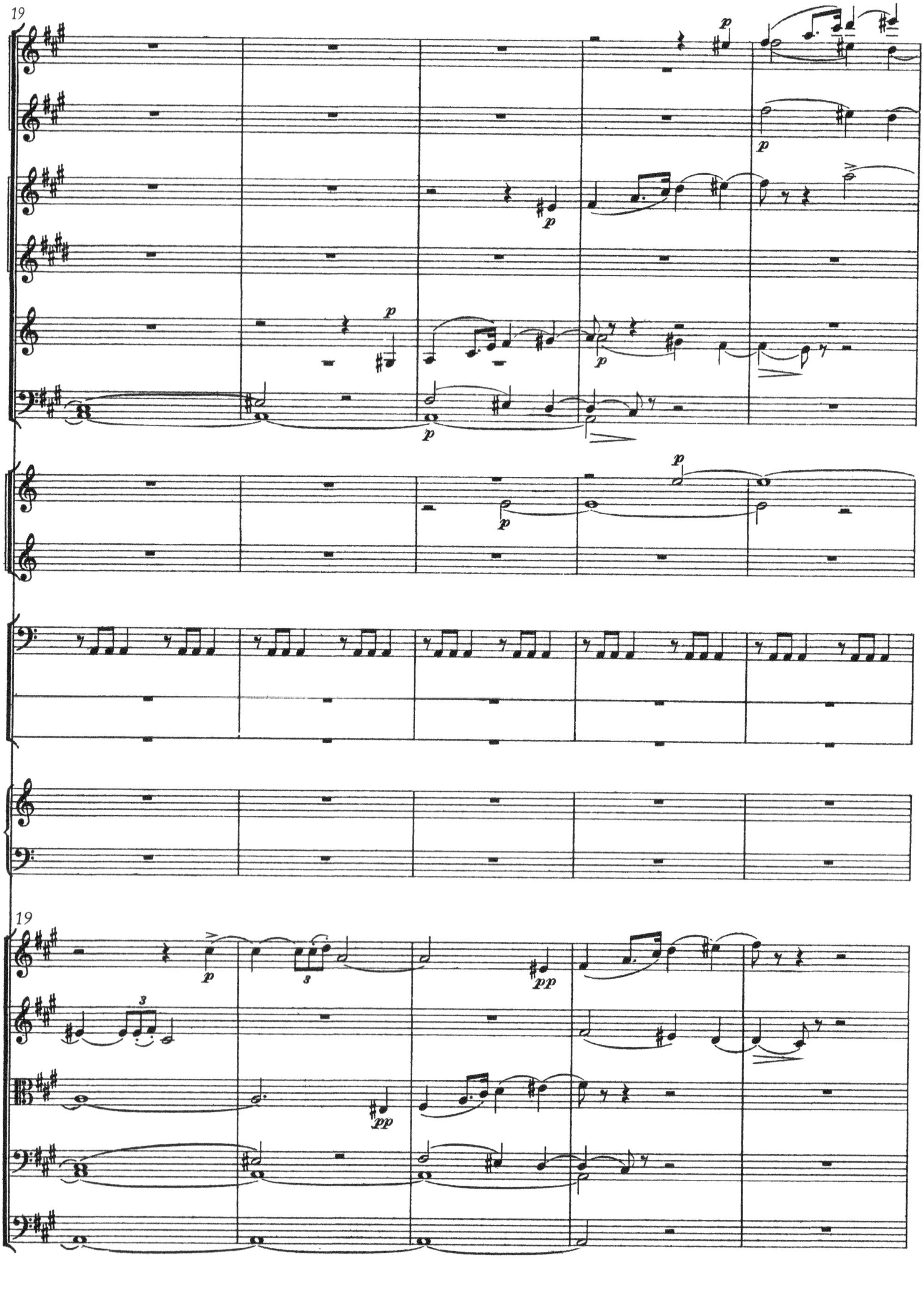
19
19

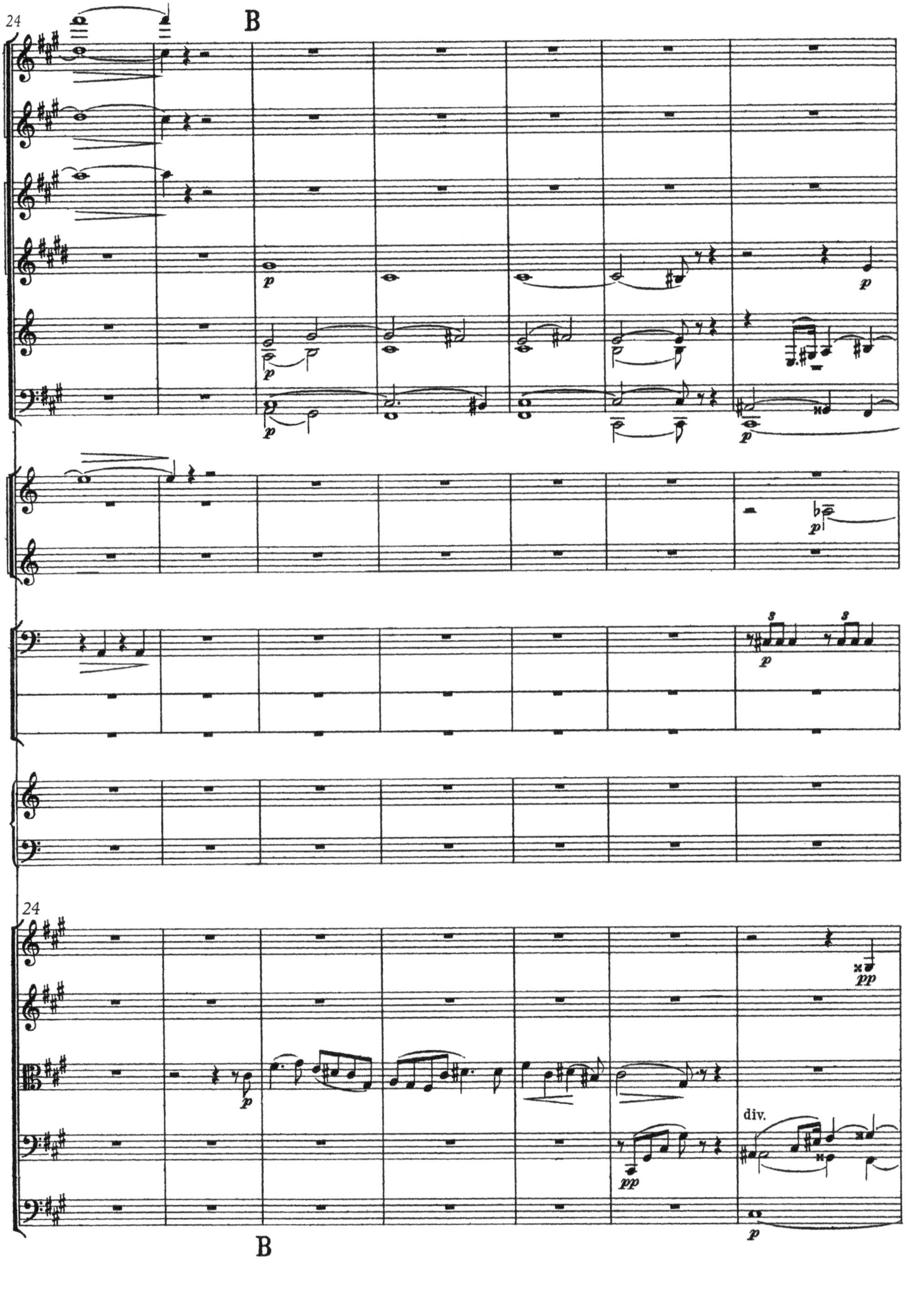
24
B
p
p
p
p
p
p
8
8
p
24
pp
p
div.
pp
p
B

C

muta Cis in D

C

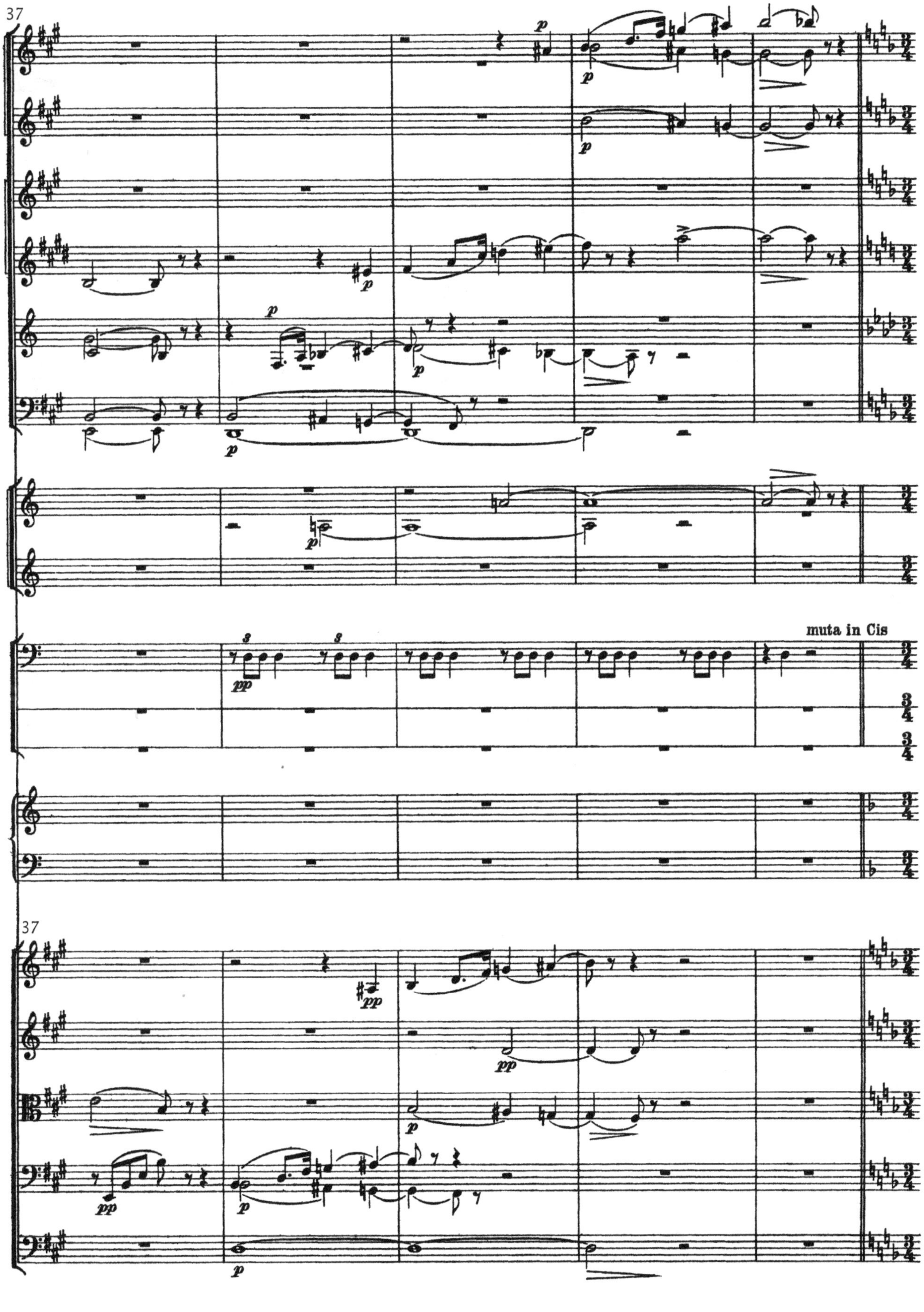
37
muta in Cis
37

Allegro giocoso
42
Fl. I Solo
p
Cor. I II
pp
Arpa
f
pp
42
Viol. I
pp leggiero
Allegro giocoso
48
p
48
53
53

58
D
Clar.
fz
cresc. poco a poco
cresc. poco a poco
cresc. poco a poco
58
cresc. poco a poco
D
63
mf
63
68
f
E
68
Vle.
con sordini
pp
Vcell.
con sordini
pp
Cb.
con sordini
E
pp

73
Viol. II
con sordini
p
p
p
p
77
con sordini
p
p
cresc.
cresc.
cresc.
cresc.
cresc.
81

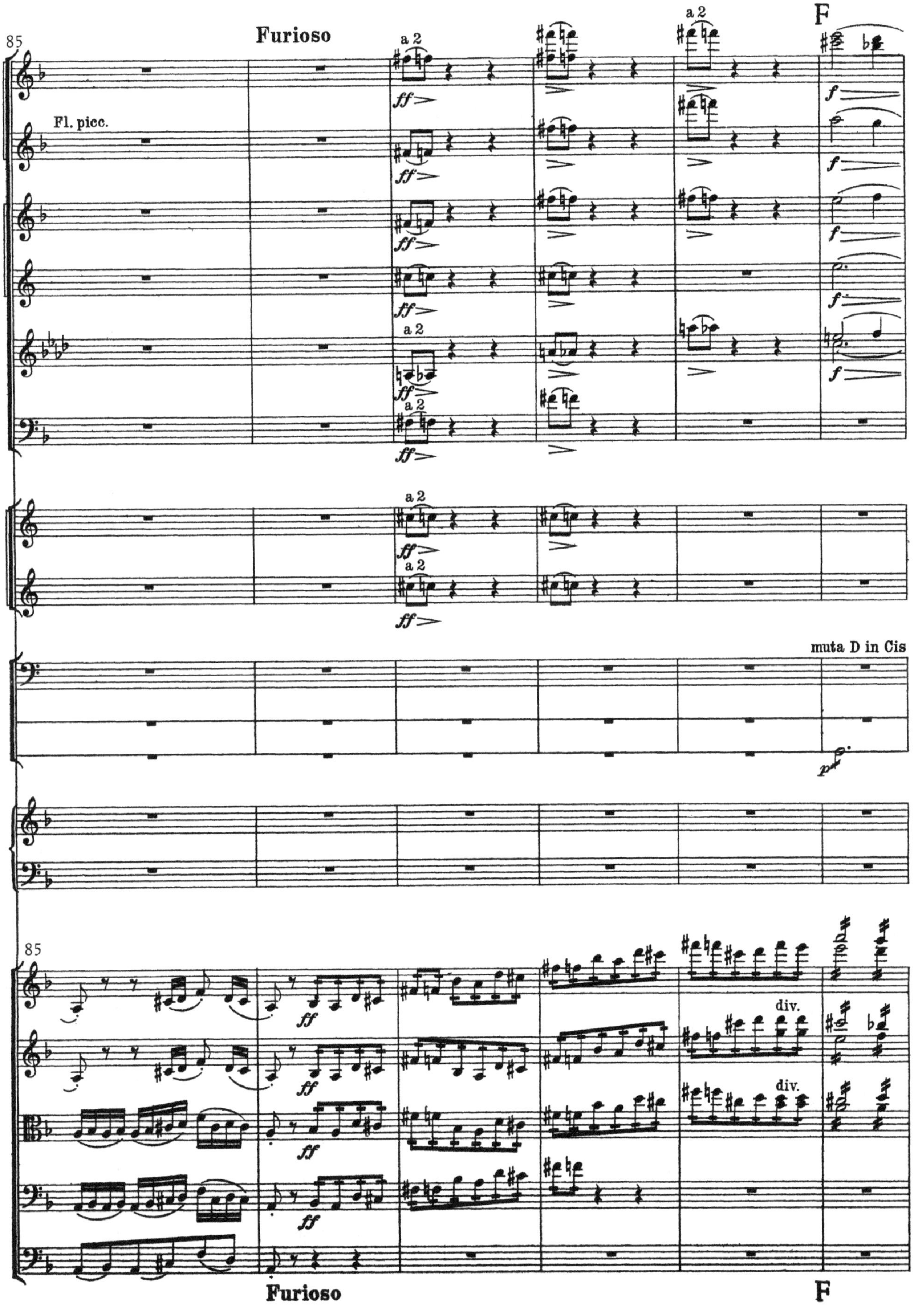
85
Furioso
F
Fl. picc.
a 2
ff
f
p
muta D in Cis
div.
Furioso

91
a 2
ff
ff
ff
ff
ff
bouchez
f
bouchez
f
f
colla bacchetta
mf
91
ff
ff
ff
f
f

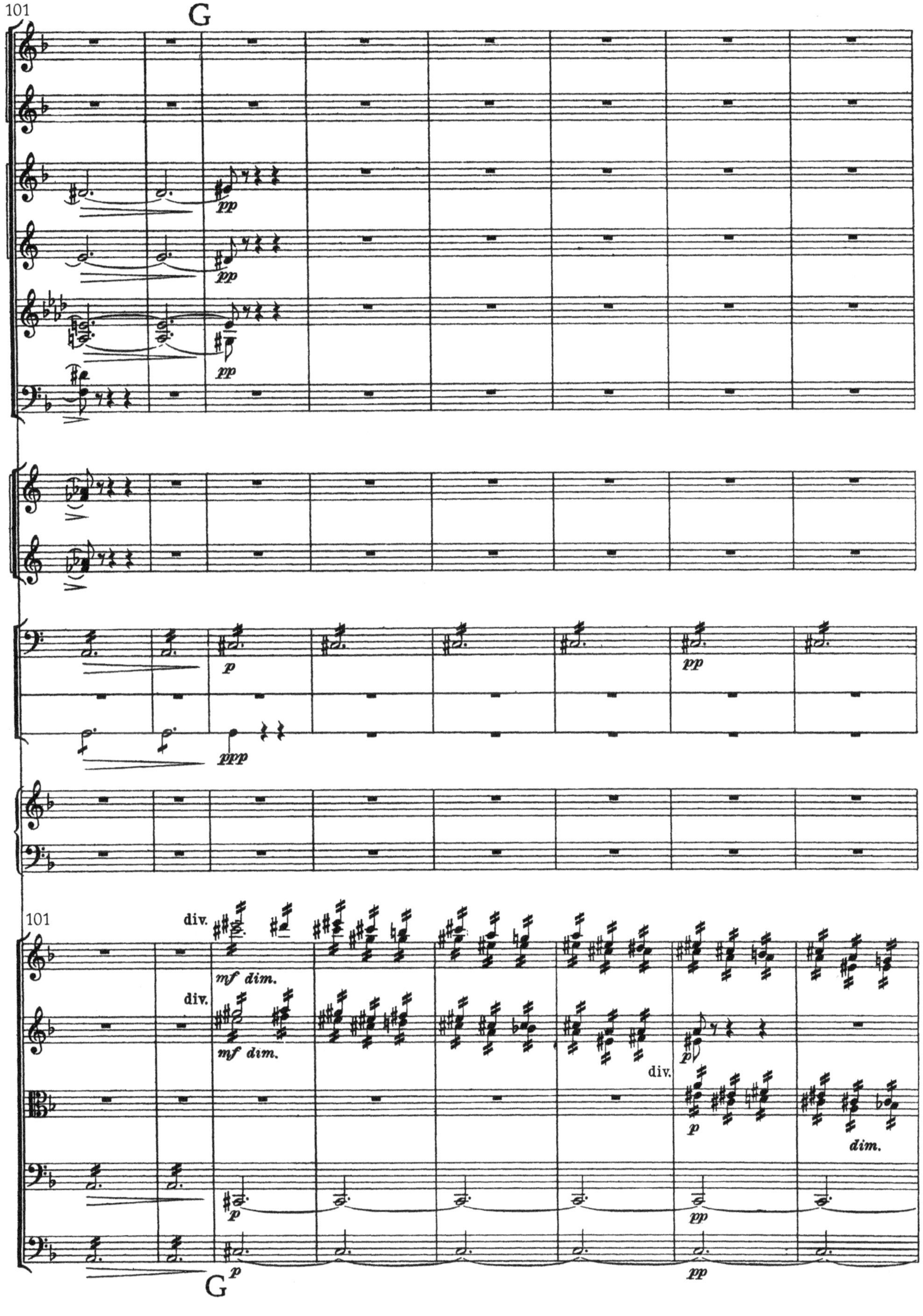
101
G
pp
pp
pp
p
pp
ppp
101
div.
mf dim.
div.
mf dim.
div.
p
dim.
p
pp
pp
G
p

109
ppp
pp
unis.
pp
pp
114
perdendosi
perdendosi
Adagio
a piacere
118
Fl. Solo
p
Largo Tempo I
Cor. ingl.
p
Clar.
p
Fag.
p
118
Vle.
senza sordini
p
Vcell.
senza sordini
pp
Adagio
Largo Tempo I

123
Allegretto vivace
pp
Fl. III
Clar. I in B
Clar. II in A
Cor.
Timp. muta A in B, Cis in Es, F in Fis
Arpa
p
Viol. I
sempre con sord.
div.
ppp
Viol. II
sempre con sord.
div.
Allegretto vivace
131
Ob.
Fag.
a 2
Vcell.
pizz.

139
H
pp
pp
pp
pp
pp
p
139
con delicat.
pp
con delicat.
pp
con sord. div.
pizz.
p
H

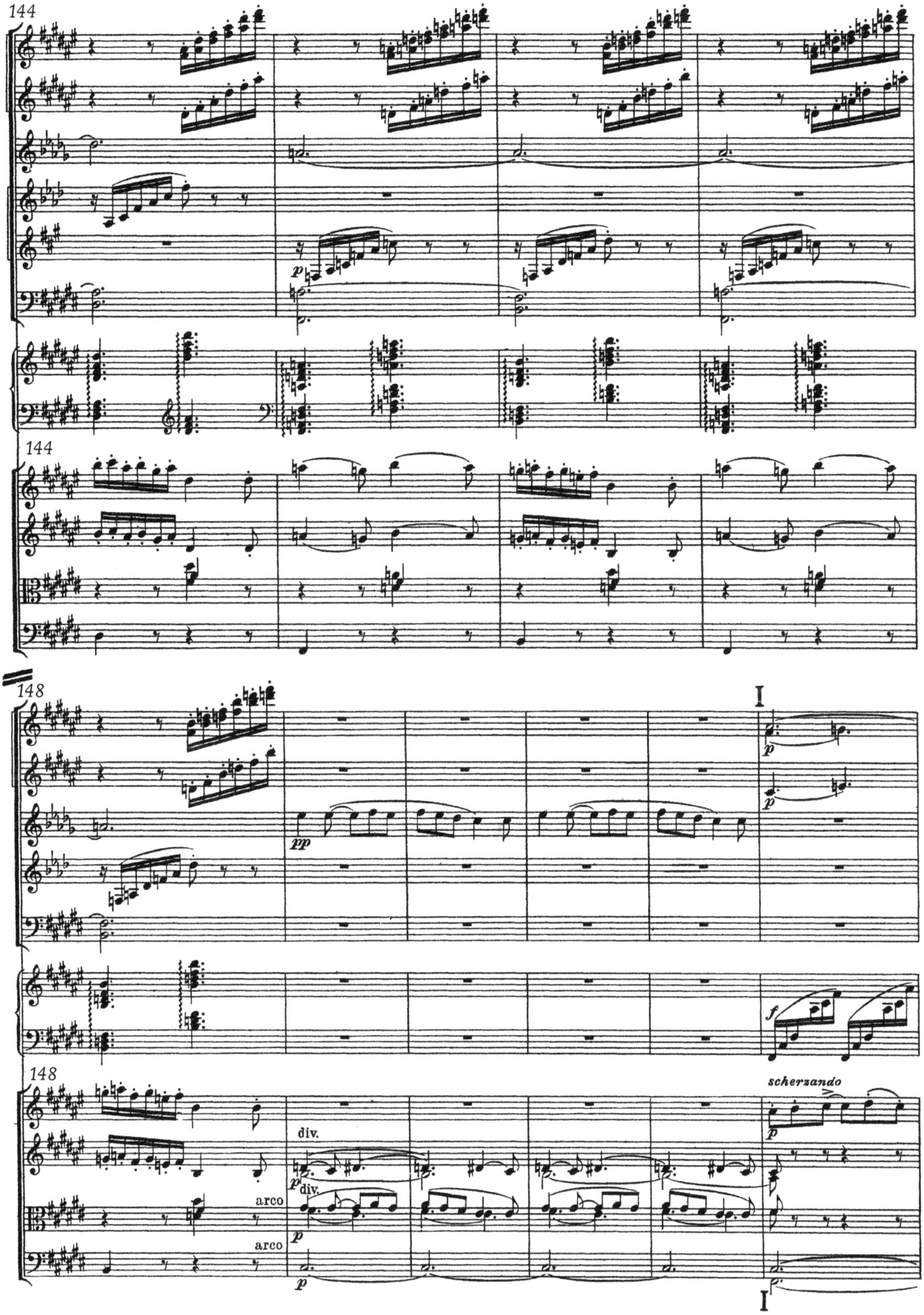
144
144
148
148
I
div.
div.
arco
arco
scherzando
I

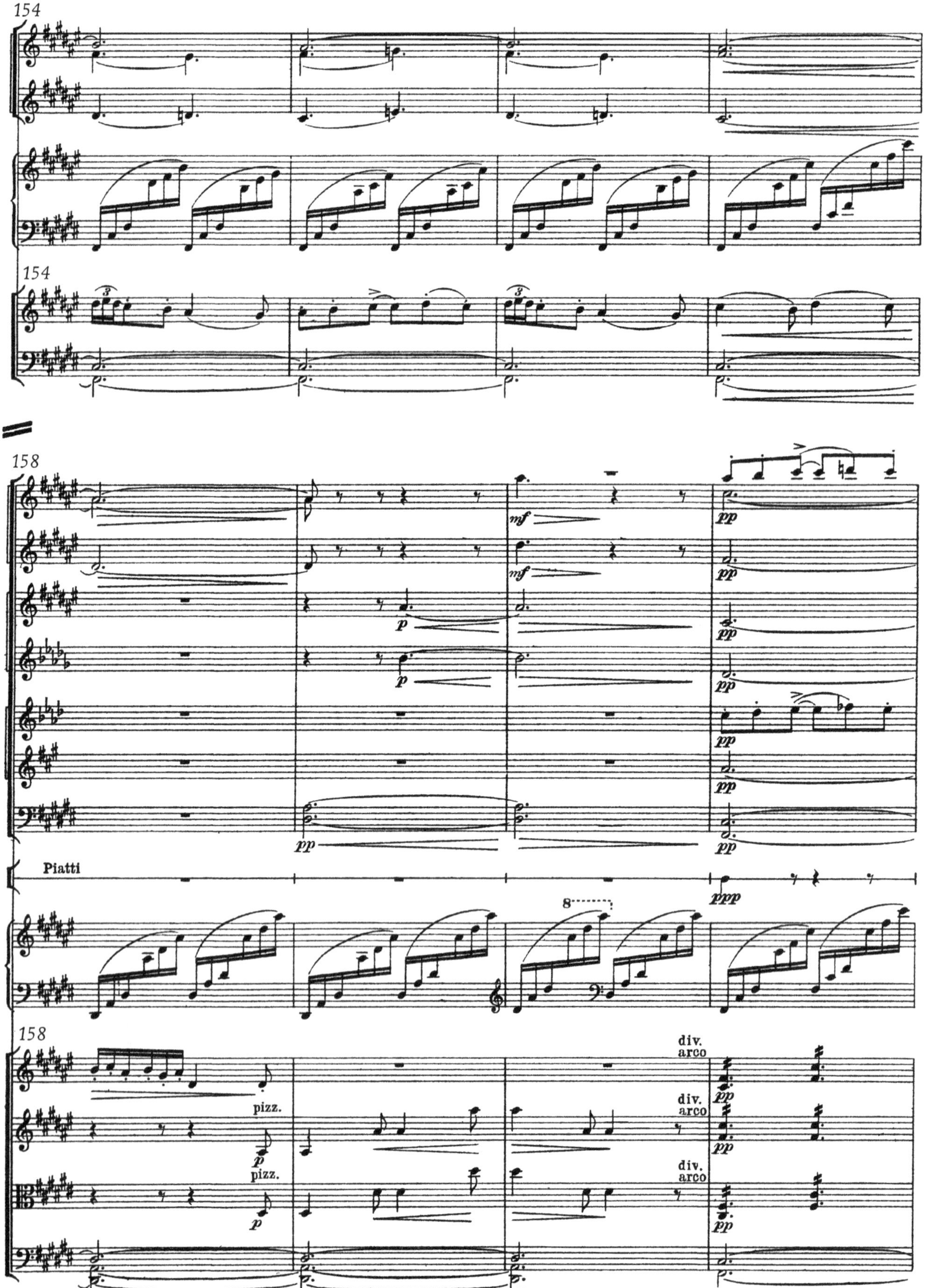
154
154
158
mf
pp
p
Piatti
ppp
8
158
div.
arco
pizz.

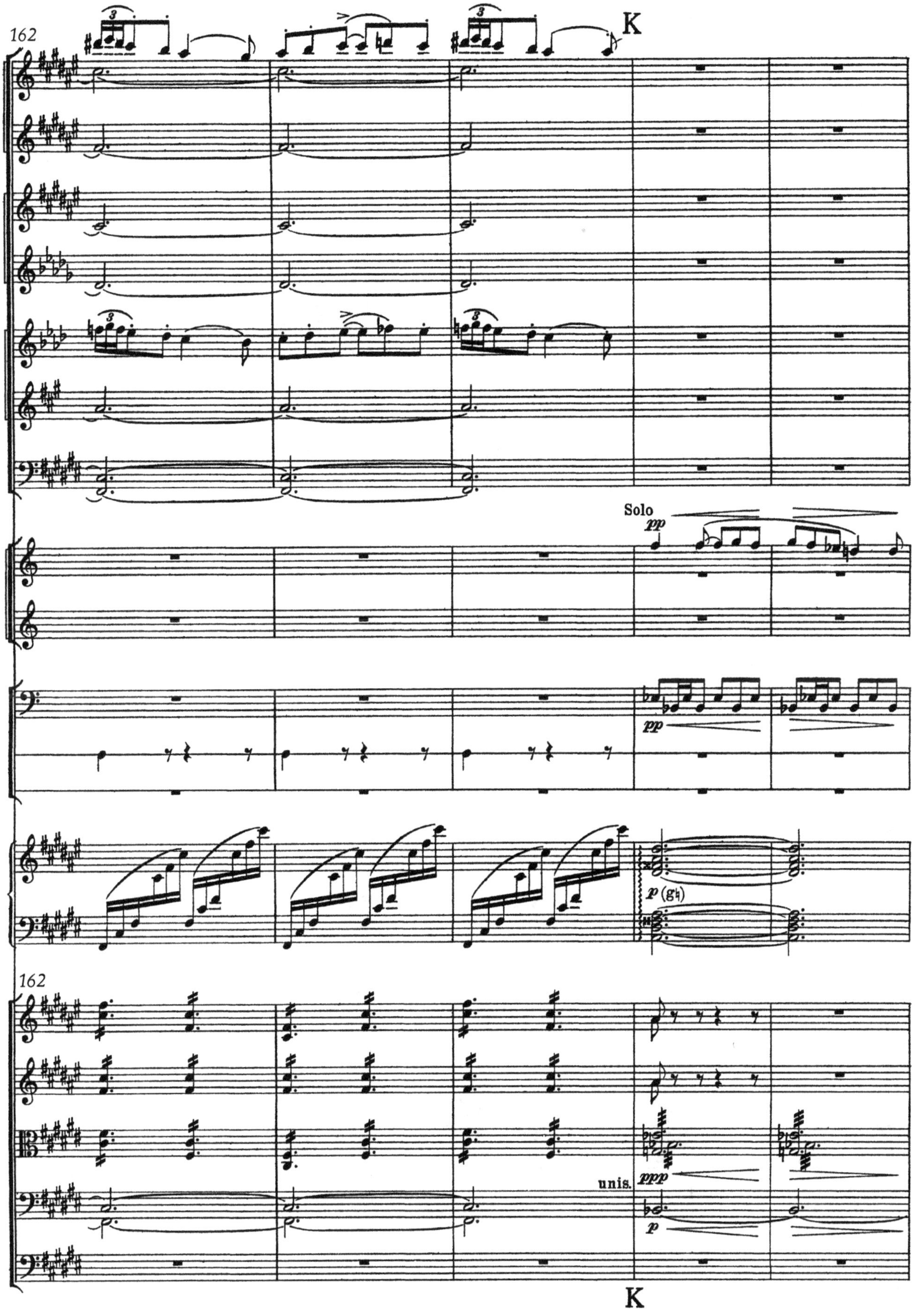
162
K
Solo
pp
pp
p (g♮)
162
unis.
ppp
p
K

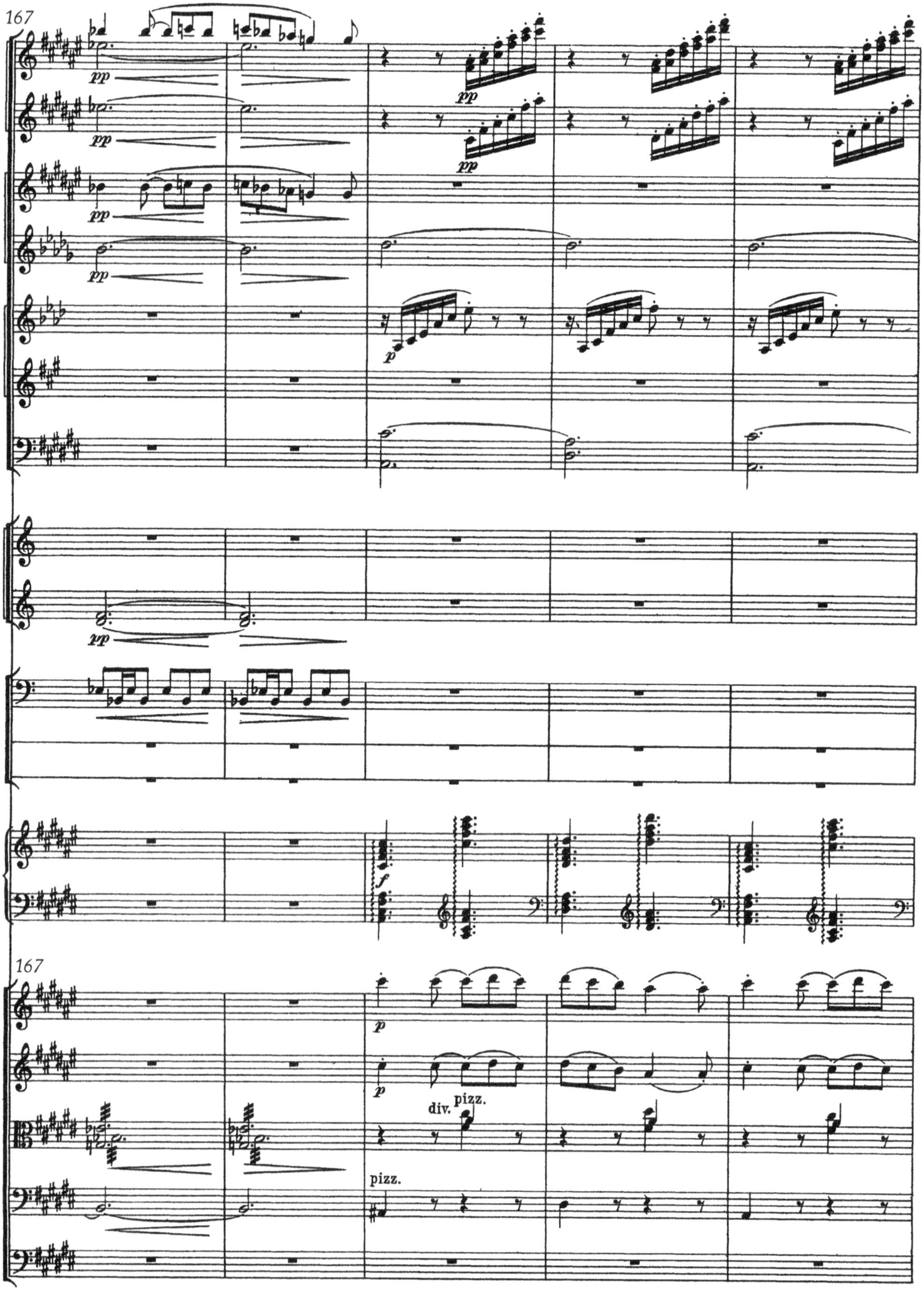
167
pp
pp
pp
pp
pp
p
pp
f
167
p
p
div.
pizz.
pizz.

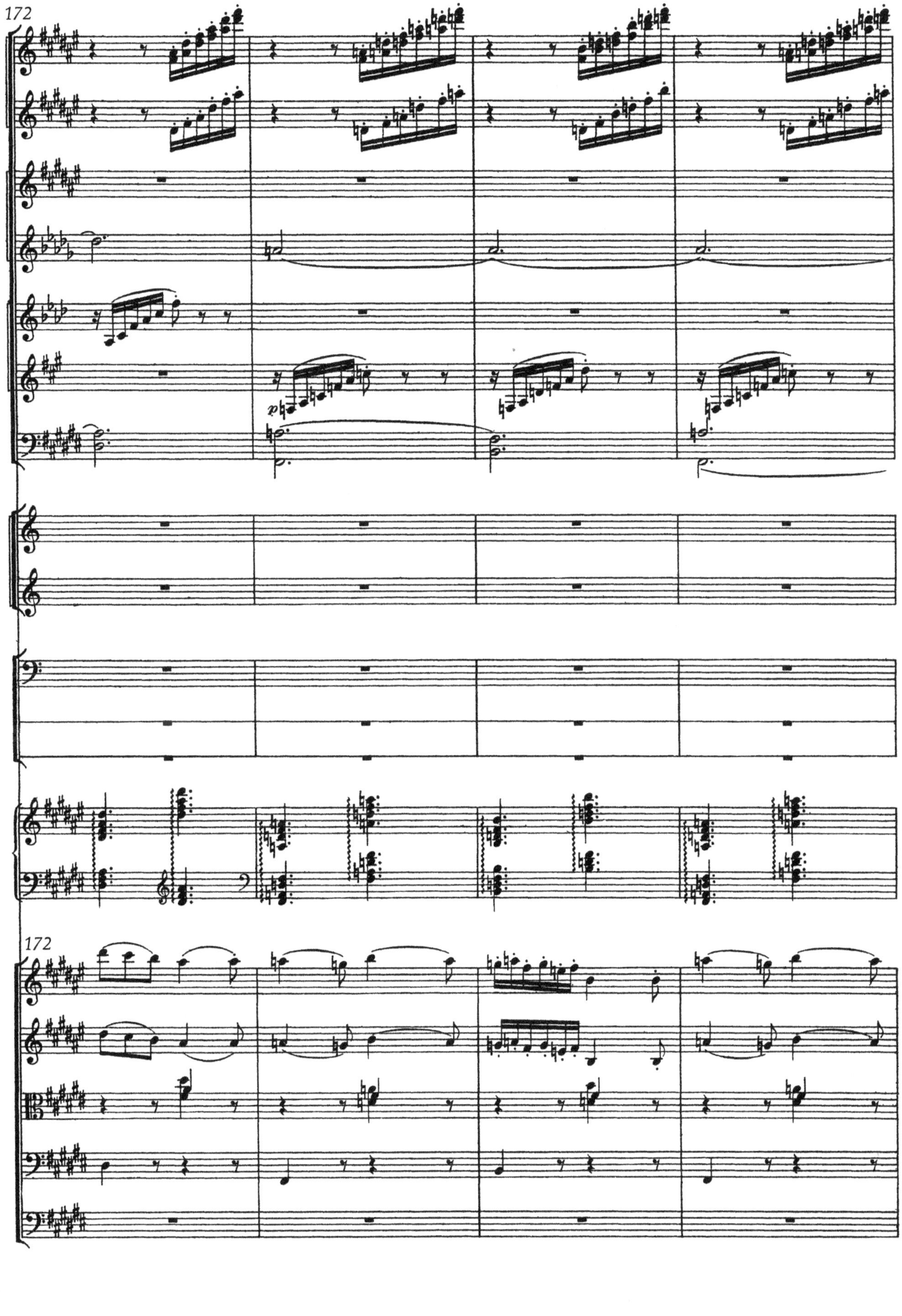
172
p
172

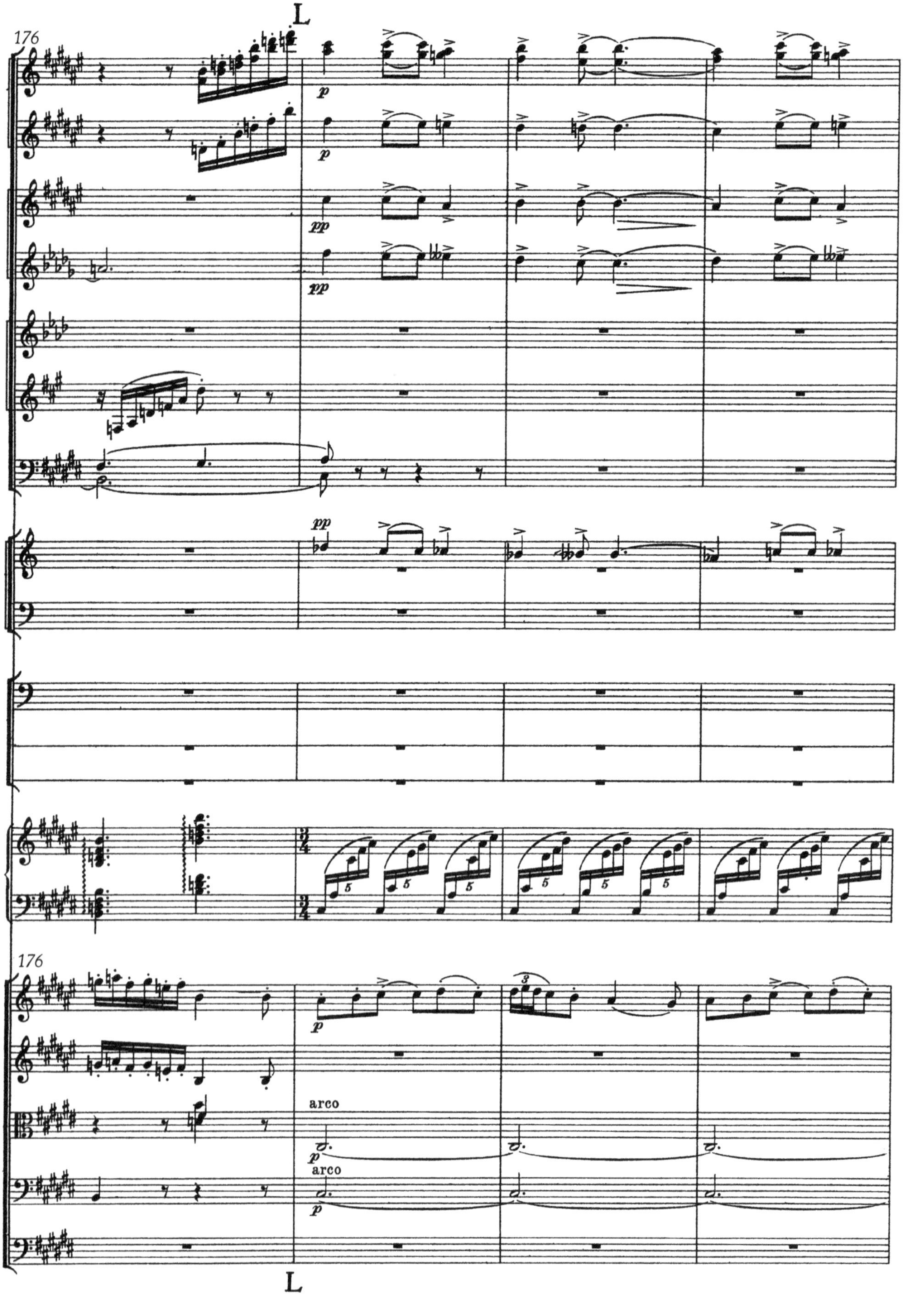
L
176
p
pp
arco
L

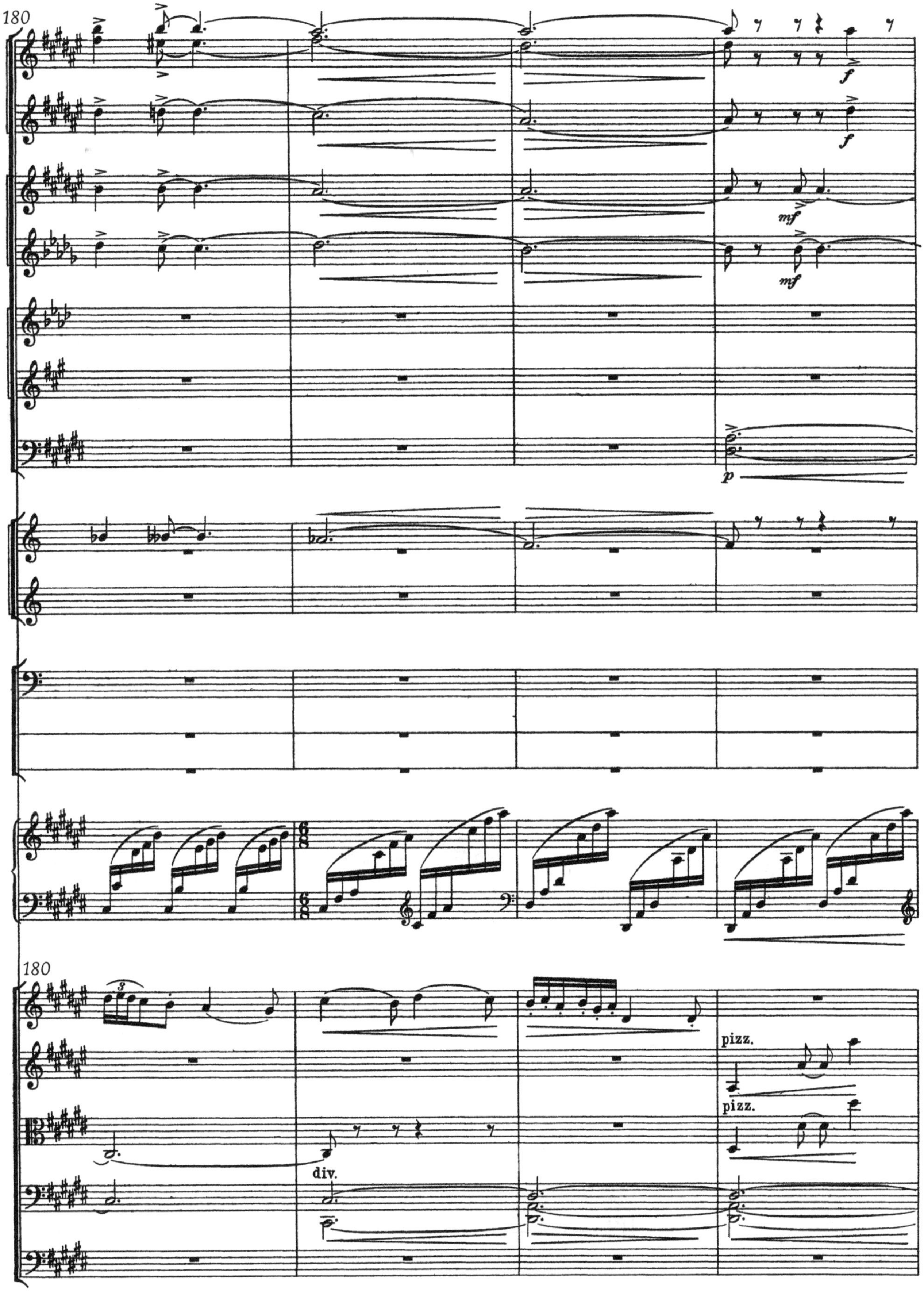
180
f
mf
p
180
pizz.
pizz.
div.

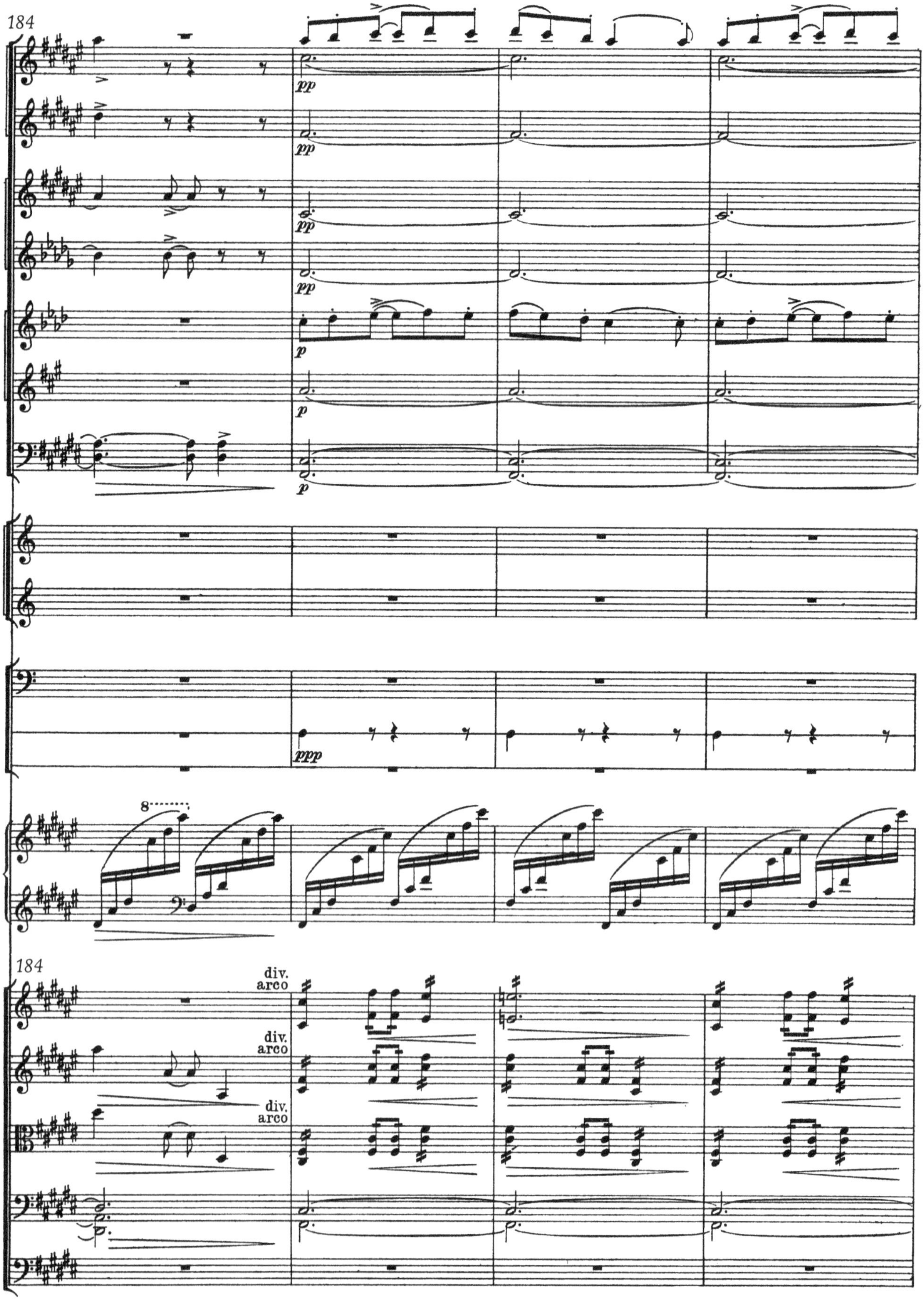
184
pp
pp
pp
pp
p
p
p
ppp
8
184
div.
arco
div.
arco
div.
arco

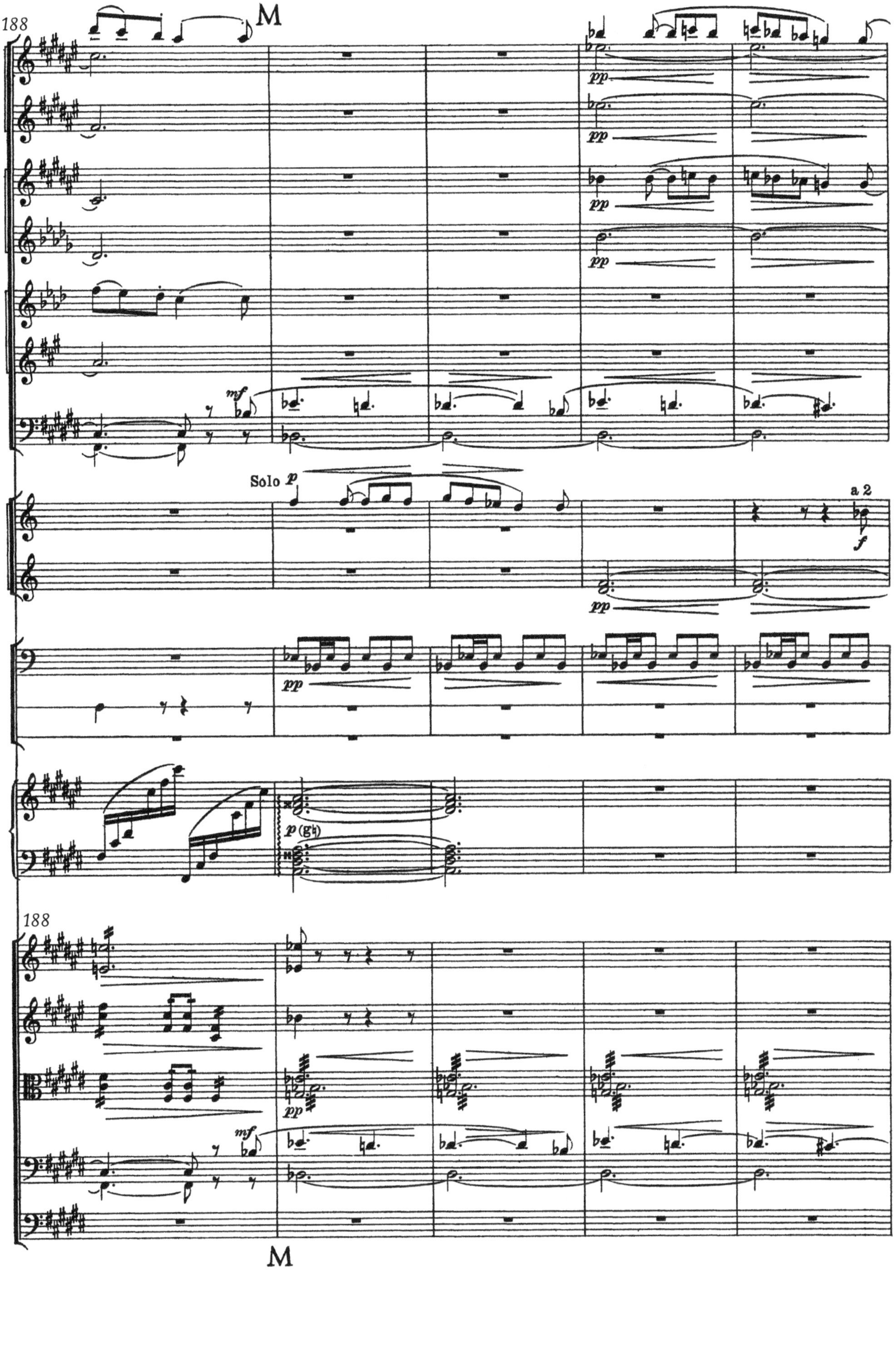
188
M
pp
mf
Solo p
a 2
f
p (g♮)
188
M

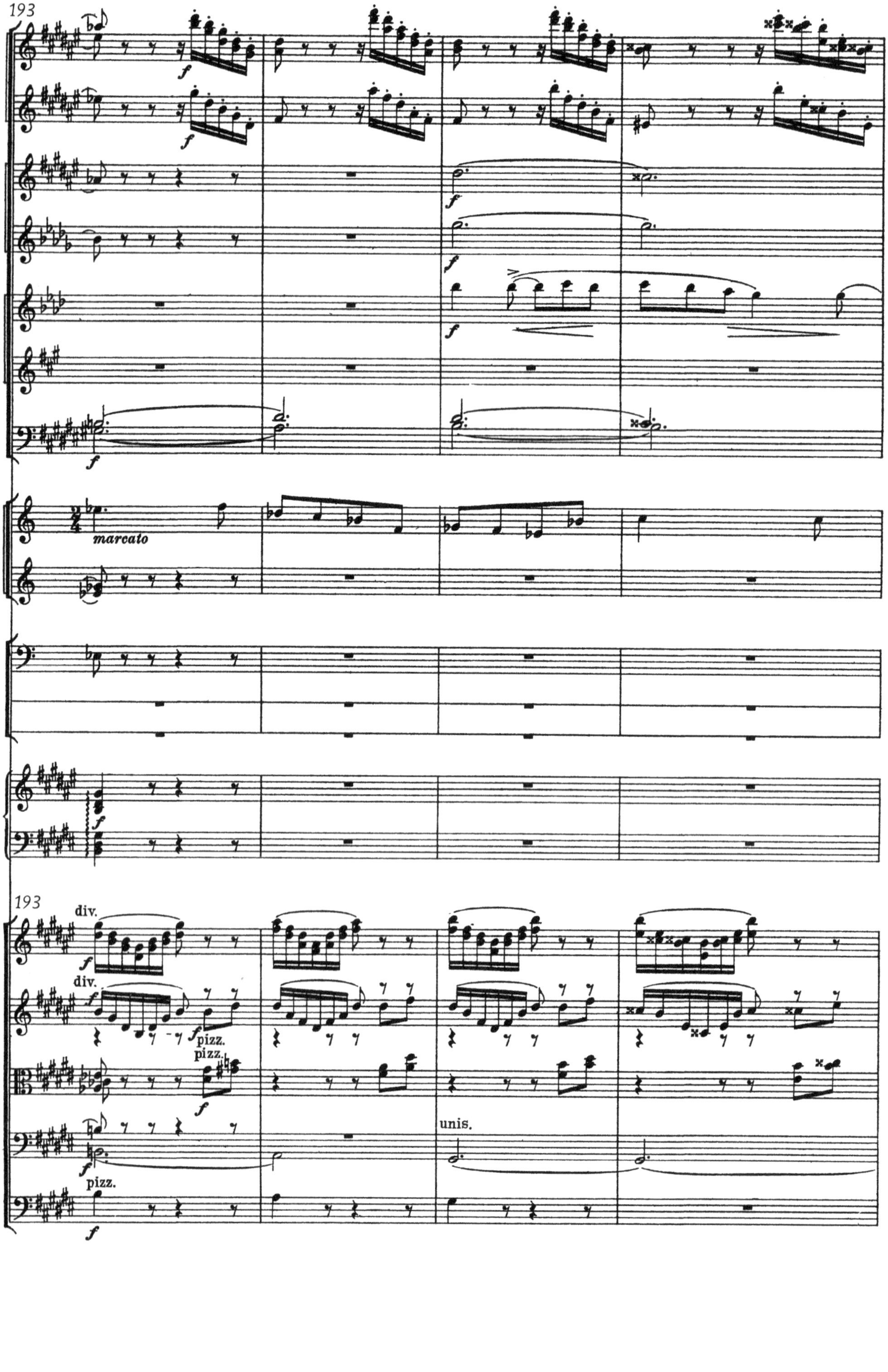
193
marcato
193
div.
div.
pizz.
pizz.
unis.
pizz.

197
f
f
197
ff
arco
unis.
ff
arco
ff
dim.
div.
dim.
dim.
f dim.
arco
f dim.
unis.

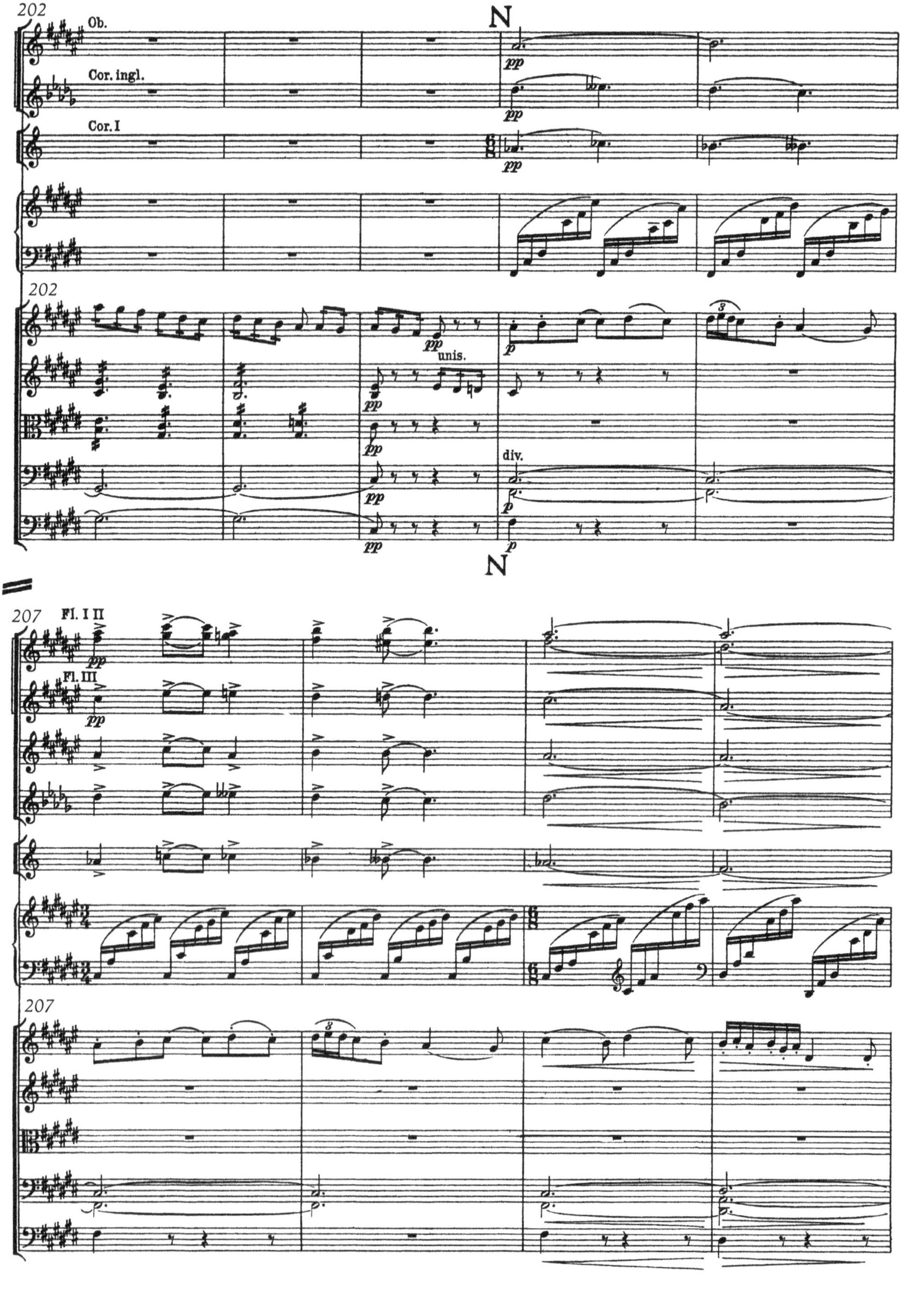
202
Ob.
Cor. ingl.
Cor. I
N
pp
unis.
div.
p
207
Fl. I II
Fl. III

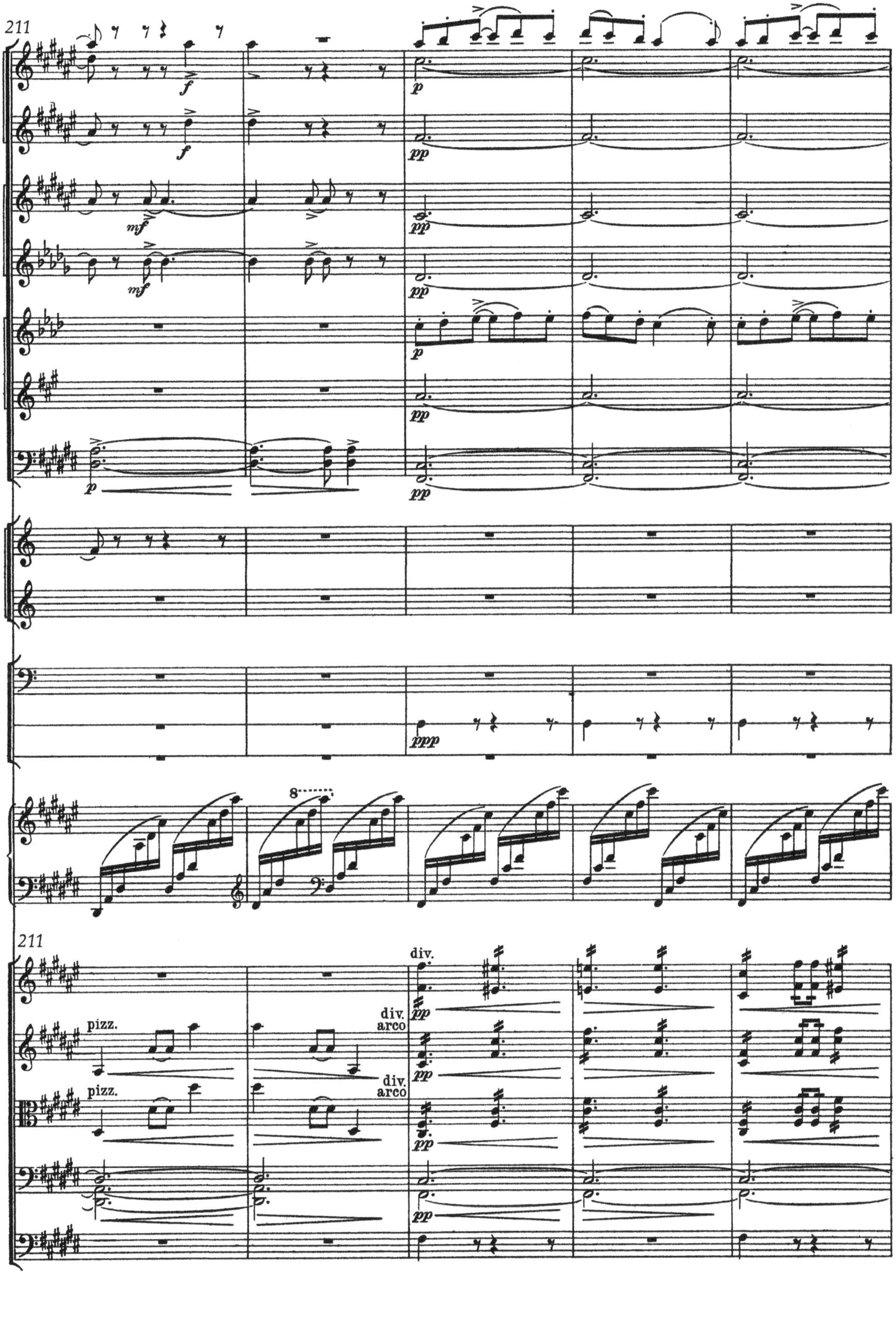
211
f
mf
p
pp
ppp
8
div.
pizz.
arco

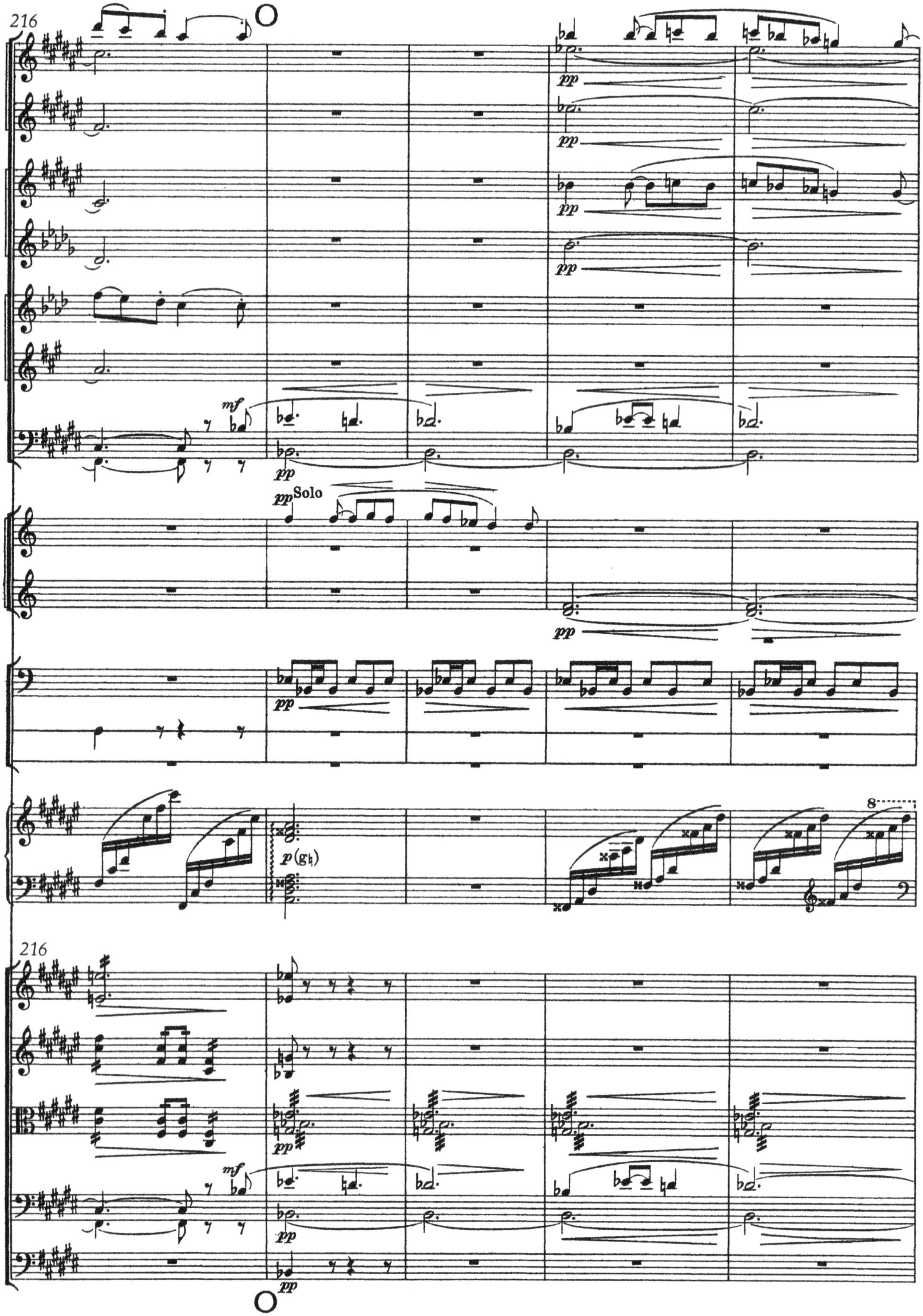
216
O
Solo
pp
mf
p (g♮)
8
216
O

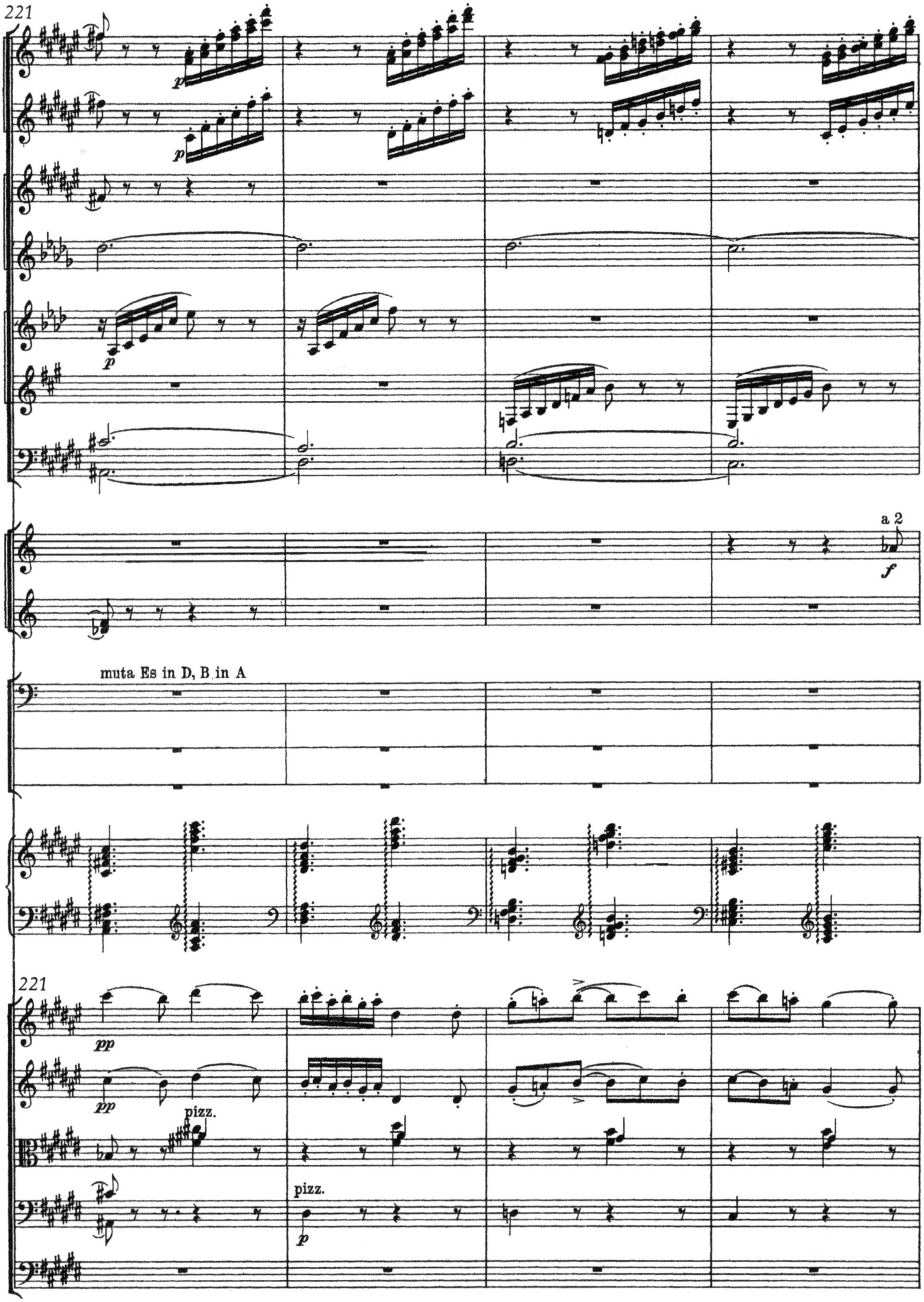
221
a 2
muta Es in D, B in A
221
pizz.
pizz.

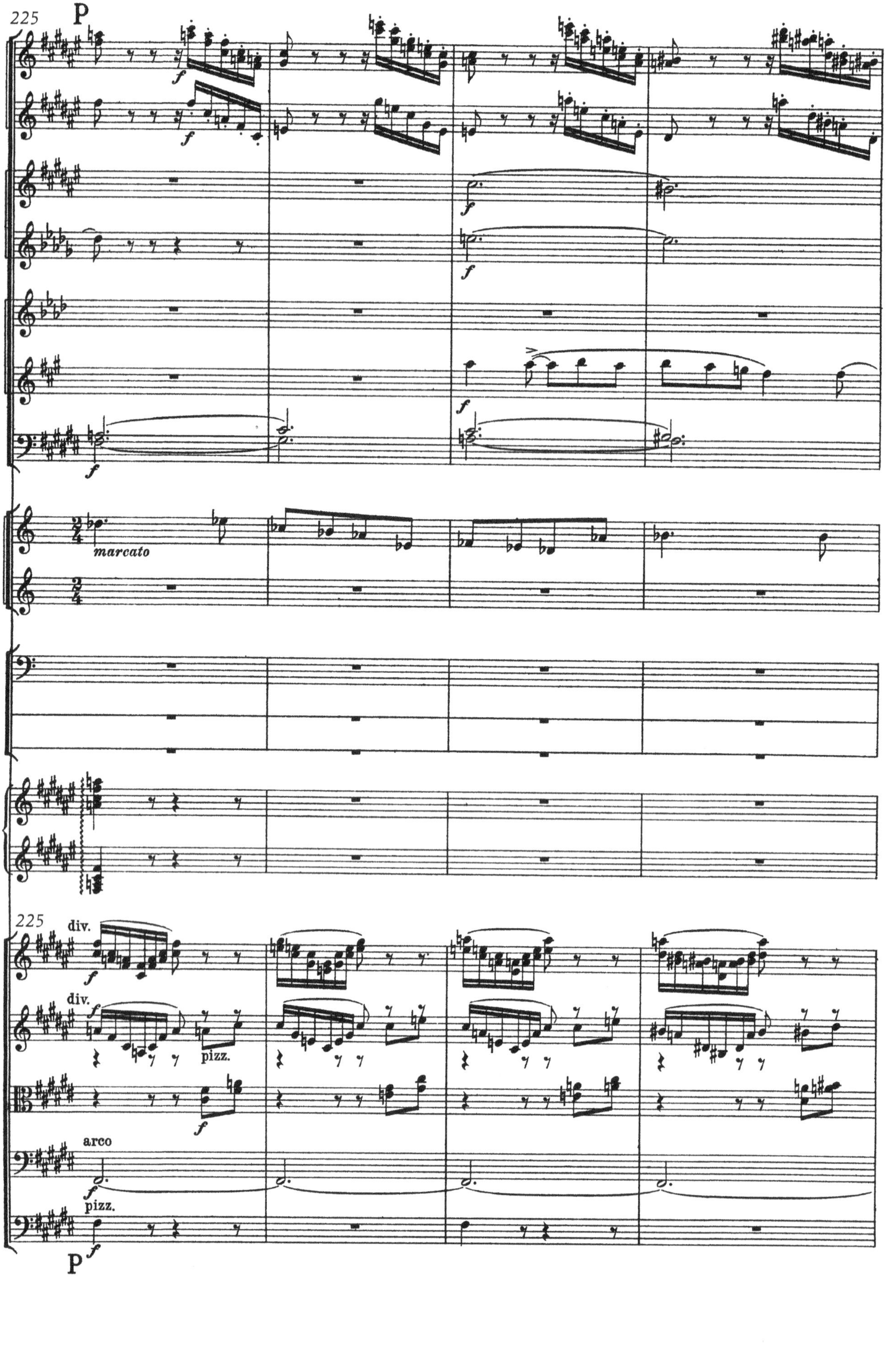
225
P
marcato
225
div.
div.
pizz.
arco
pizz.
P

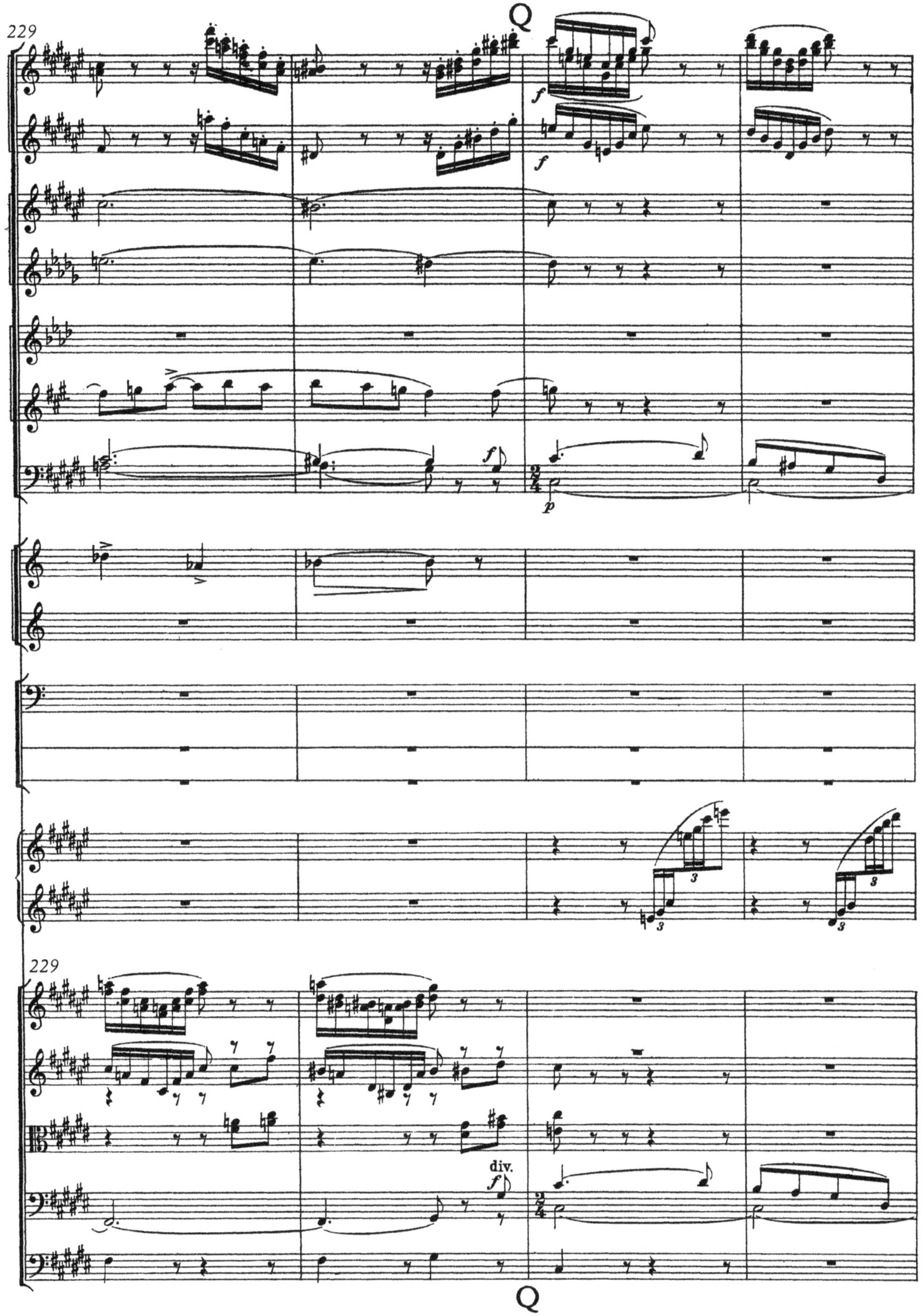

229
Q
f
f
p
229
div.
f
Q

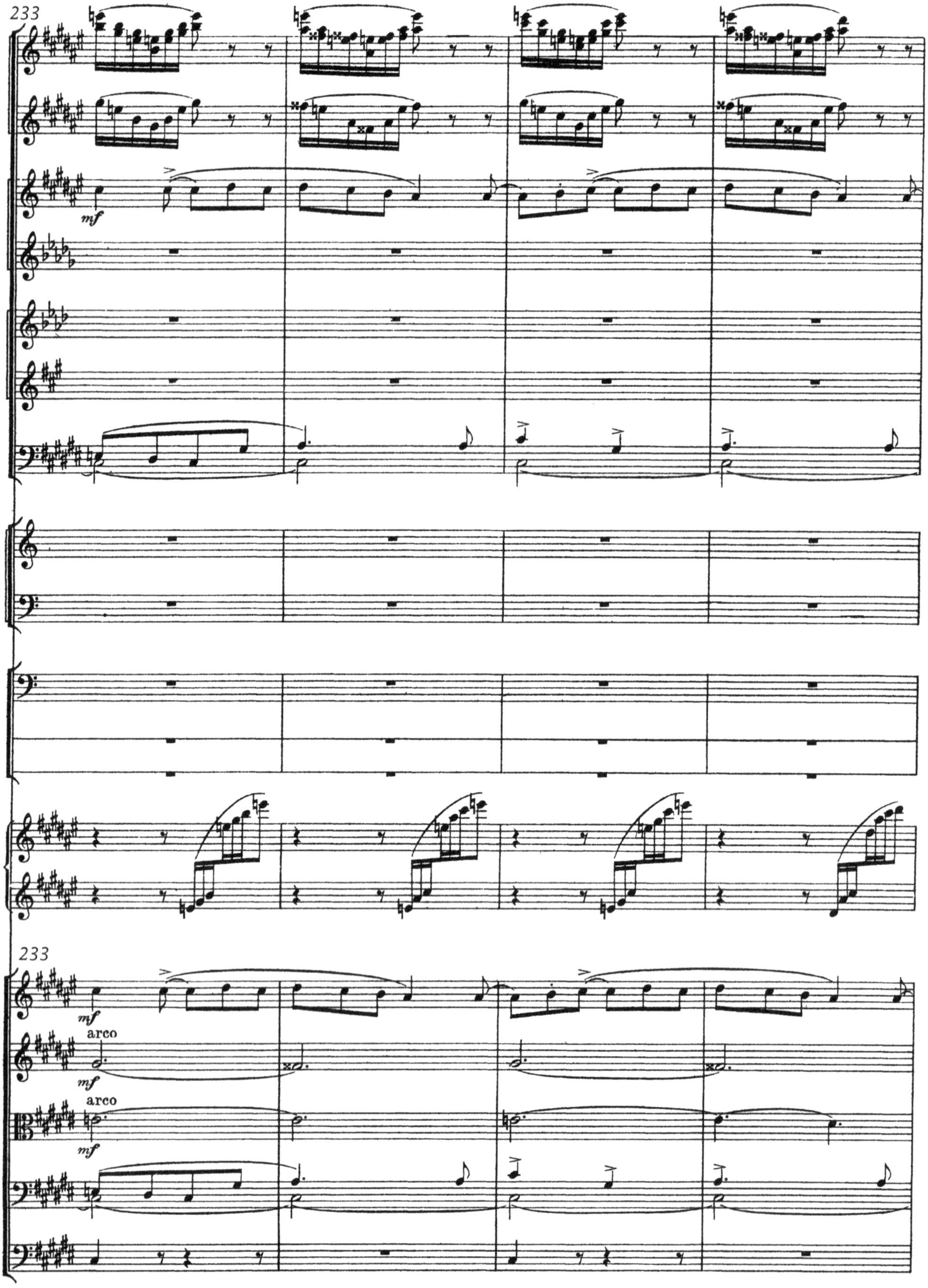
233
mf
233
mf
arco
mf
arco
mf

237
f
f dim.
muta in A
muta in Fis, Ges, Ais, B, Cis, Des, E
237
div.
ùnis.
ff
dim.
pp
arco

Adagio

Adagio

244
R
a tempo
a tempo
pp
I in A
Solo
a piacere
dolce espress.
a piacere
a piacere
Due Viol. I soli
div.
div.
arco
arco
a tempo
a tempo

249
a tempo
ritard.
pp
ppp
Altri Viol. I
p
pp
pp
pp
pp
pizz.
p
pizz.
p
ritard.
a tempo

254
S Allegretto vivace
pp
pp
pp
in A
pp
a 2
pp
pp
pp
p
mf
254
pp
pp
divisi
pizz.
p
pp
pp
S Allegretto vivace

259
Fl. I II
pp
Fl. III
pp
Ob.
Clar. in A
pp
Fag.
Cor. I II
Arpa
mf
dim.
259
Vcell.
mf
Cb.
267
Fl. I II
pp
Clar.
8
perd.
267
Viol. II
pizz.
pp
Vle
p
Vcell.

Largo Tempo I
273
Fag.
Cor. III IV
Timp.
273
Viol. II senza sord.
Vle senza sord.
Vcell.
Cb.
divisi
arco
arco
arco
arco
I
I
Largo Tempo I
279
Fl. I II
Fl. III
Ob.
Clar. in A
Cor. I II
279
Viol. I
senza sord.

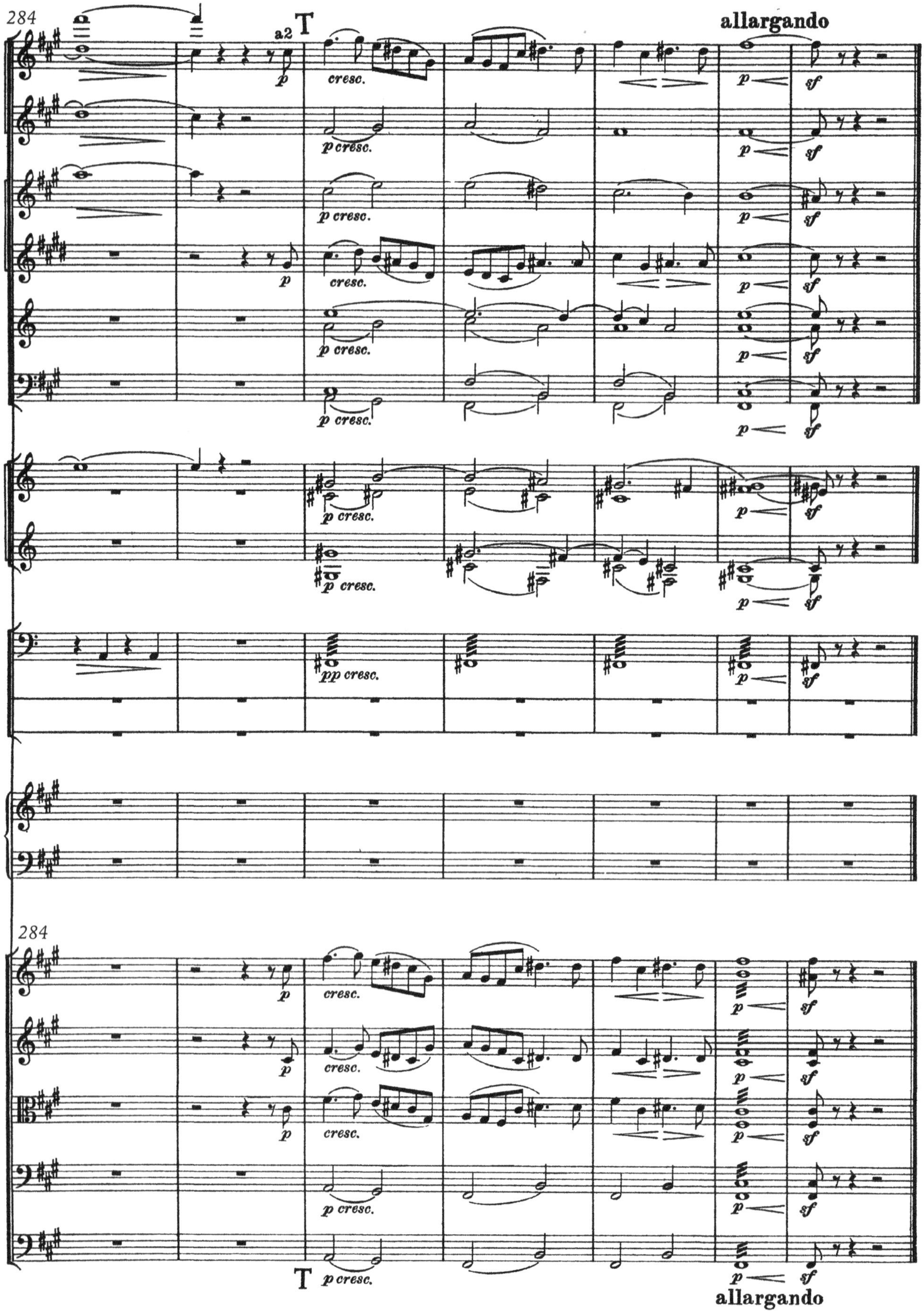

II

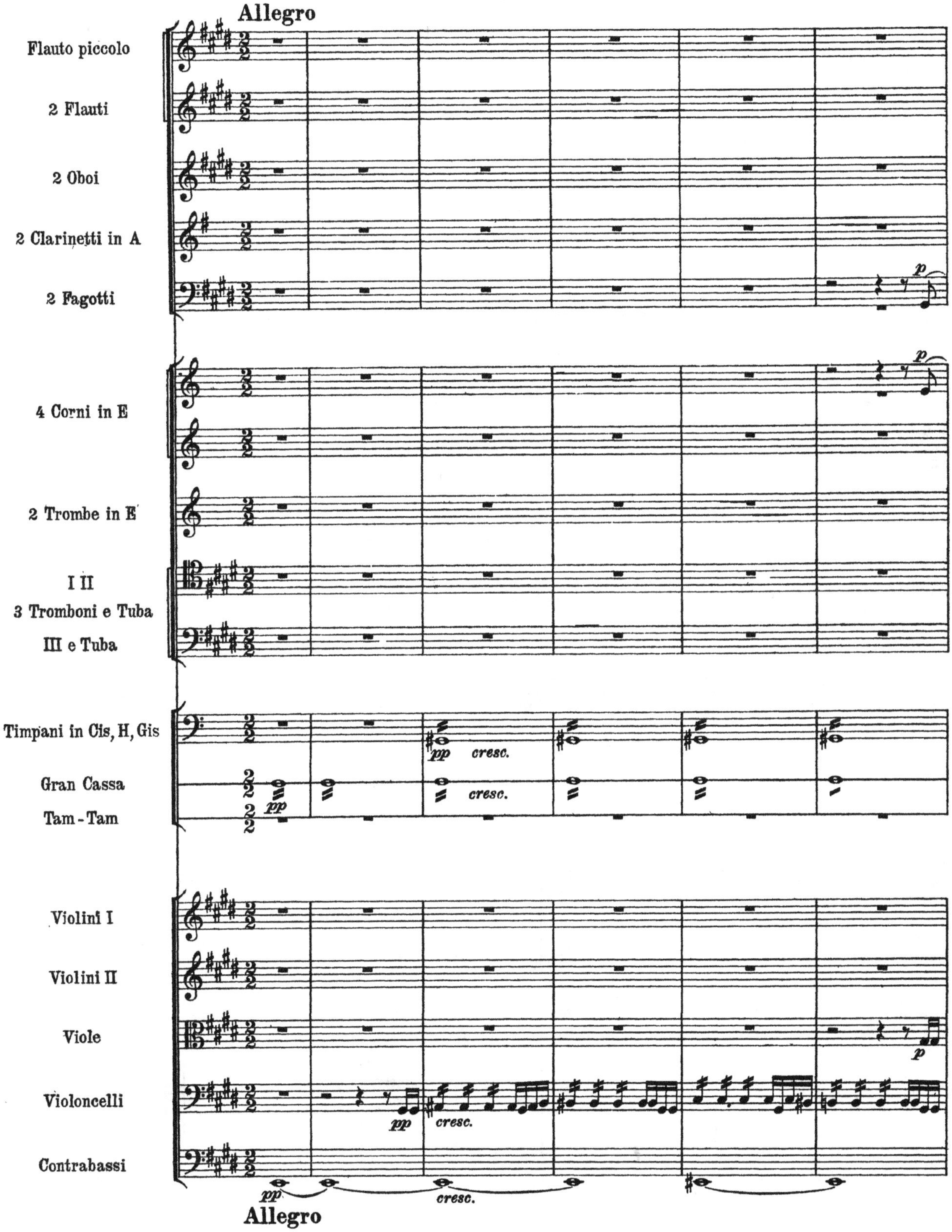
Allegro
Flauto piccolo
2 Flauti
2 Oboi
2 Clarinetti in A
2 Fagotti
4 Corni in E
2 Trombe in E
I II
3 Tromboni e Tuba
III e Tuba
Timpani in Cis, H, Gis
Gran Cassa
Tam-Tam
Violini I
Violini II
Viole
Violoncelli
Contrabassi
p
pp
cresc.
Allegro

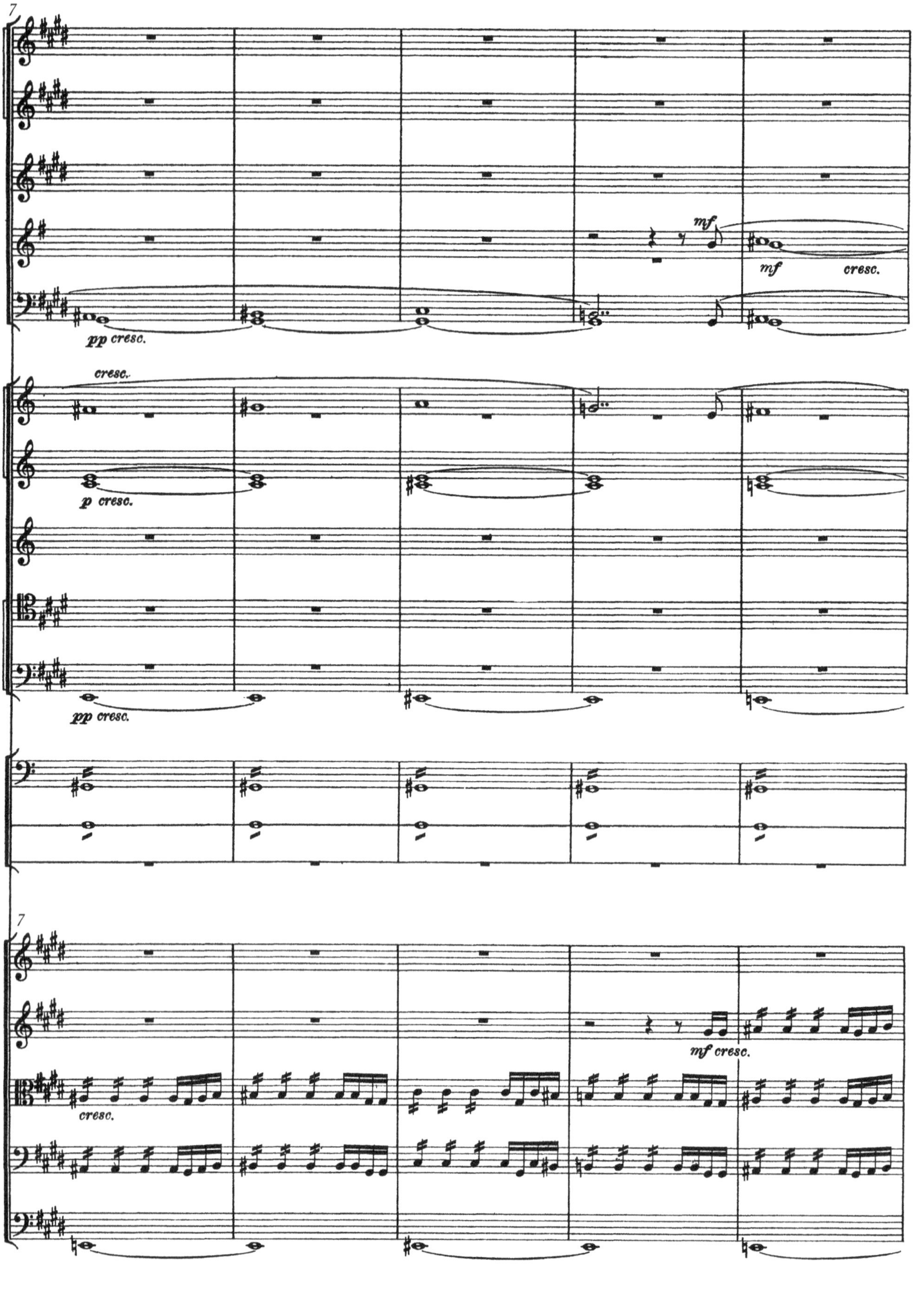
7
mf
mf
cresc.
pp cresc.
cresc.
p cresc.
pp cresc.
7
cresc.
mf cresc.

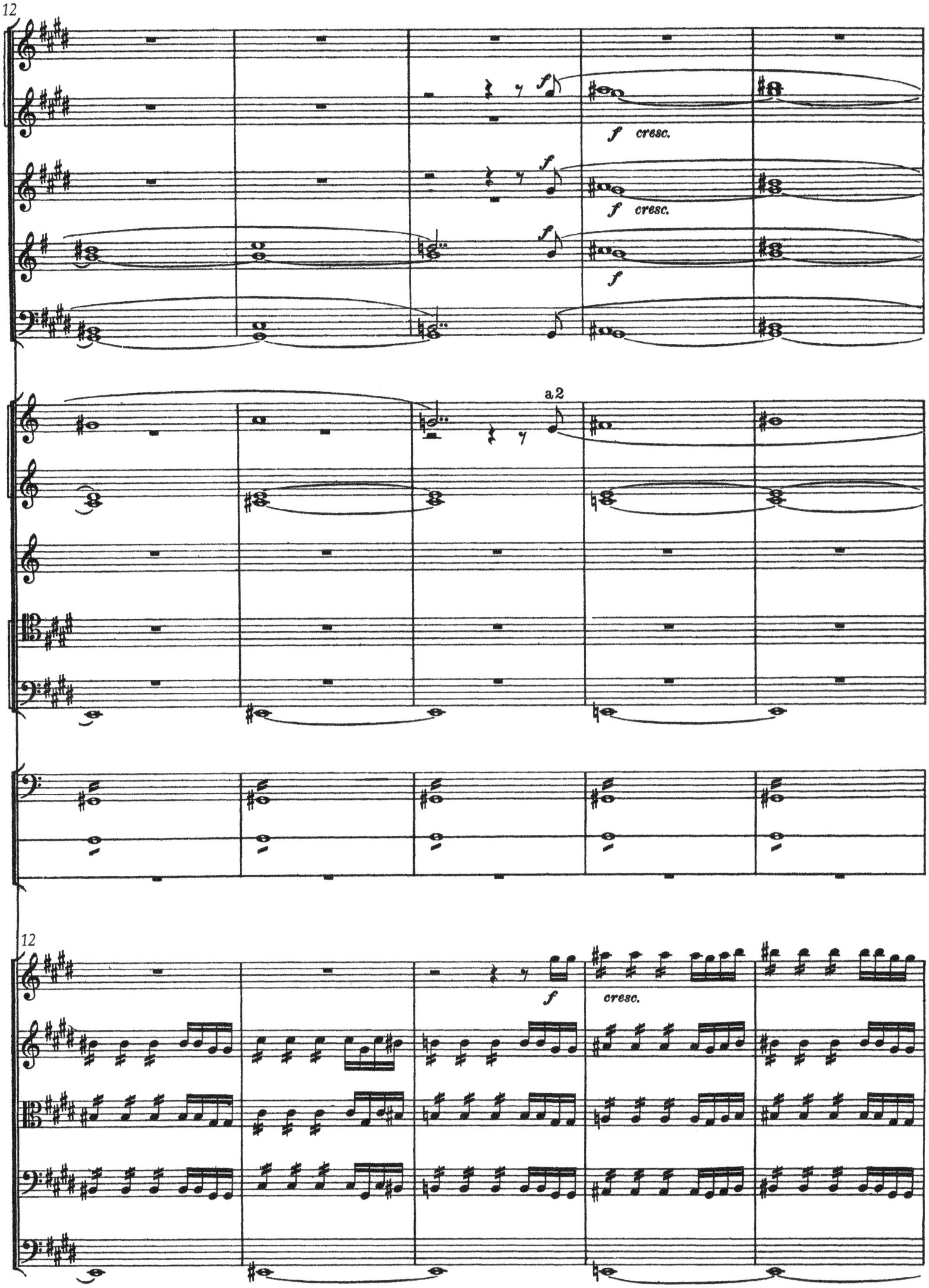
12
f
cresc.
f
cresc.
f
f
a 2
12
f
cresc.

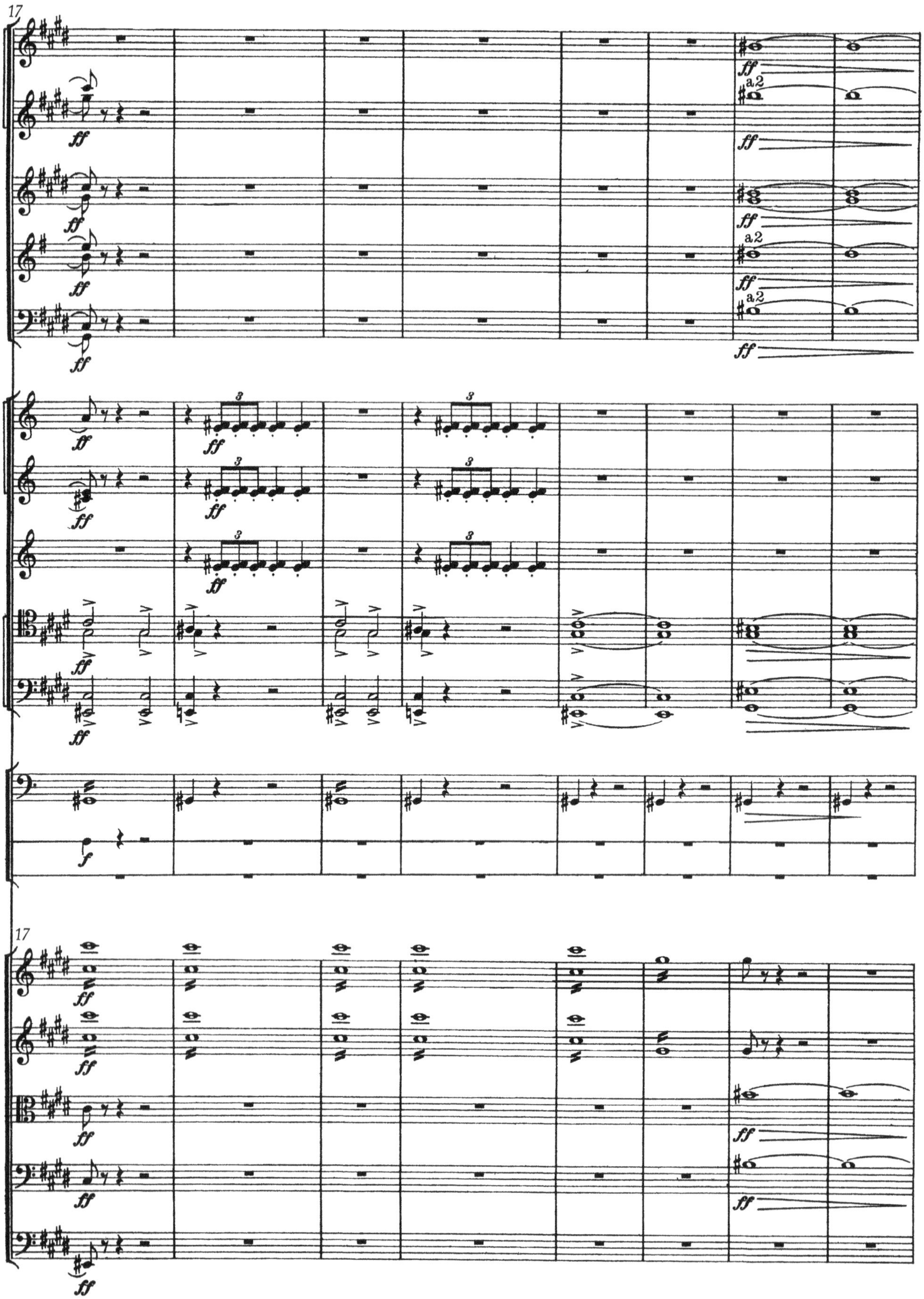
17
a2
ff
3
f

25
A
Fl. picc.
Fl.
Ob.
Clar. in A
Fag.
Cor. I II in E
Trbni I II
Trbne III e Tba.
Timp.
Gr. C.
pp
pp cresc.
cresc.
25
Vle
Vcell.
pp
cresc.
p
Cb.
A pp
cresc.
31
Clar.
mf
Fag.
p cresc.
cresc.
Cor. III IV in E
p cresc.
Trbne III e Tba
pp cresc.
31
Viol. II
mf
cresc.

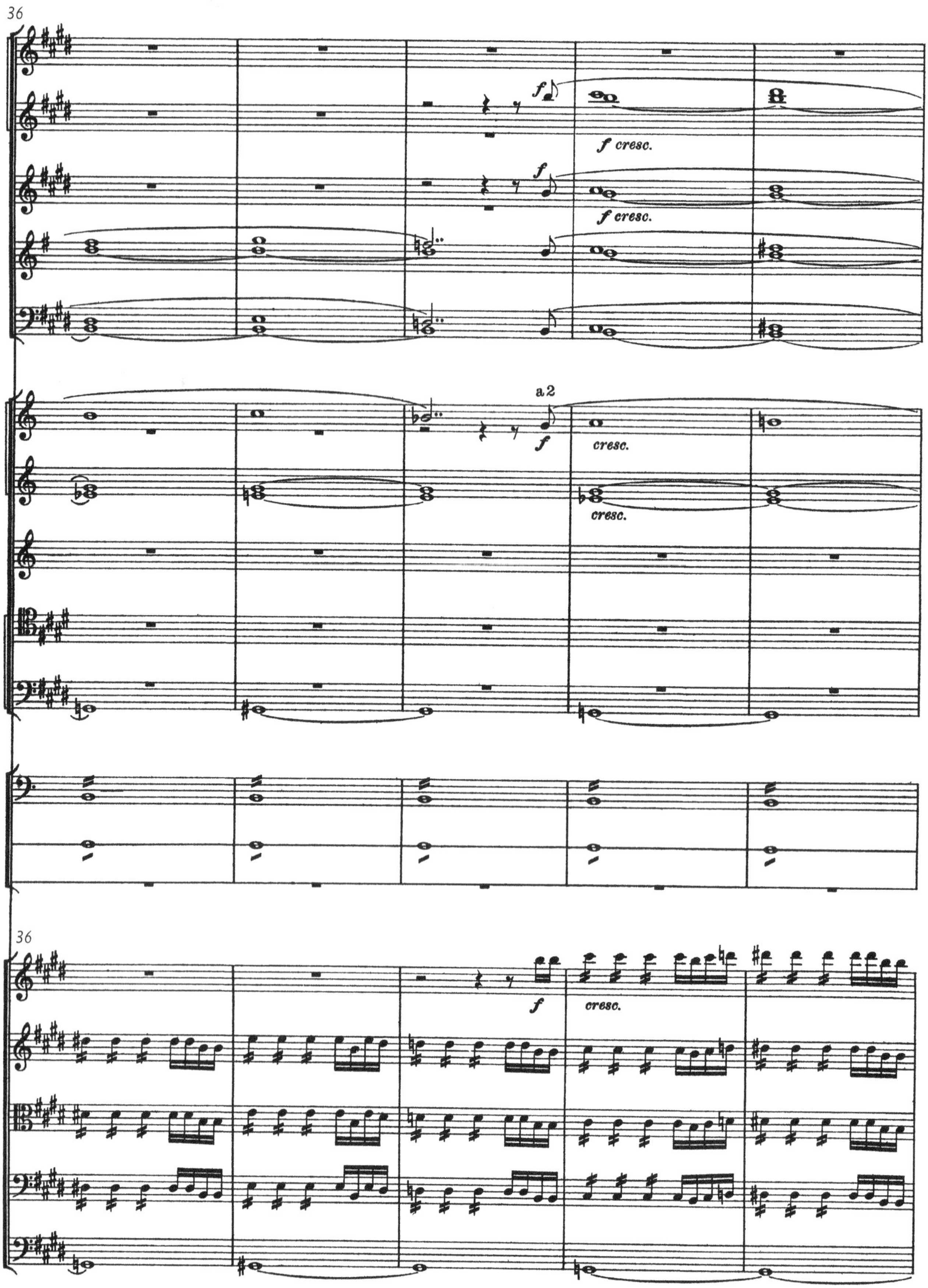
36
f
f cresc.
f
f cresc.
a 2
f
cresc.
cresc.
36
f
cresc.

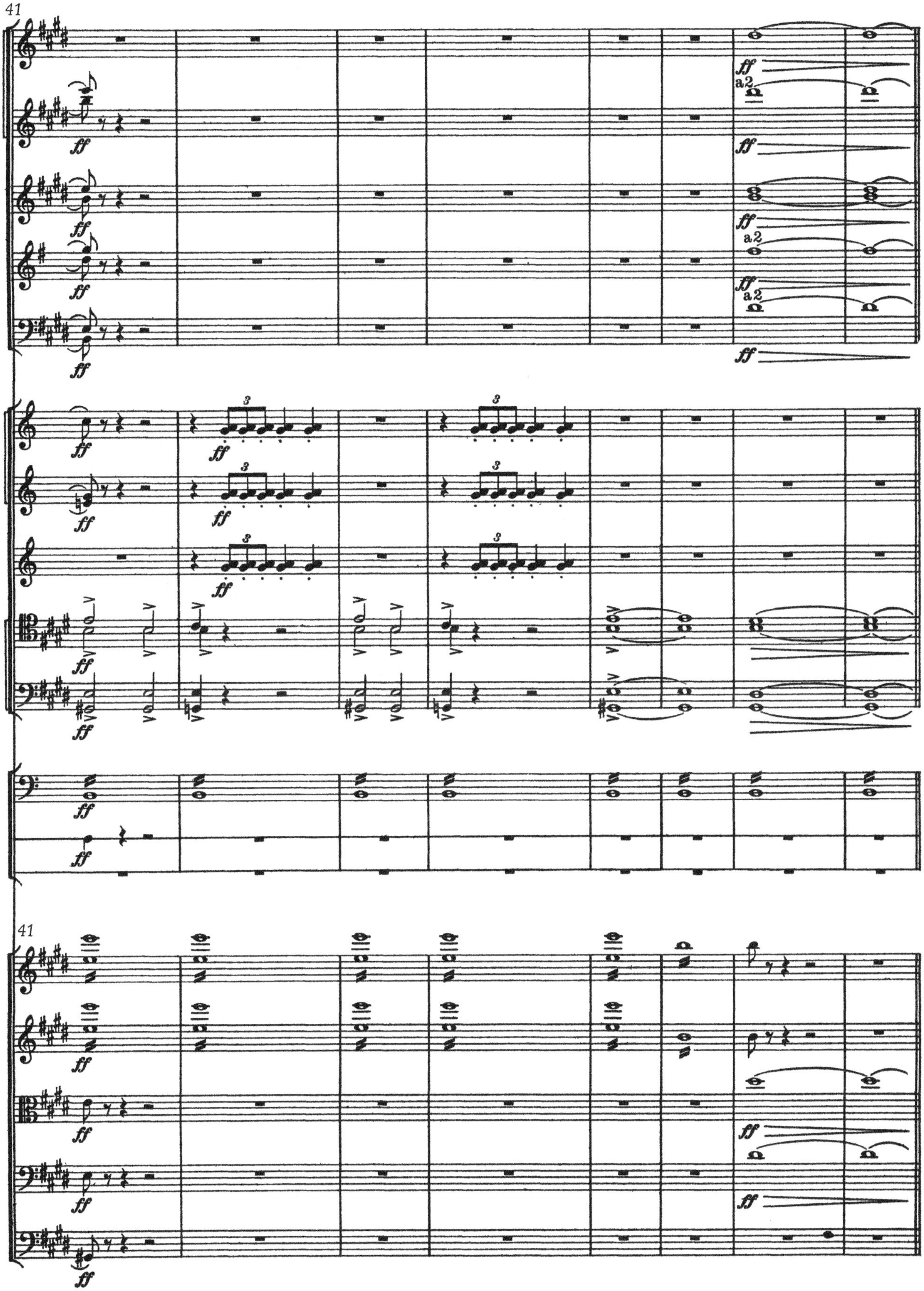
41
a2
ff
3
41

B Molto Allegro

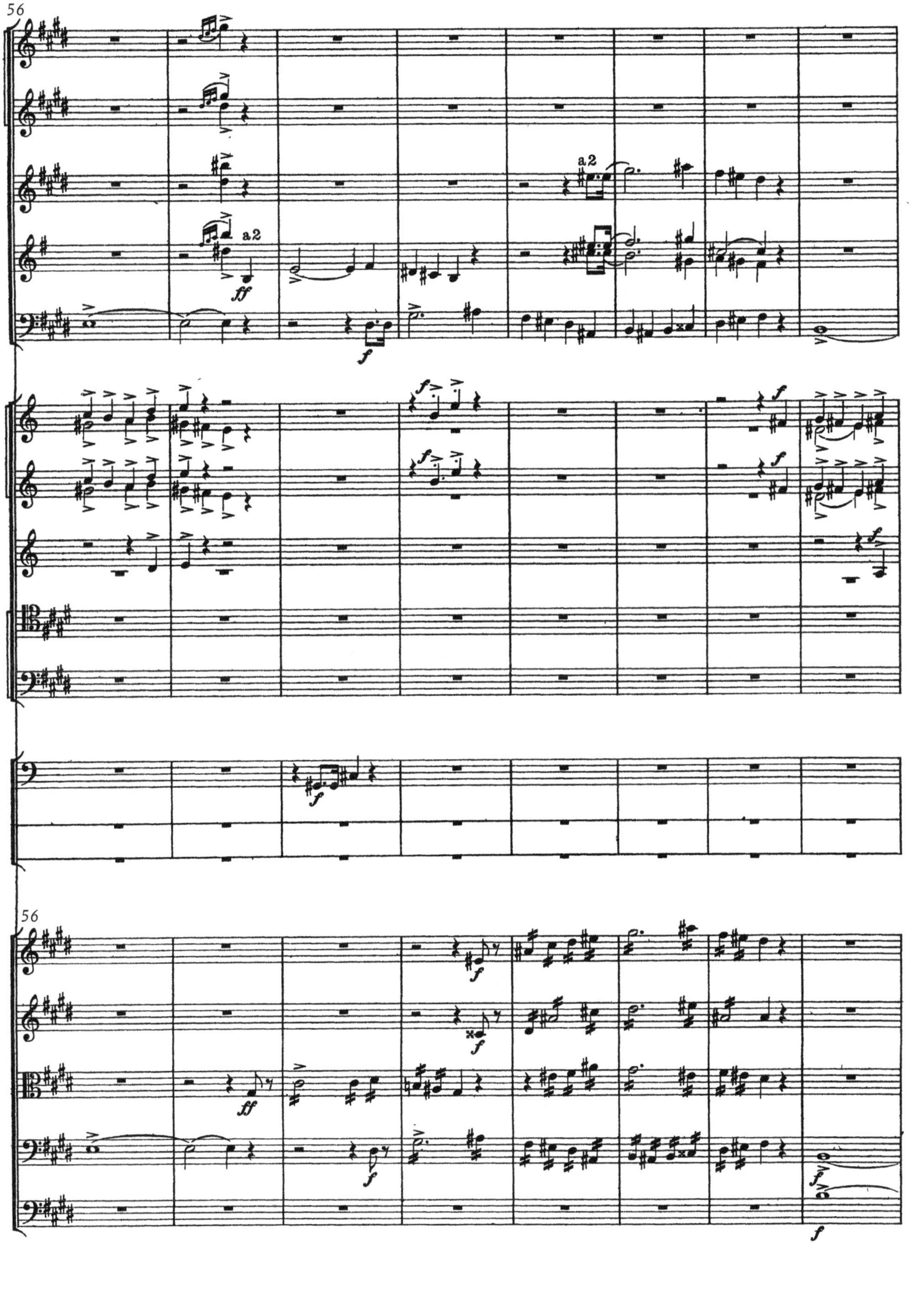
56
a2
ff
f
a2
56
ff
f

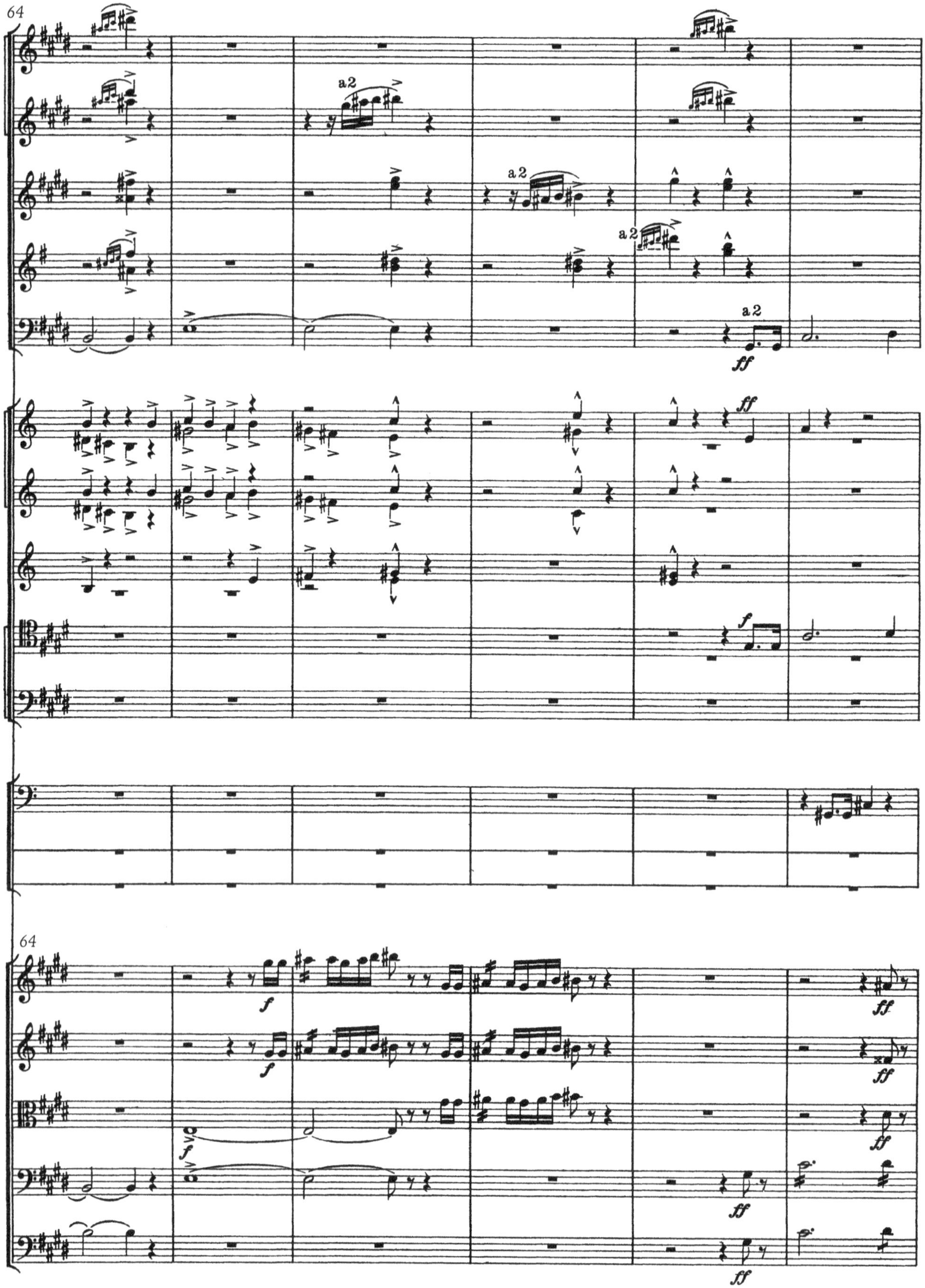
64
a2
a2
a2
a2
ff
ff
f
64
f
f
f
ff
ff
ff
ff
ff

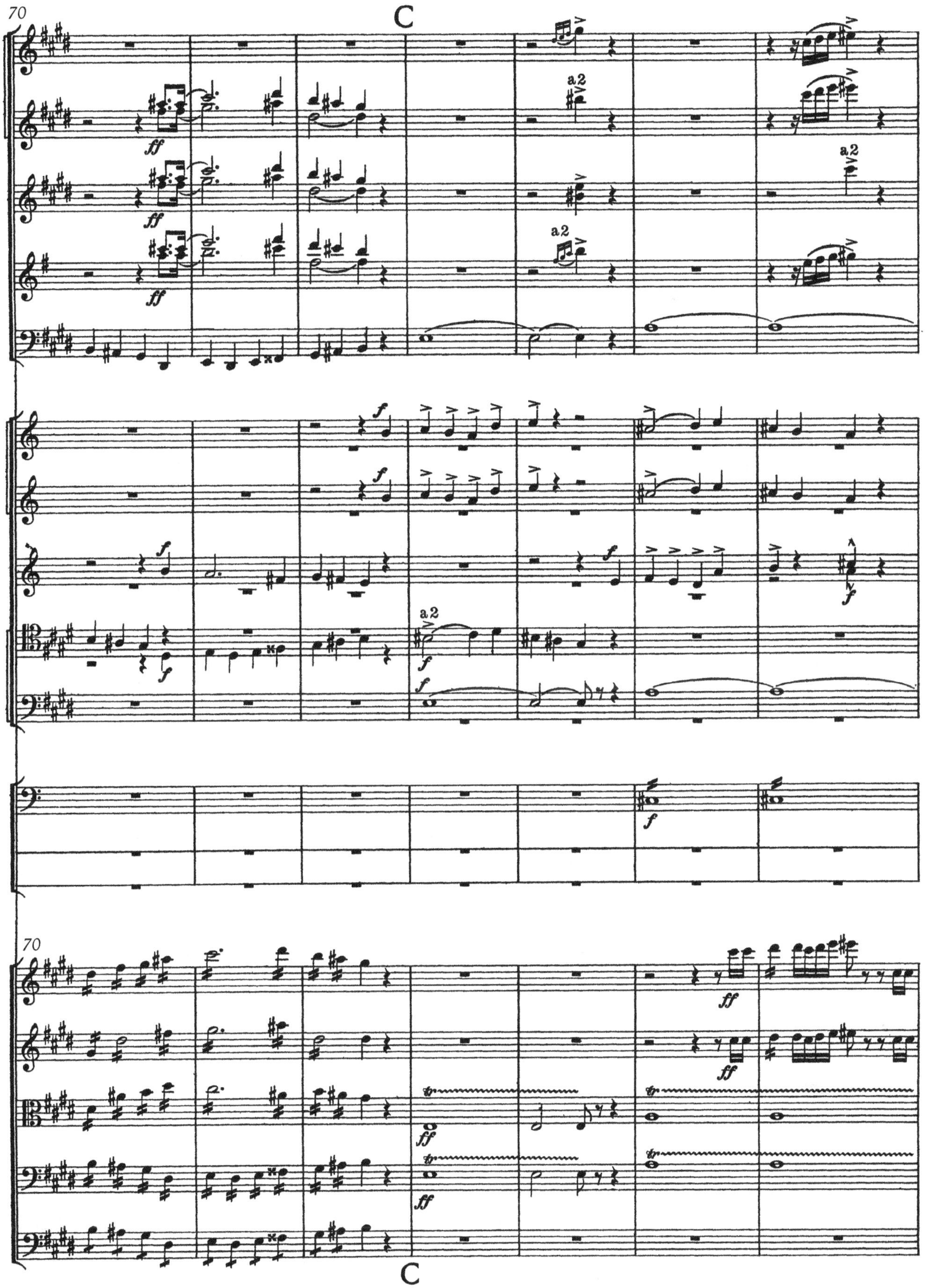
70
C
a2
ff
f
70
C

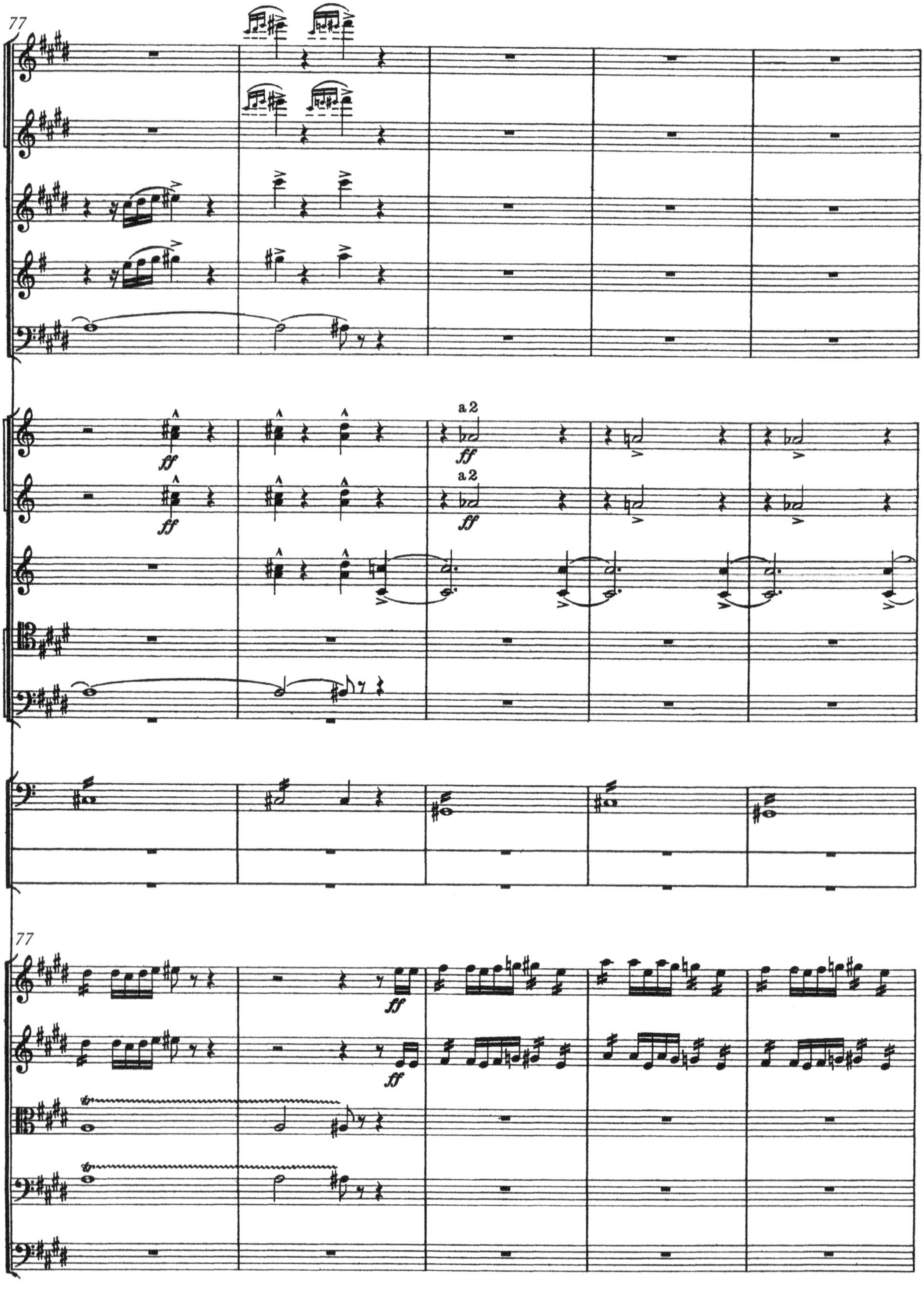
77
a 2
ff
a 2
ff
77
ff
ff

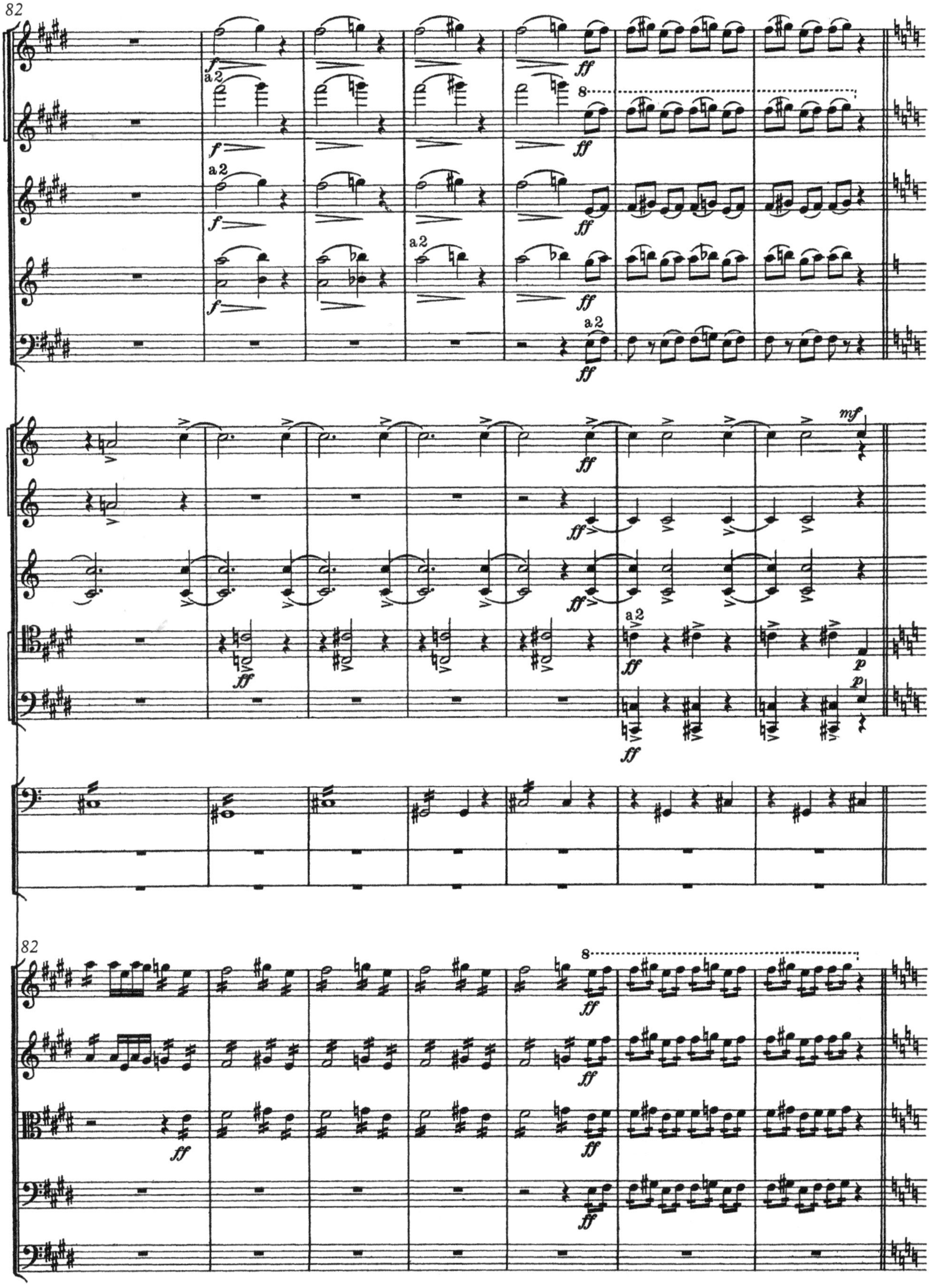
82
a 2
a 2
a 2
a 2
8
a 2
82
8

89
D
Meno mosso
allargando
a 2
a 2
a 2
f
f
f
p
pp
mf
mf
p
p
89
sul ponticello al segno
sul ponticello al segno
sul ponticello al segno
sul ponticello al segno
sfp
sfp
sfp
sfp
sfp
ff
ff
ff
ff
ff
D
allargando
Meno mosso

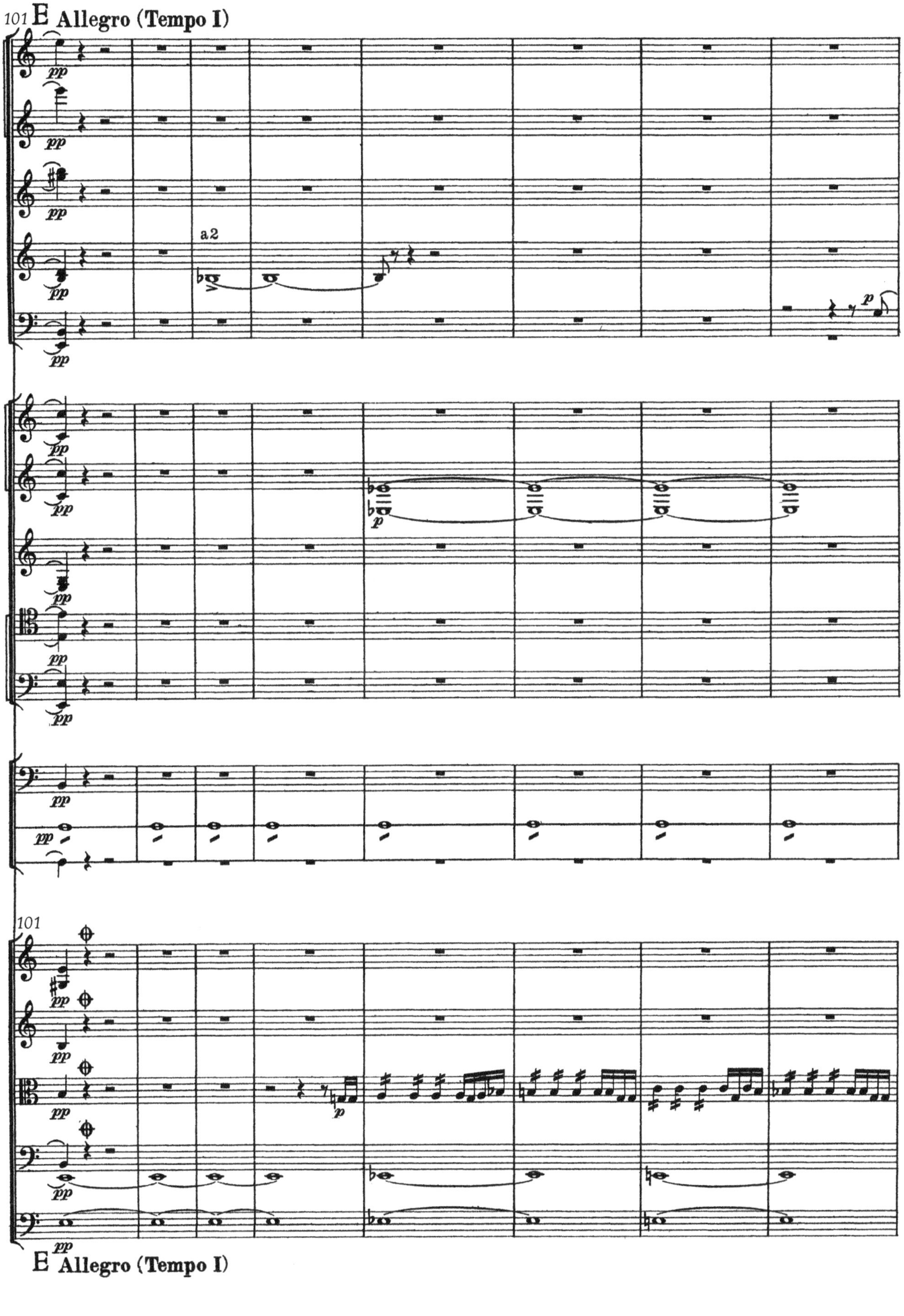
101
E Allegro (Tempo I)
pp
a2
p
101
Allegro (Tempo I)

109
p
p cresc.
p
p cresc.
p cresc.
p
cresc.
cresc.
109
p
cresc.
p
cresc.
cresc.
cresc.
cresc.

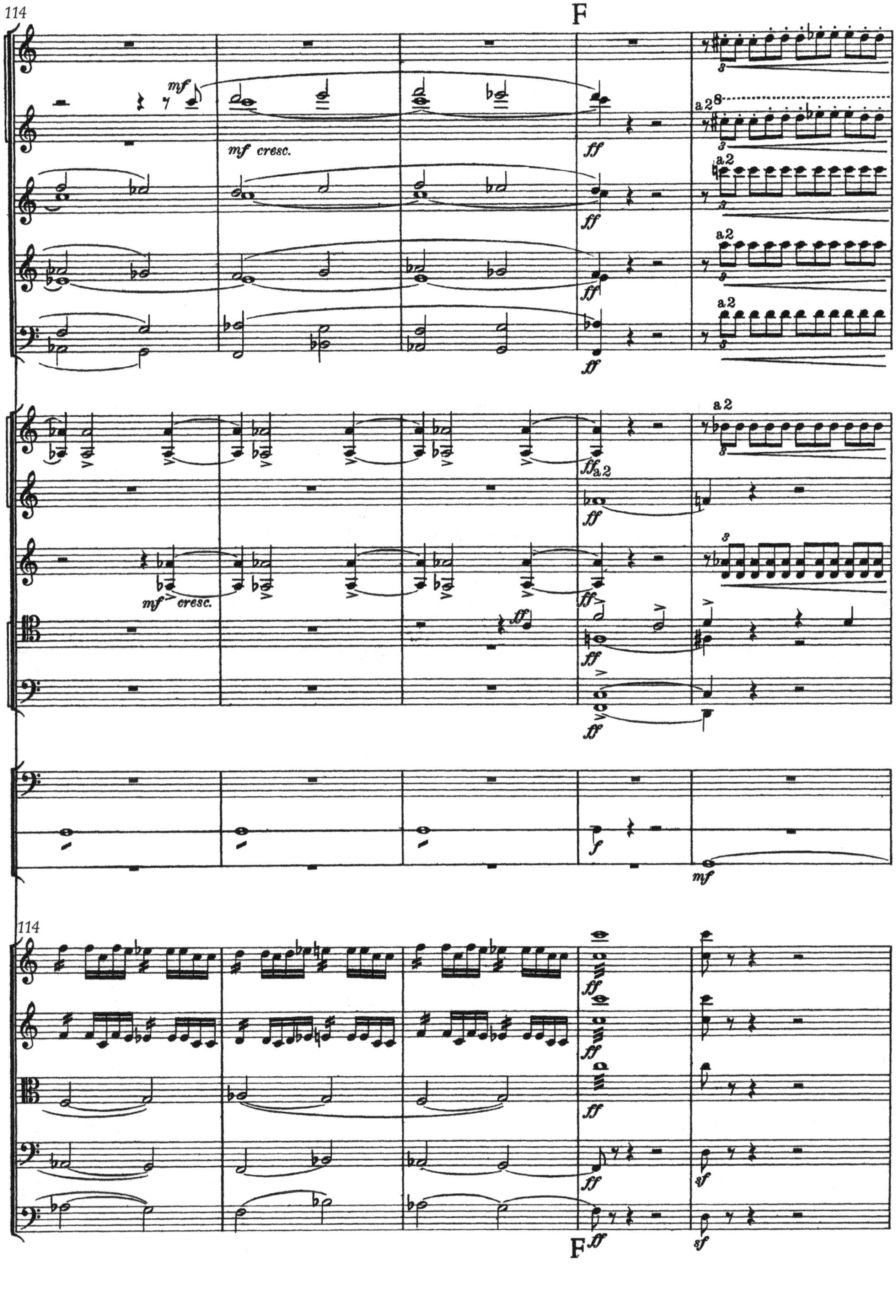
114
F
mf
mf cresc.
ff
a 2
3
mf cresc.
f
mf
sf
114
F

119

muta H in C

119

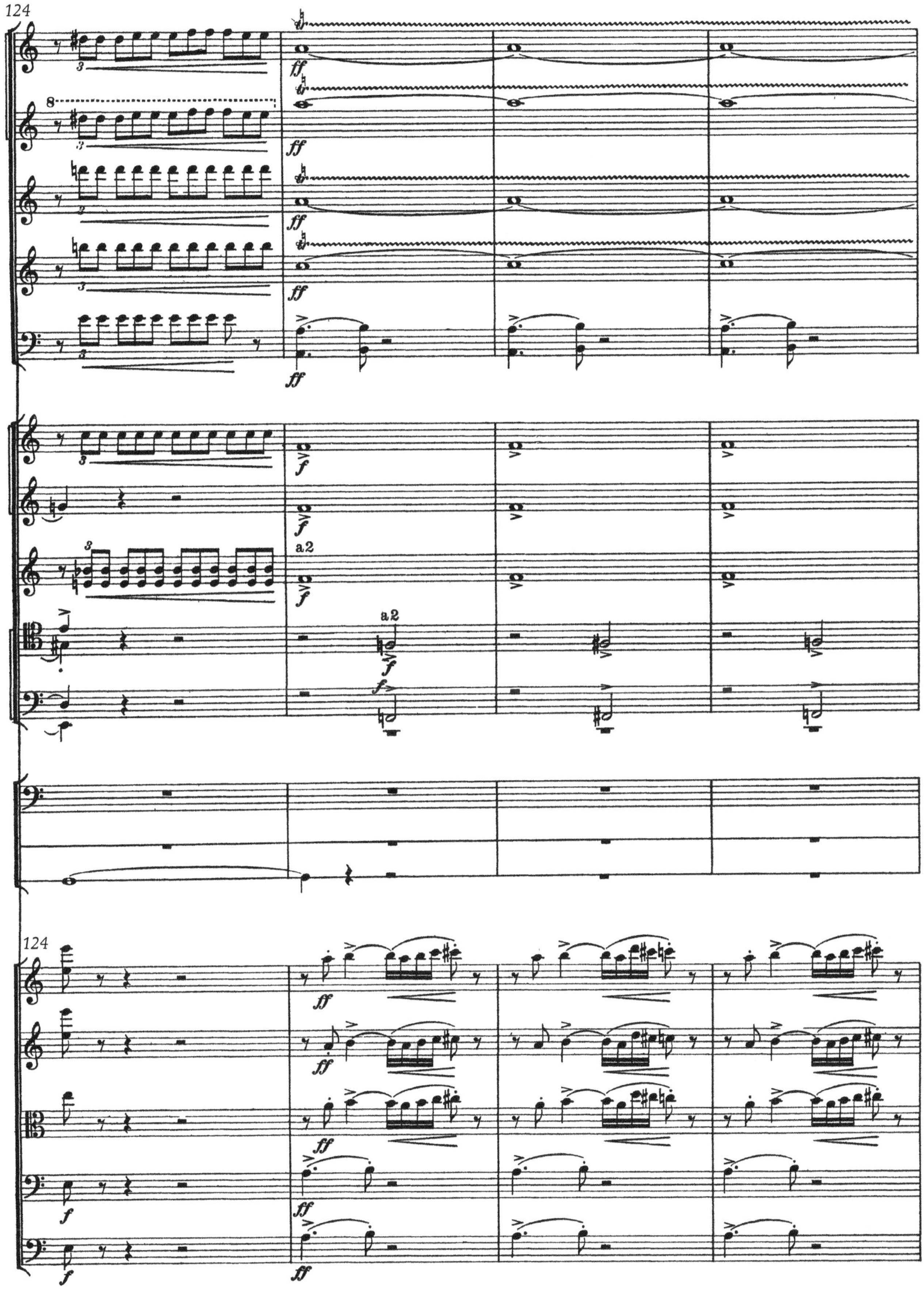
124
ff
8
a2
f
124
ff
f

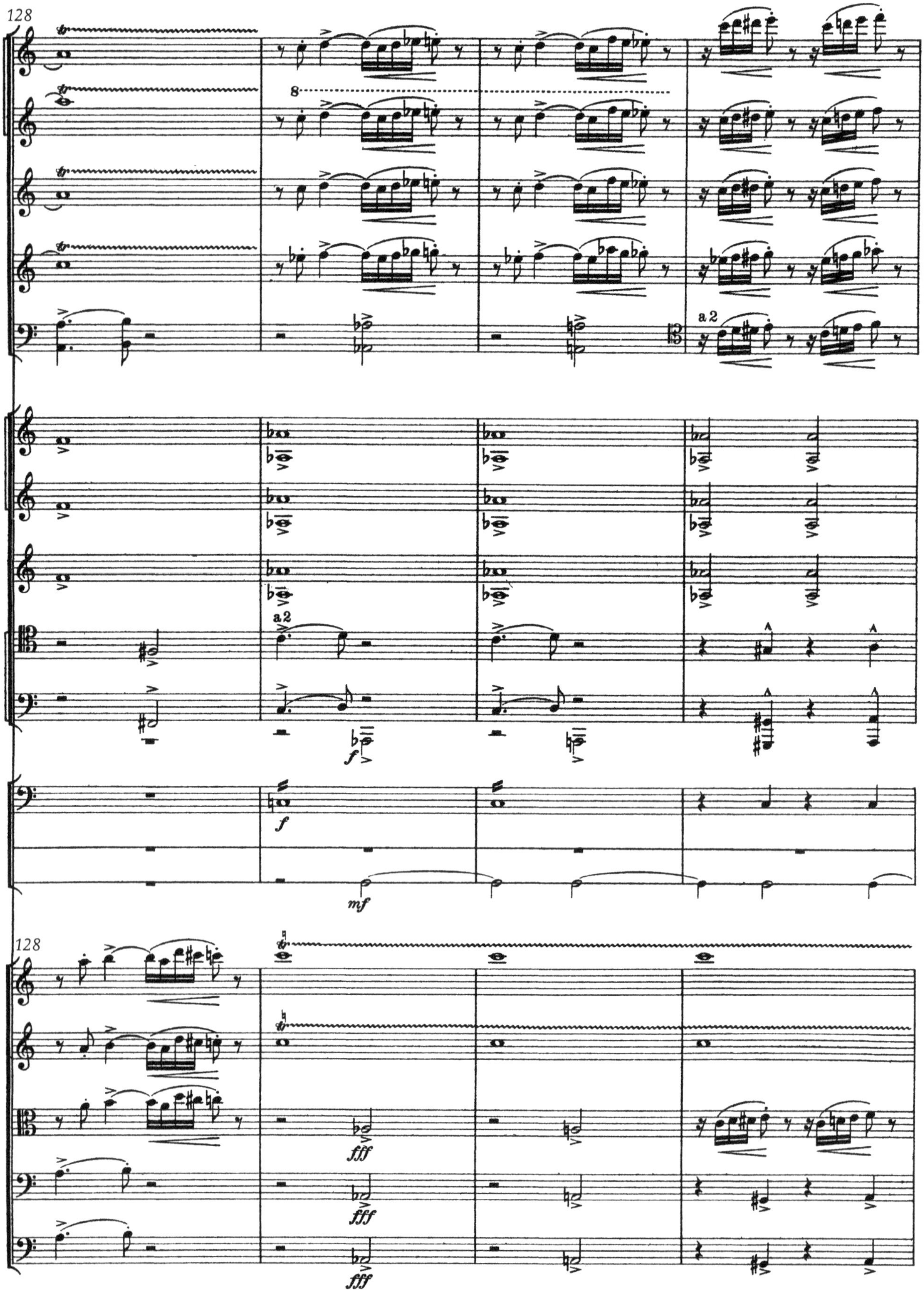
128
8
a 2
a 2
f
f
mf
128
fff
fff
fff

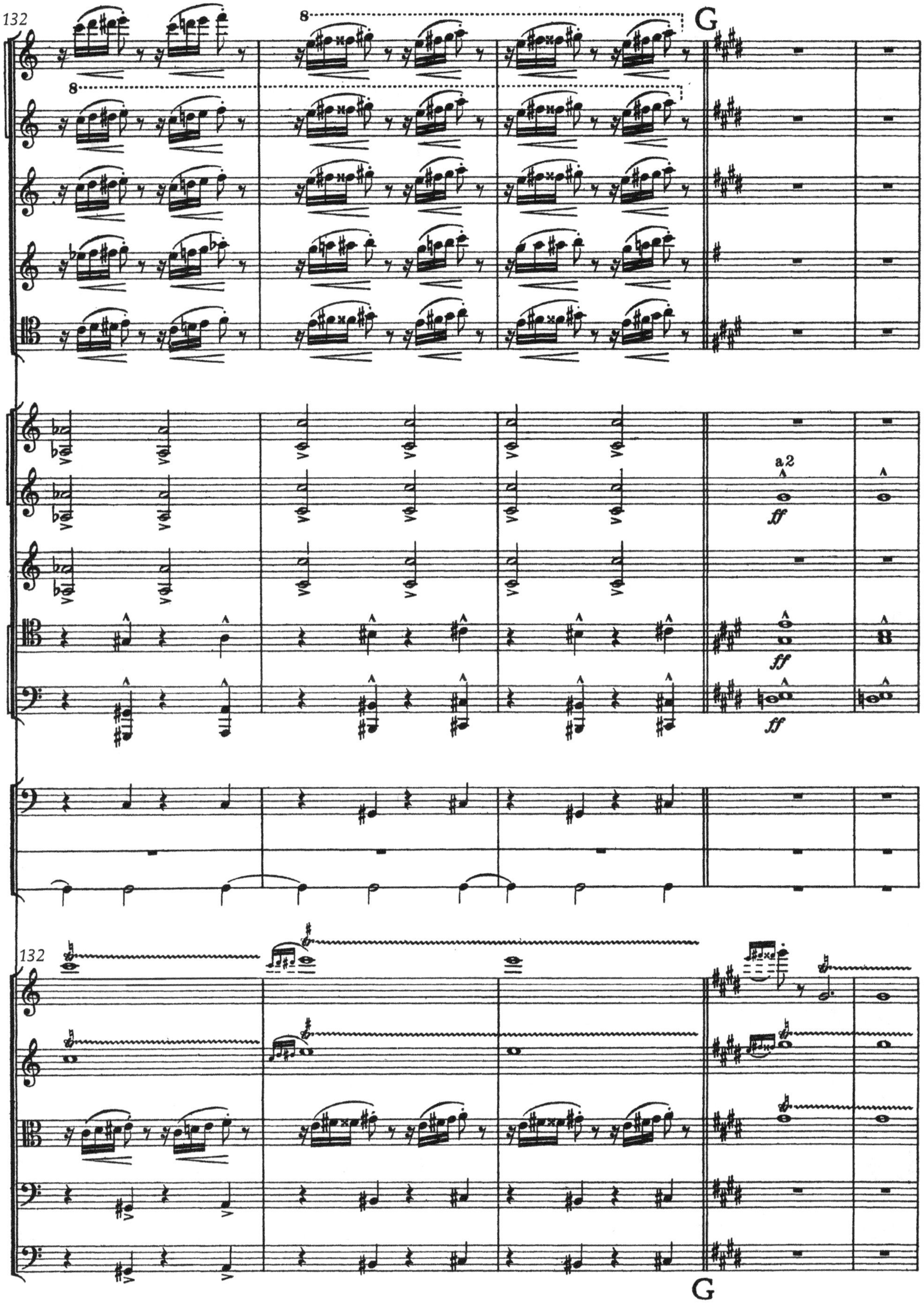
132
8
G
a2
ff
ff
ff
132
G

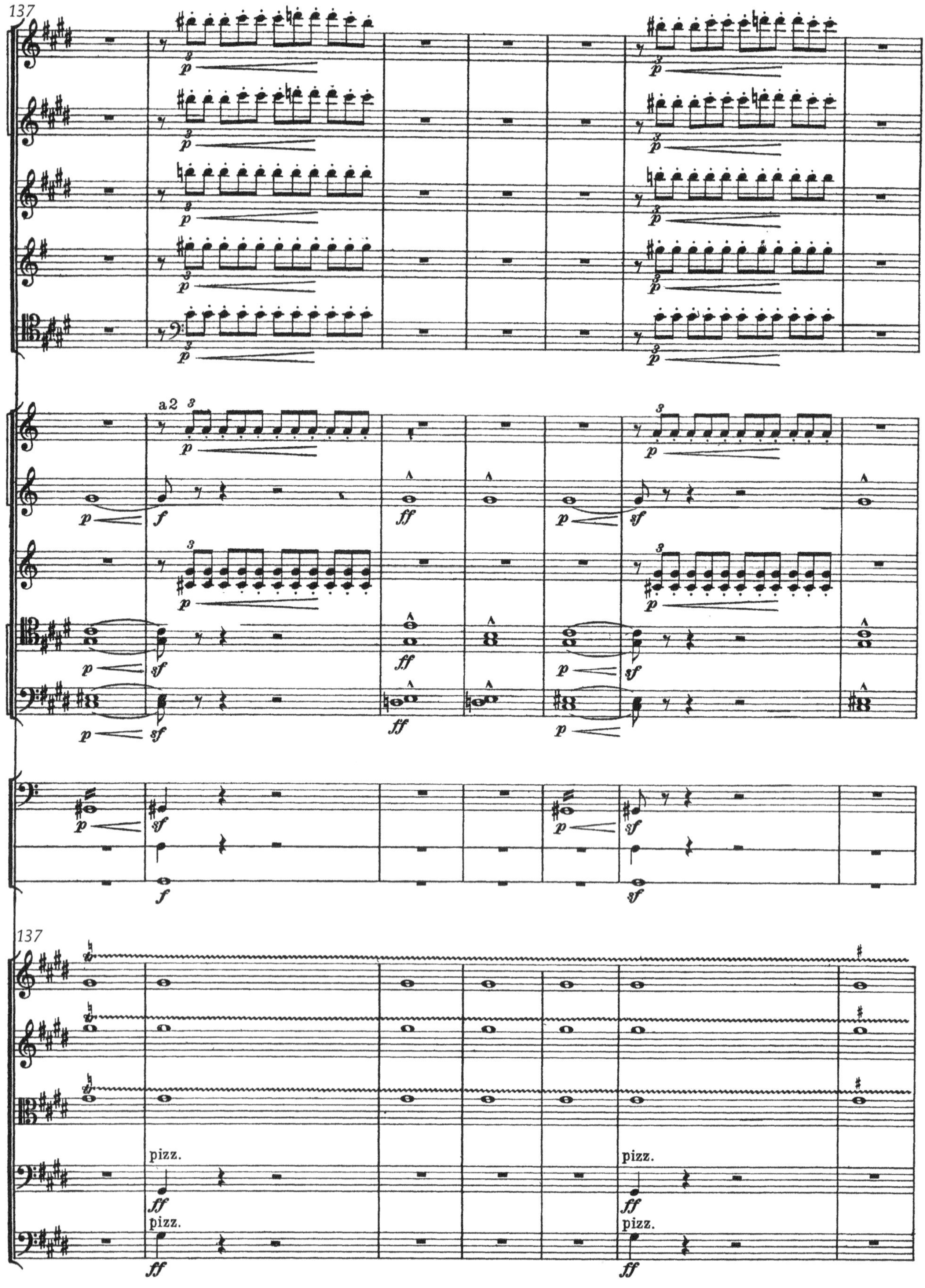
137
a2
pizz.
pizz.
pizz.
pizz.

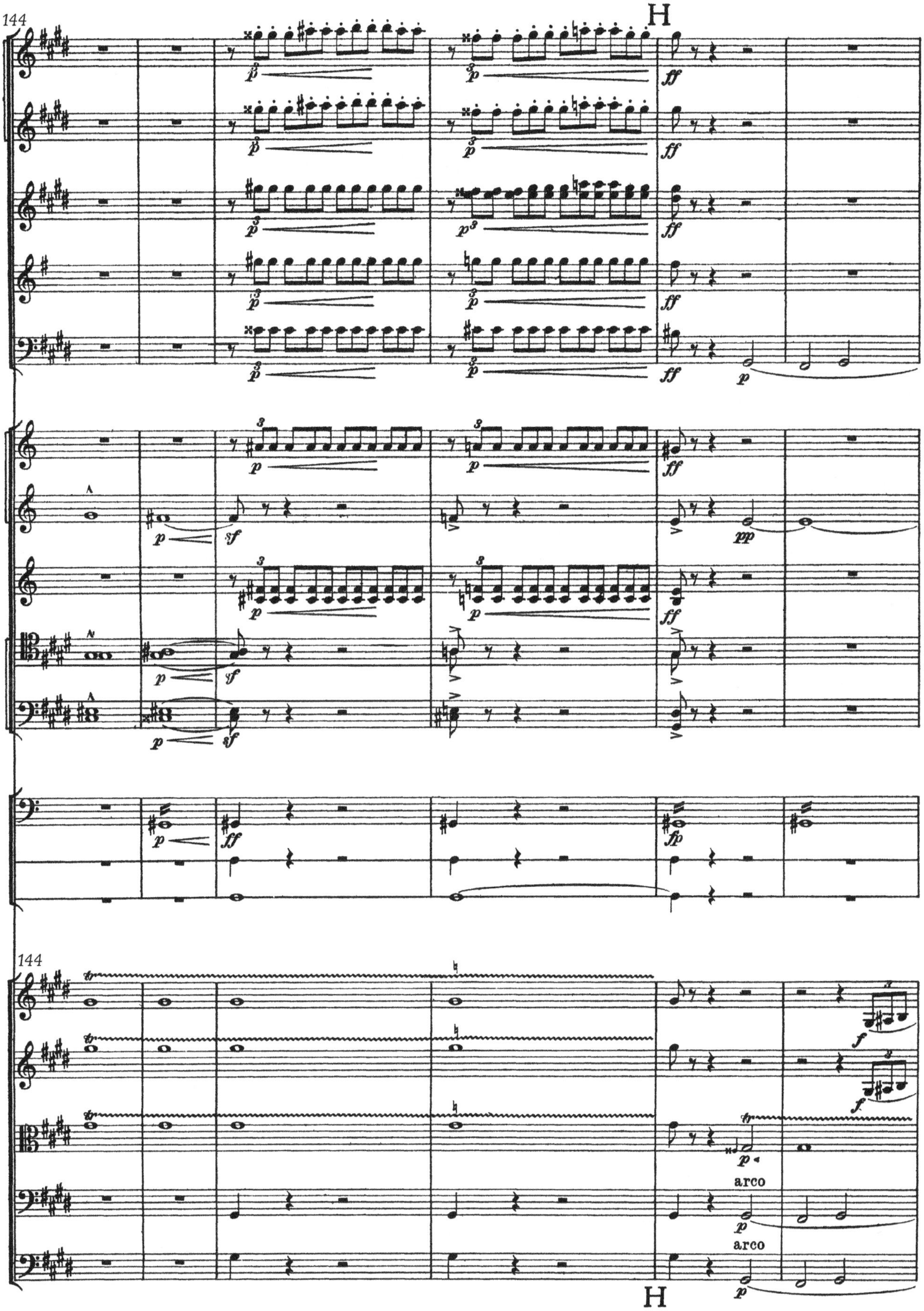
144
H
144
arco
arco
H

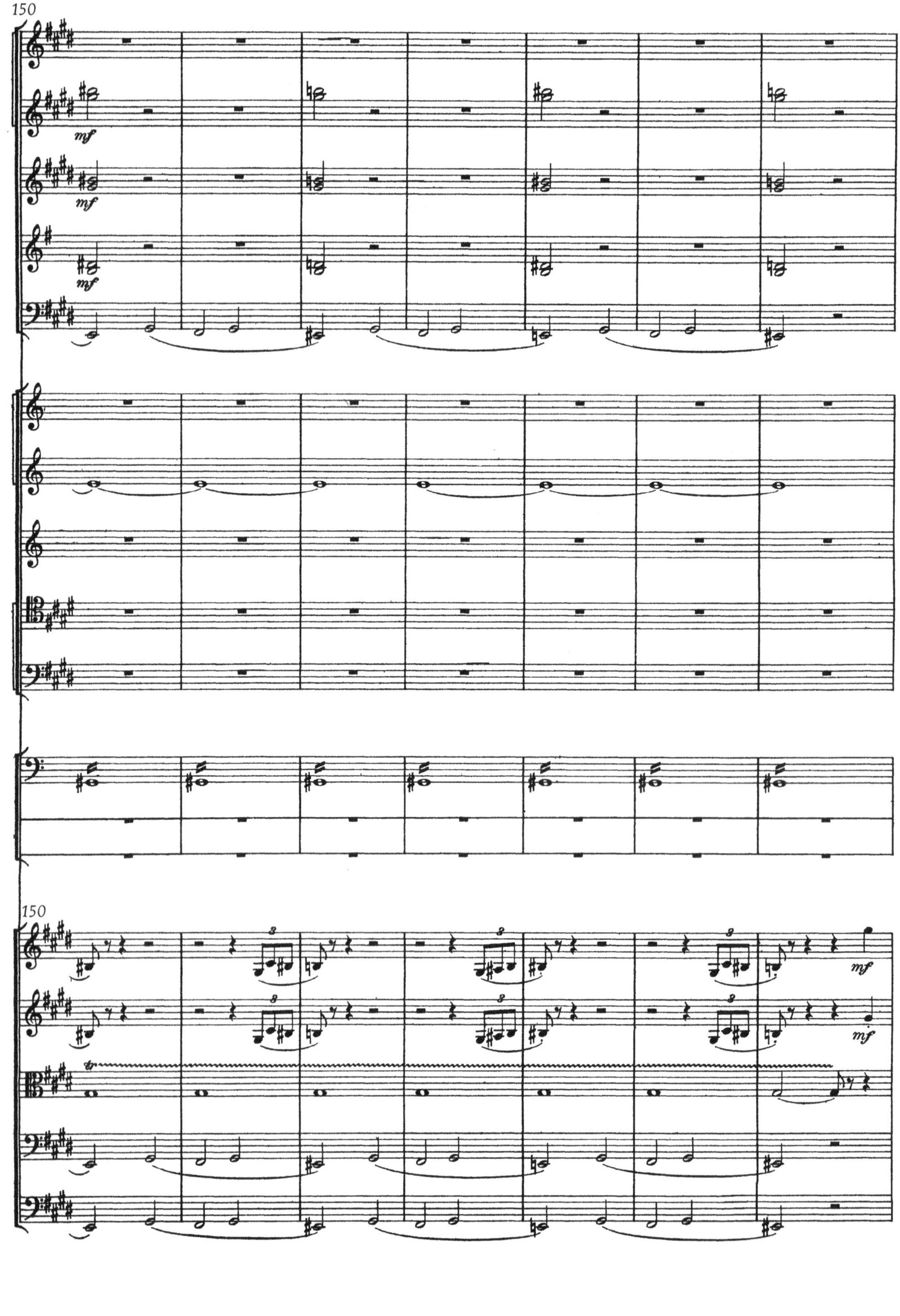
150
mf
mf
mf
150
tr
mf
mf

poco a poco stringendo
157
a 2
a 2
a 2
a 2
a 2
157
poco a poco stringendo

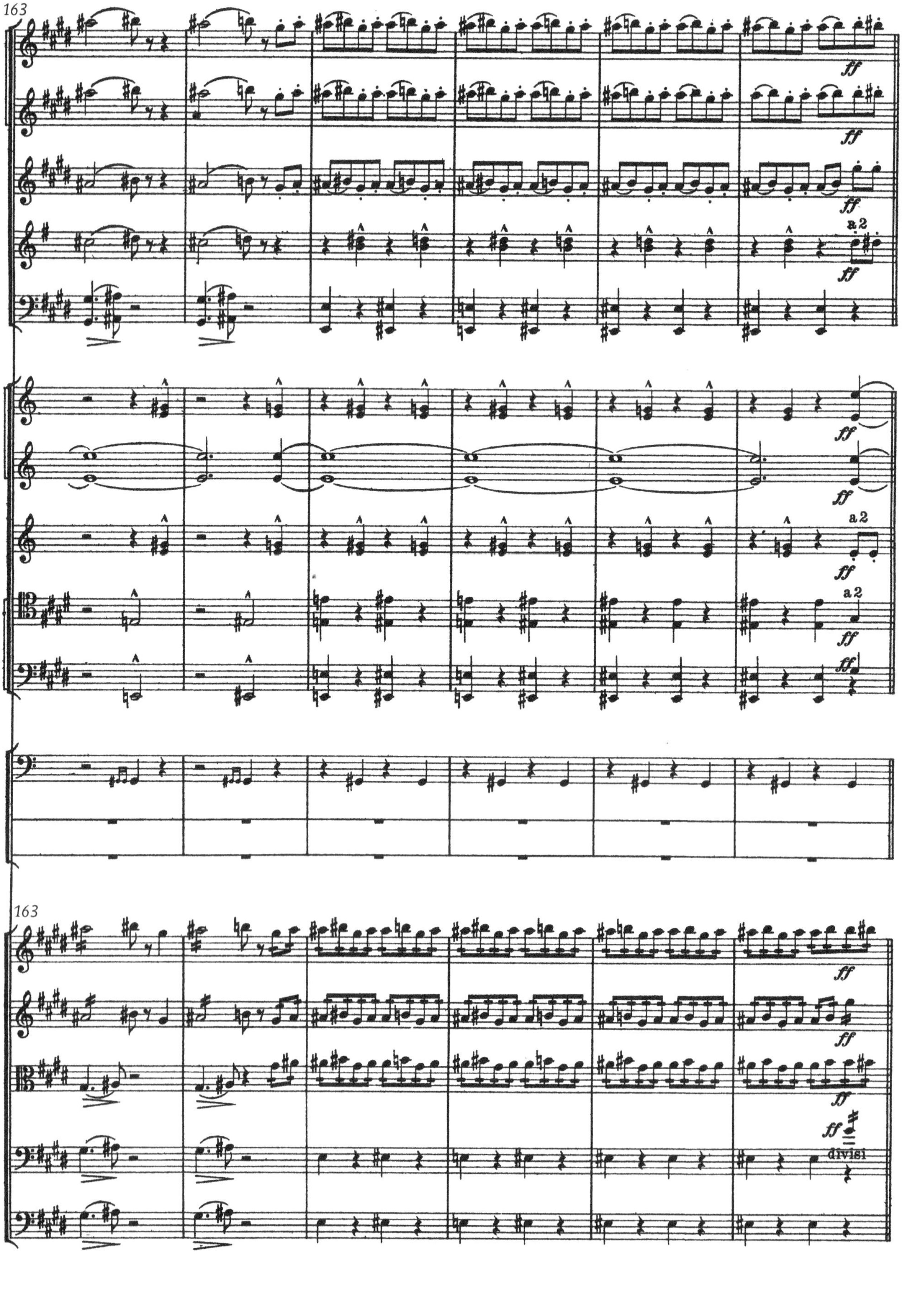
163
ff
a 2
163
divisi

I Molto Allegro
169
a 2
ff
ff
ff
169
divisi
I parte divisi
ff
ff
I Molto Allegro

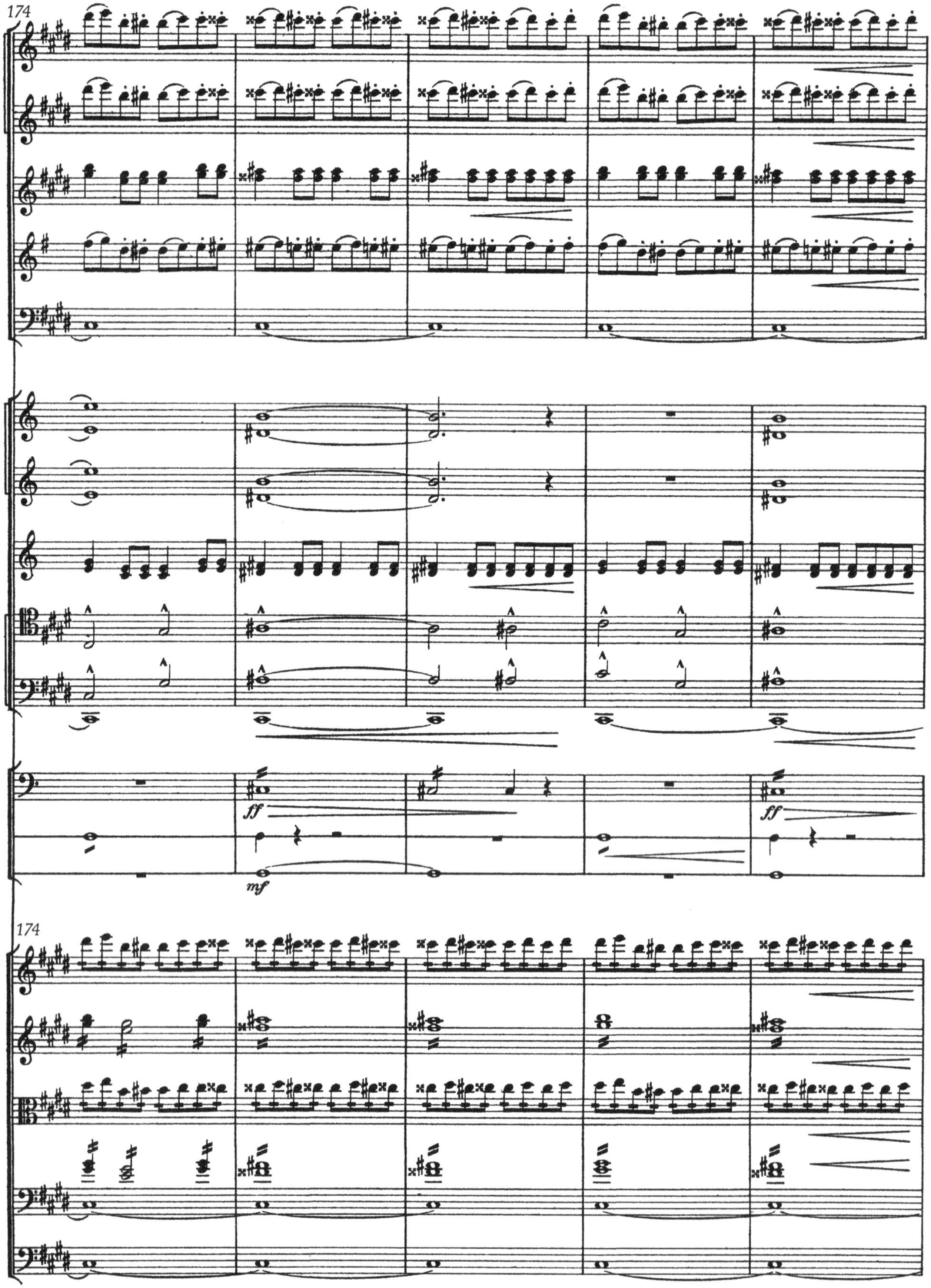
174
ff
ff
mf
174

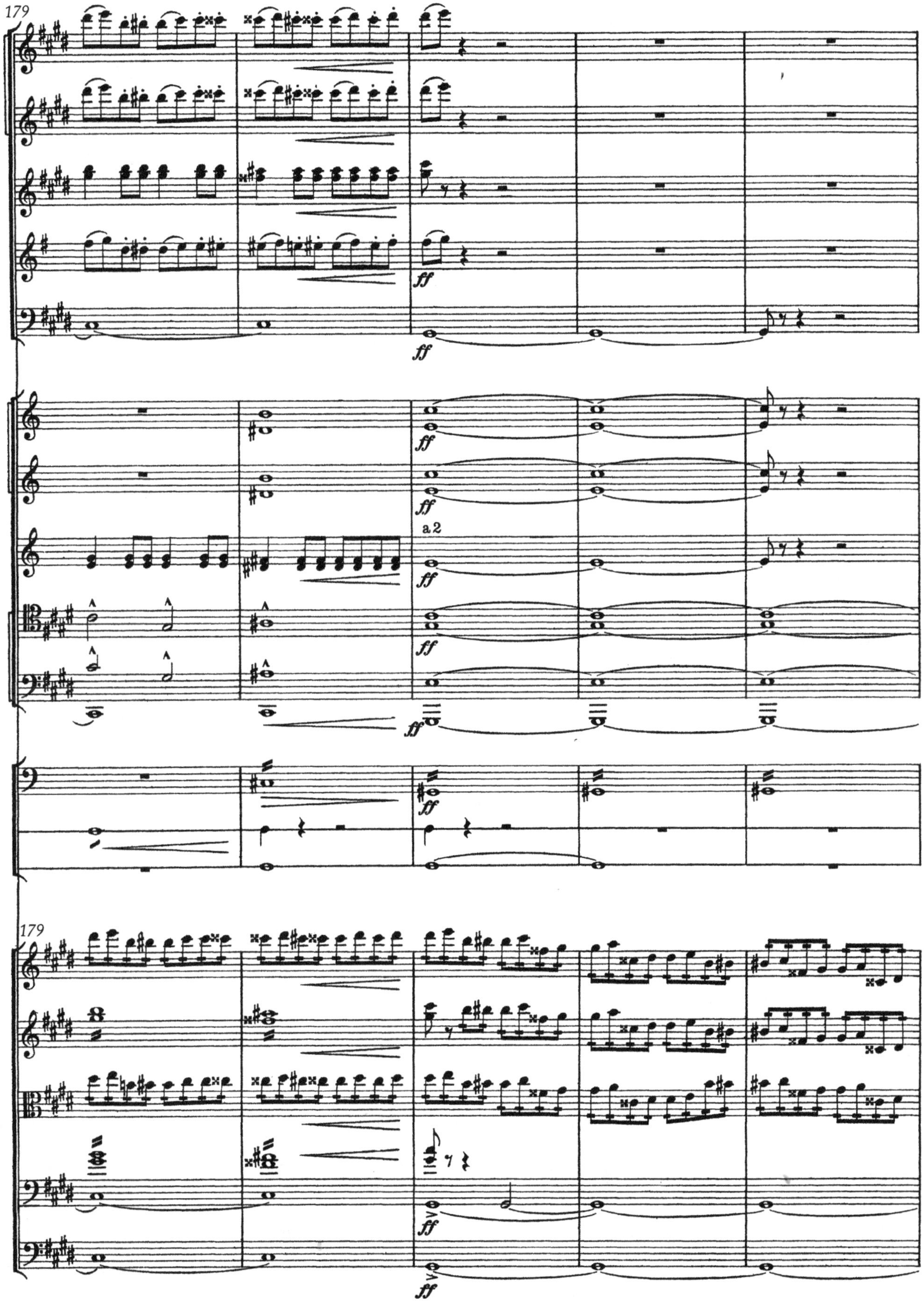
179
ff
a 2
179

184
K Poco meno mosso
p
a2
p
mf
mf
p
sf
mf
pp
p
184
f
p
crescendo poco a poco
f
p
crescendo poco a poco
K Poco meno mosso

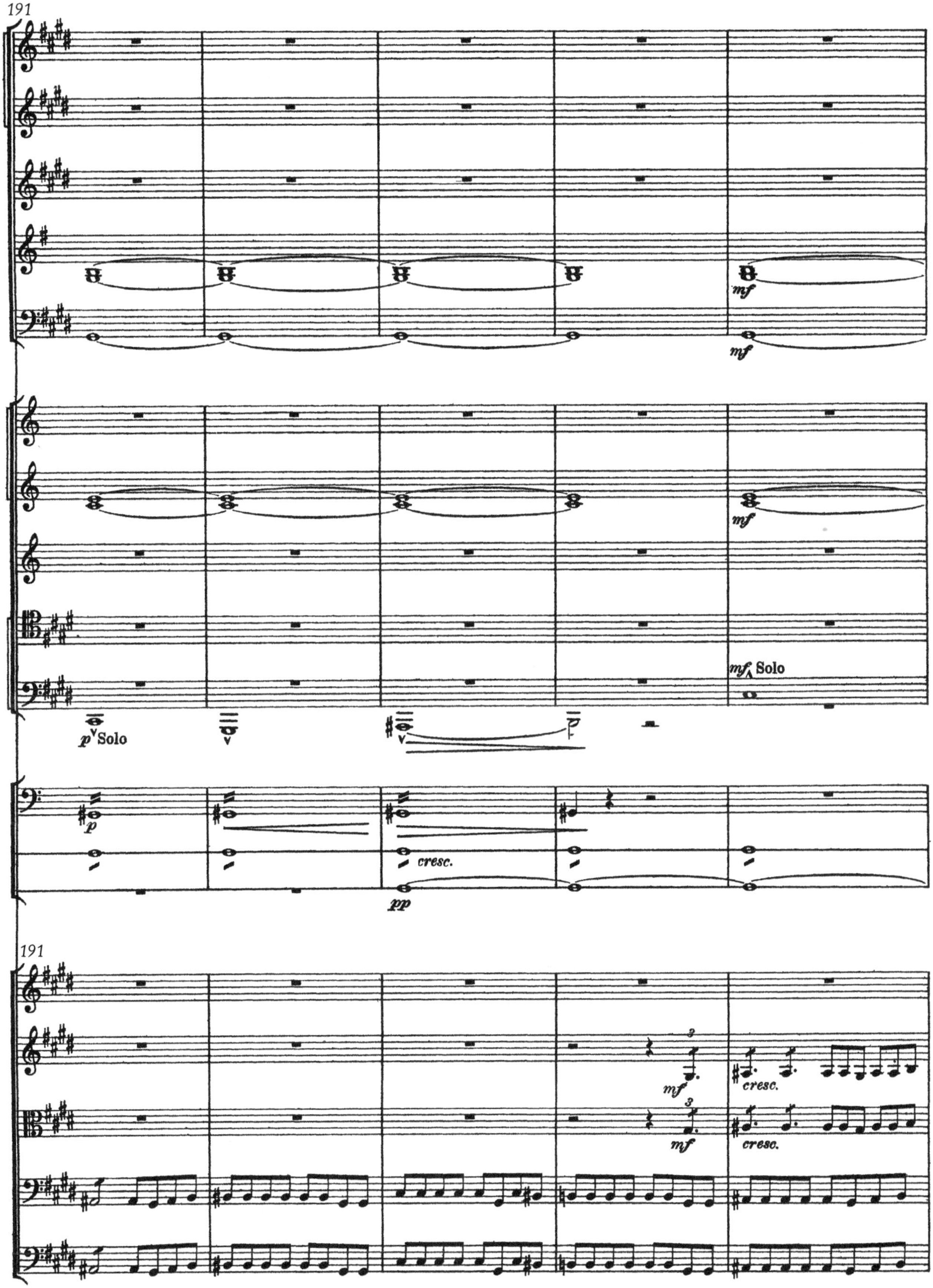
191
mf
mf
mf
mf Solo
p Solo
p
cresc.
pp
191
mf
mf
cresc.
cresc.

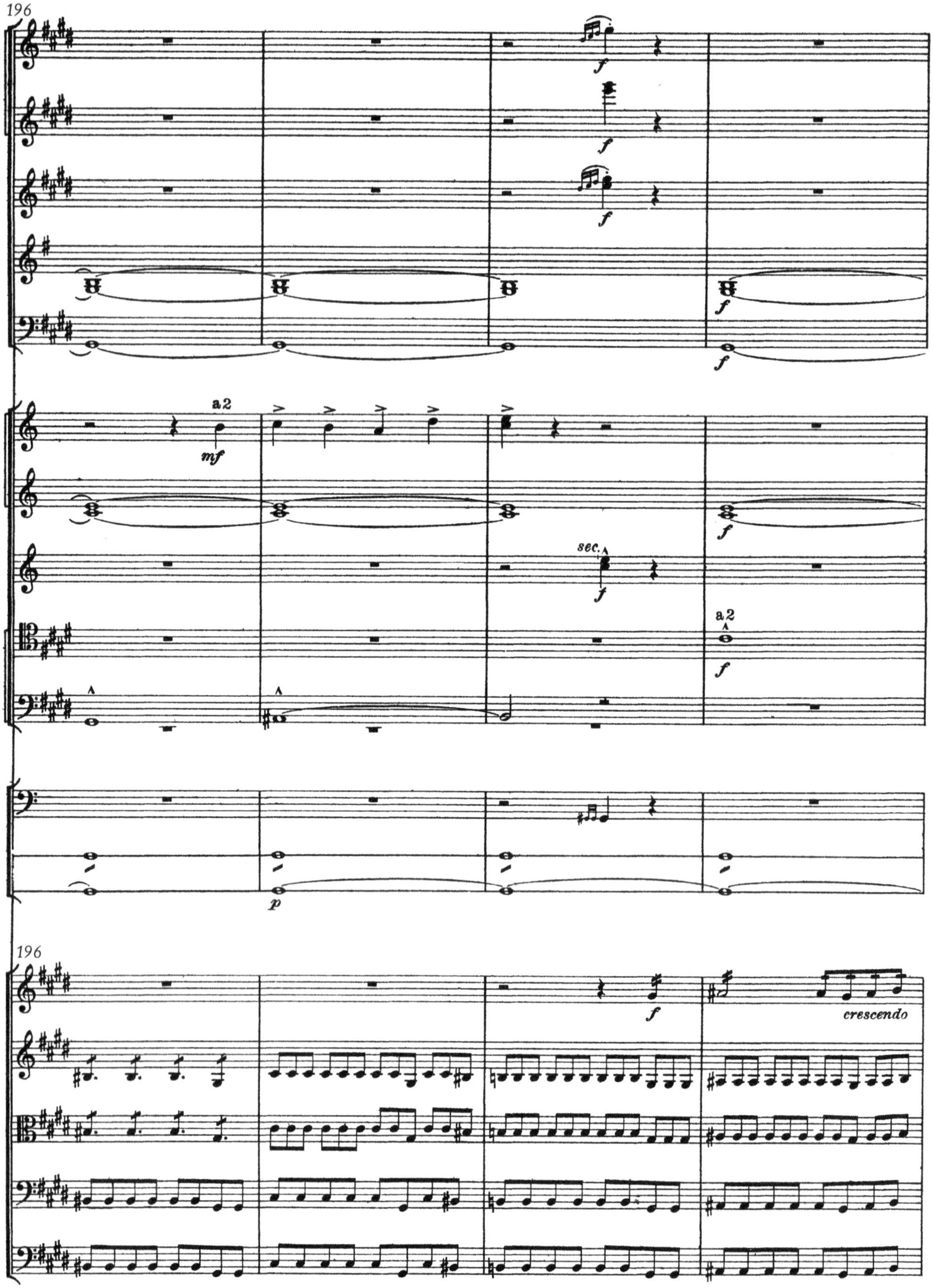
196
a2
mf
sec.
a2
p
196
crescendo

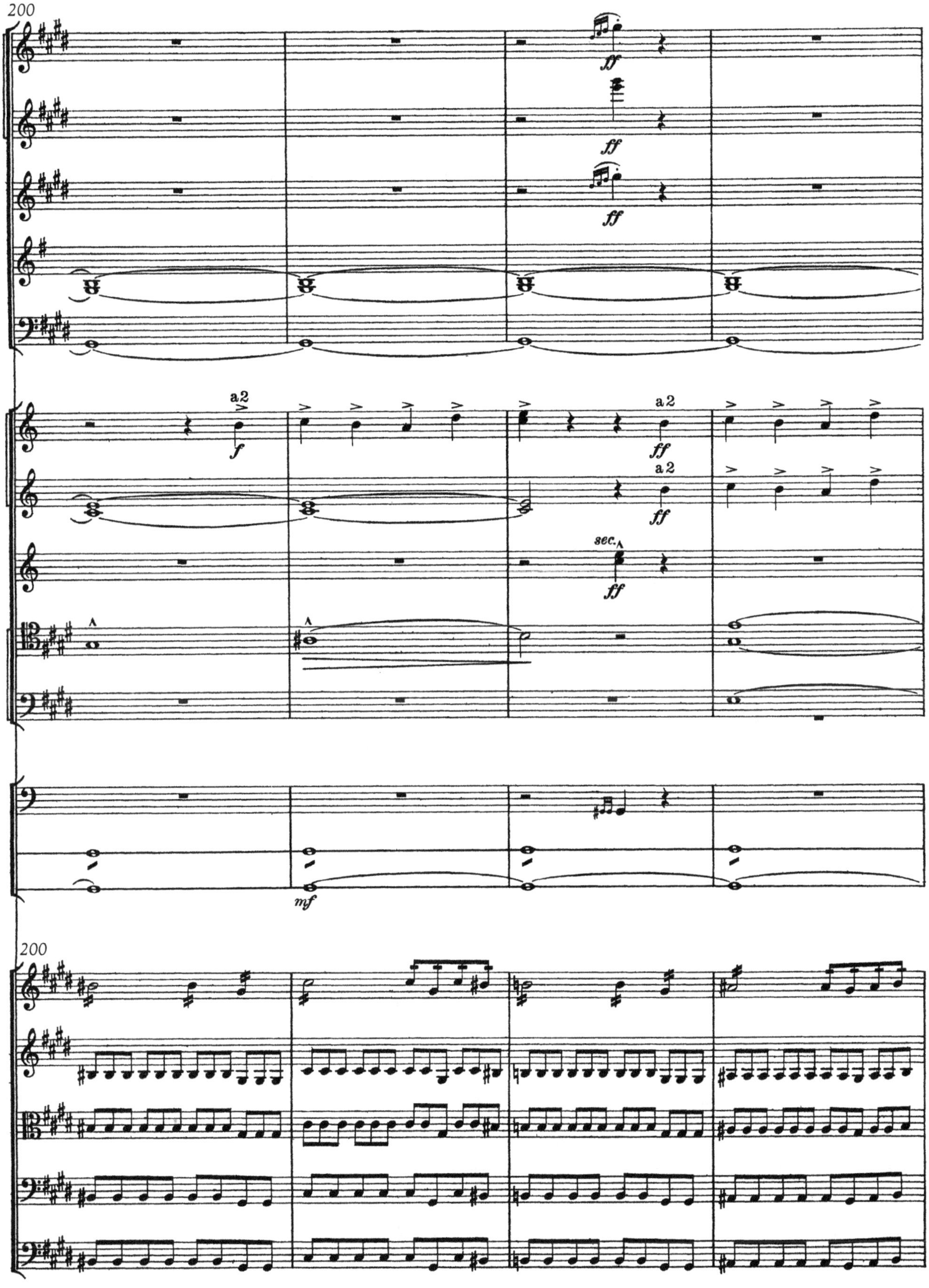
200
ff
ff
ff
a2
f
a2
ff
a2
ff
sec.
ff
mf
200

L Molto Allegro

L Molto Allegro

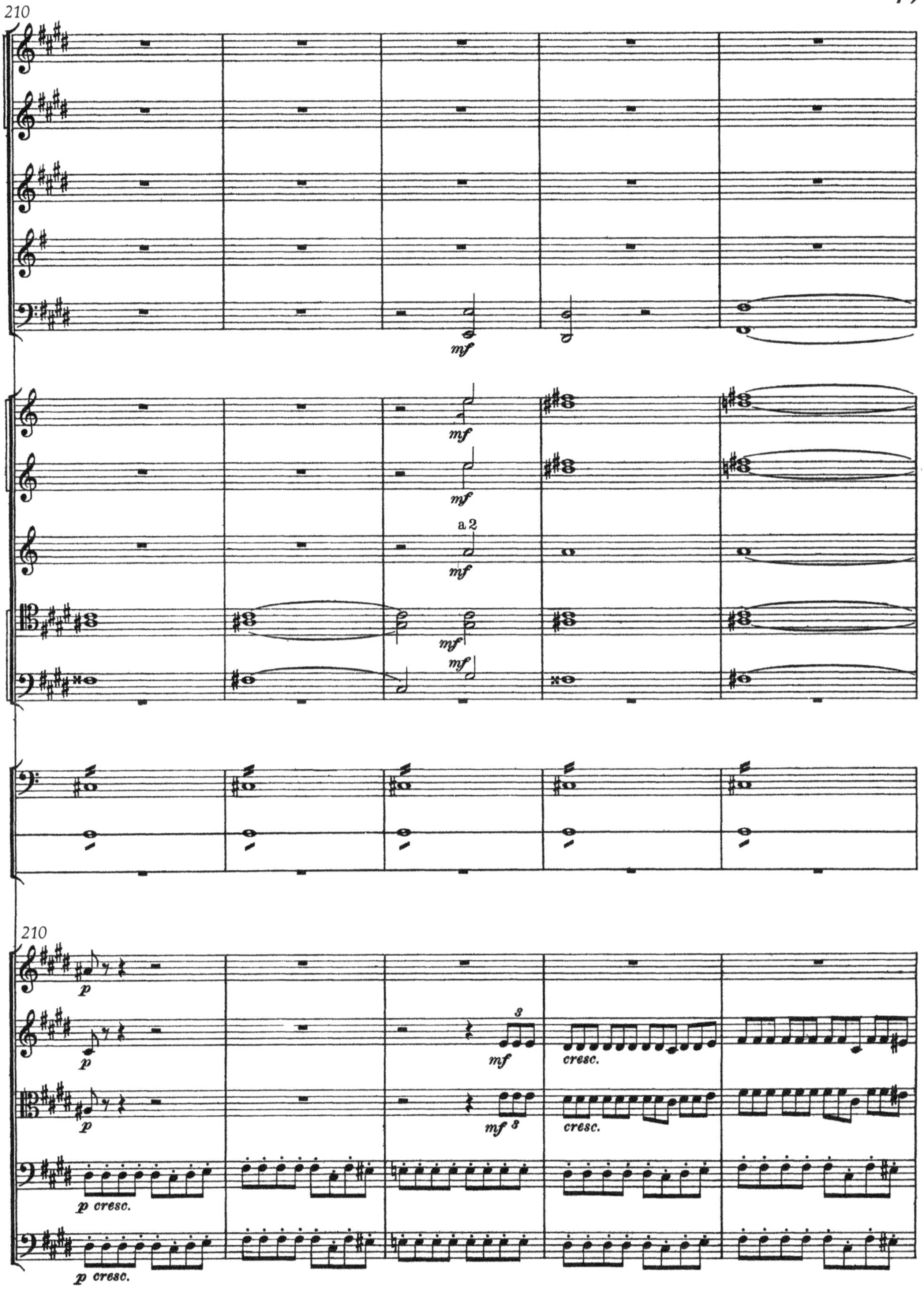
210
mf
mf
mf
a 2
mf
mf
mf
210
p
p
mf
cresc.
p
mf
cresc.
p cresc.
p cresc.

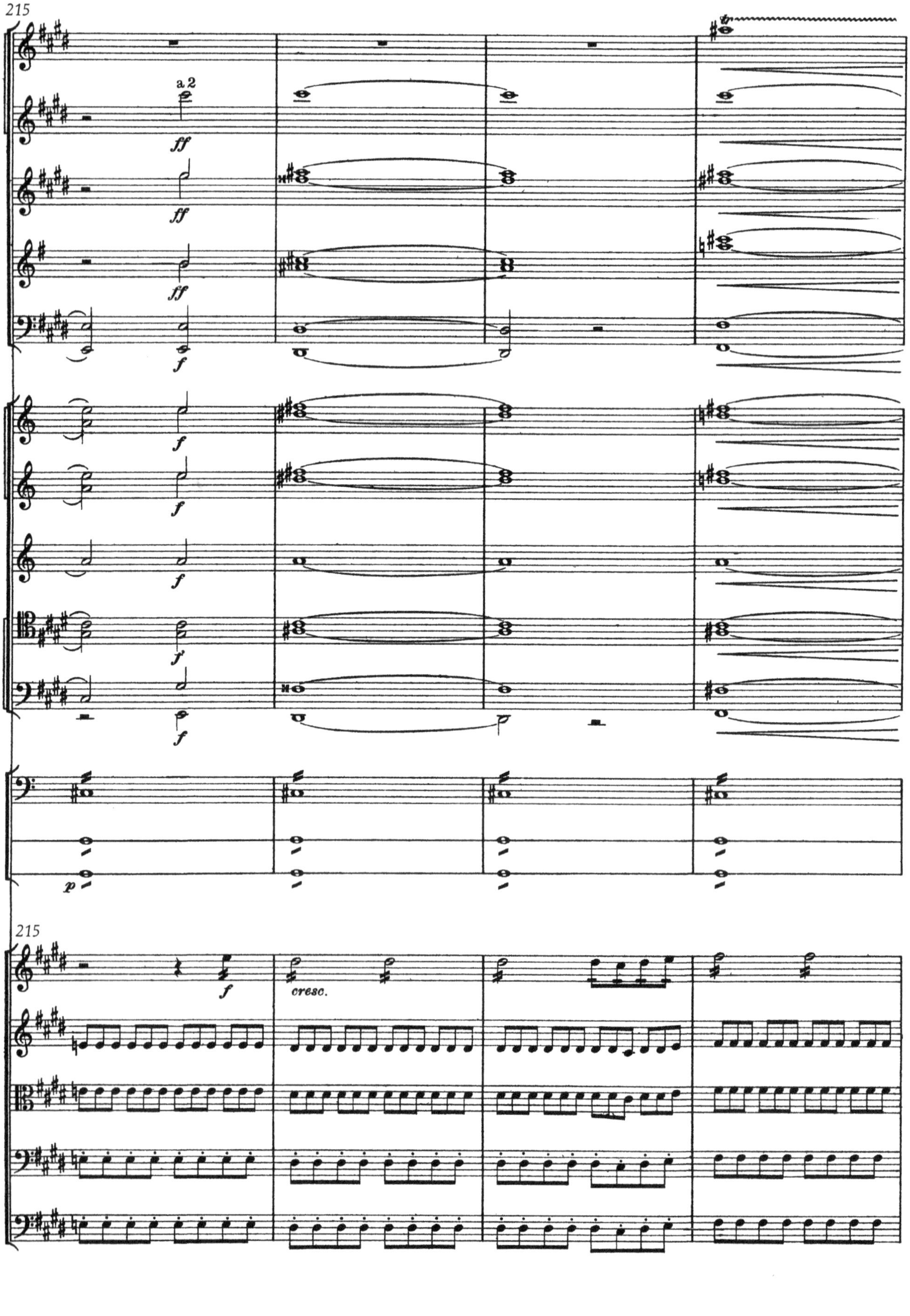
215
a 2
ff
f
p
cresc.

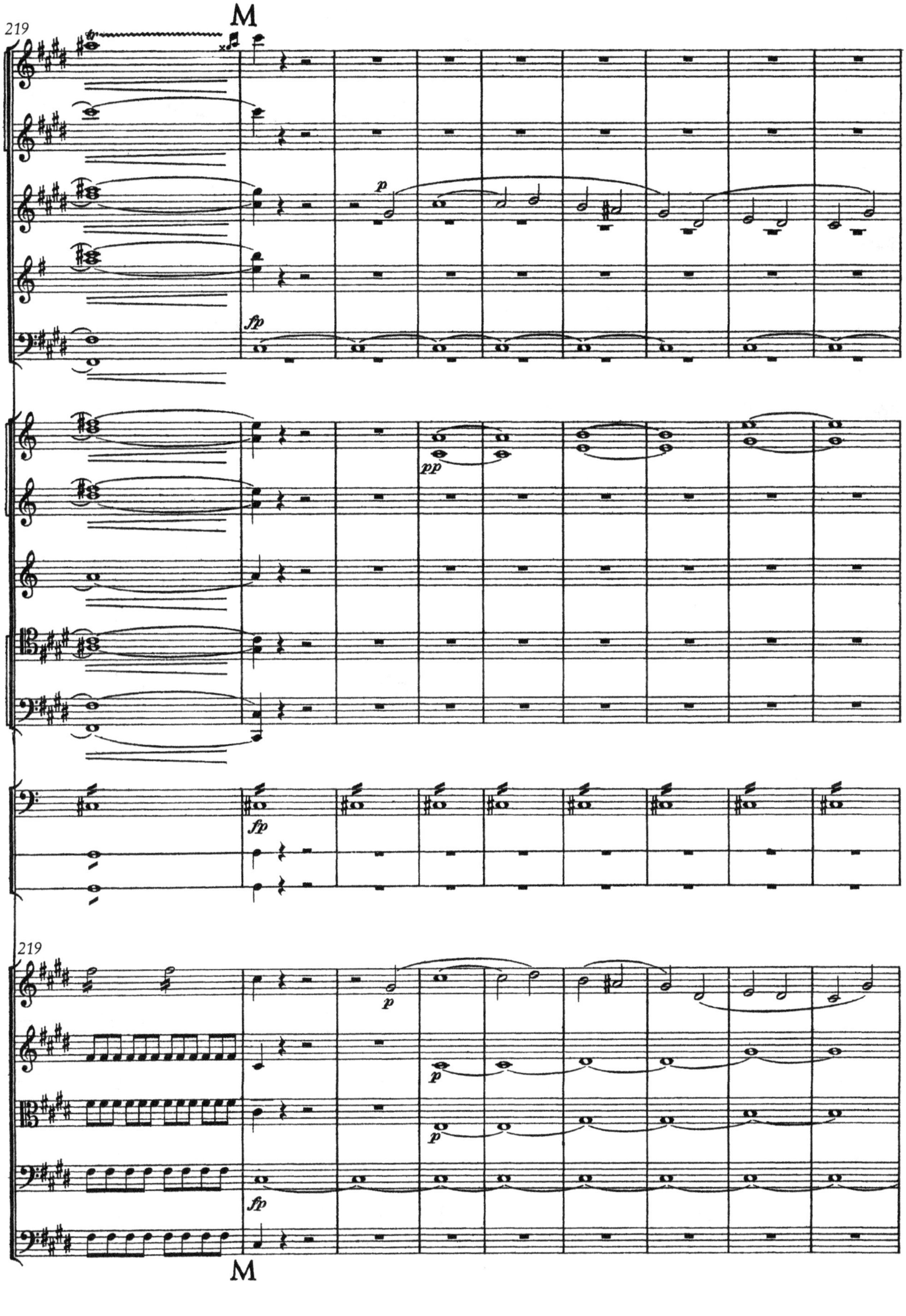
M
219
p
fp
pp
p
p
p
fp
M

poco a poco riten.

poco a poco riten.

III

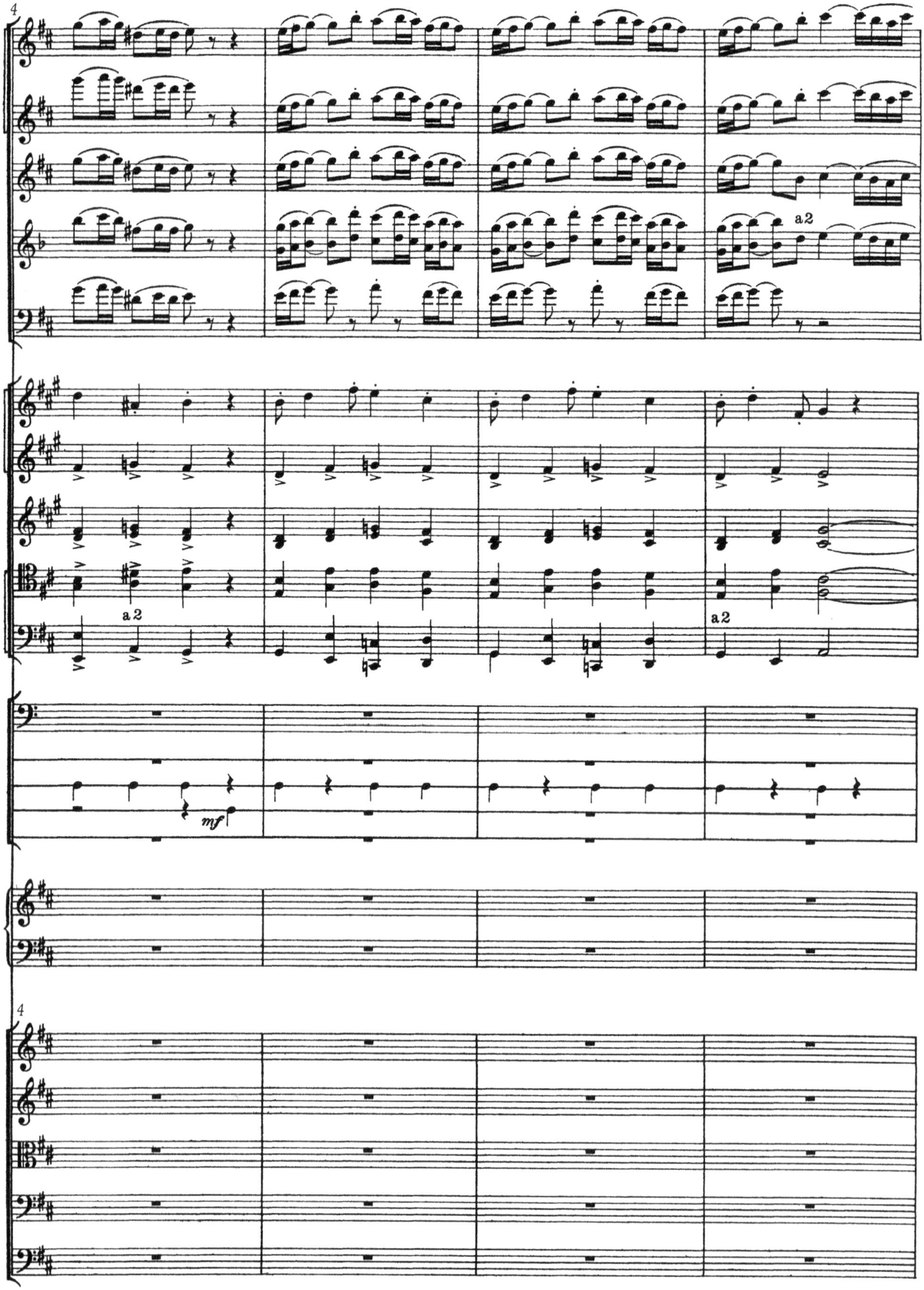
4
a2
a2
a2
mf
4

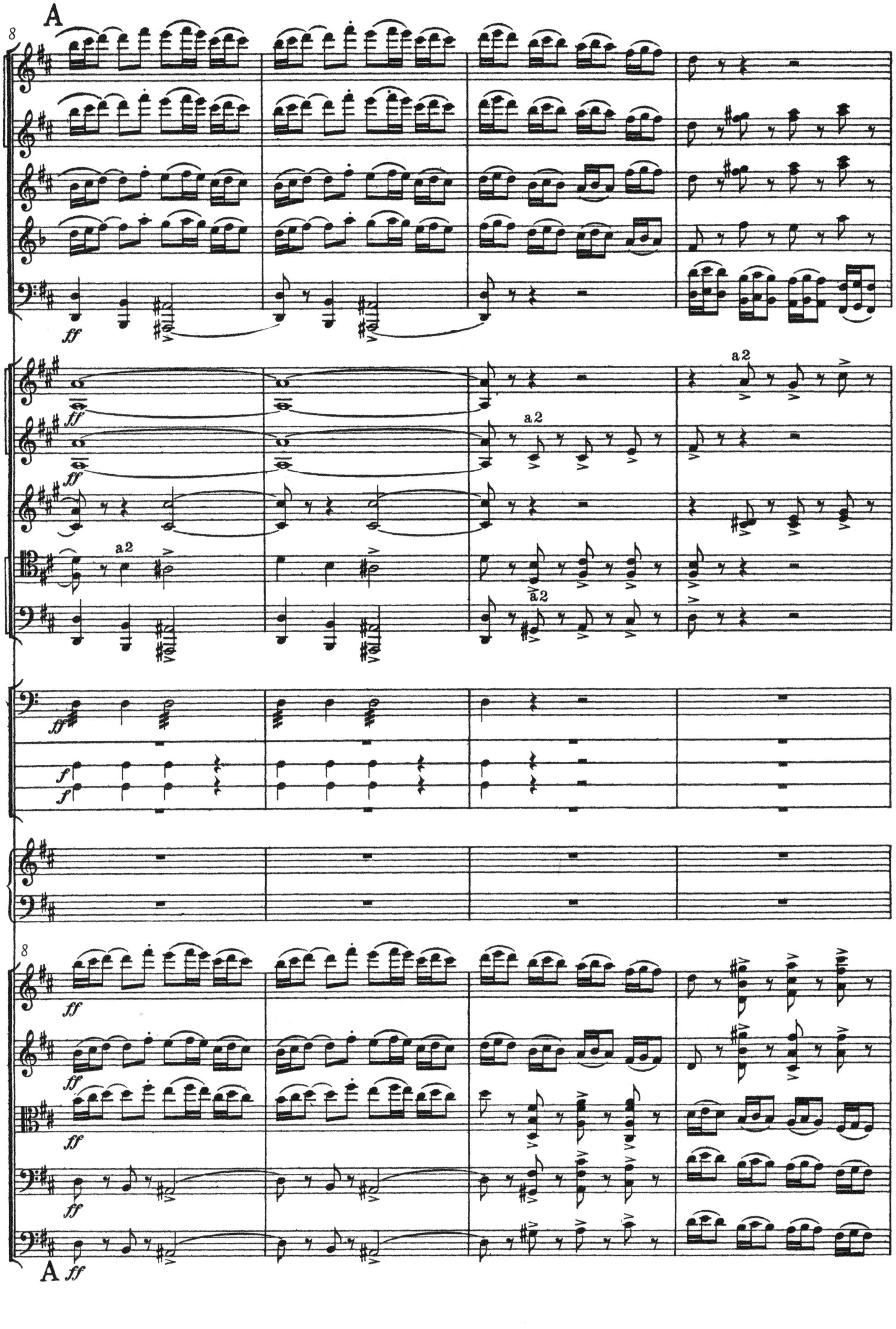
A
8
ff
a2
f
8
ff
A

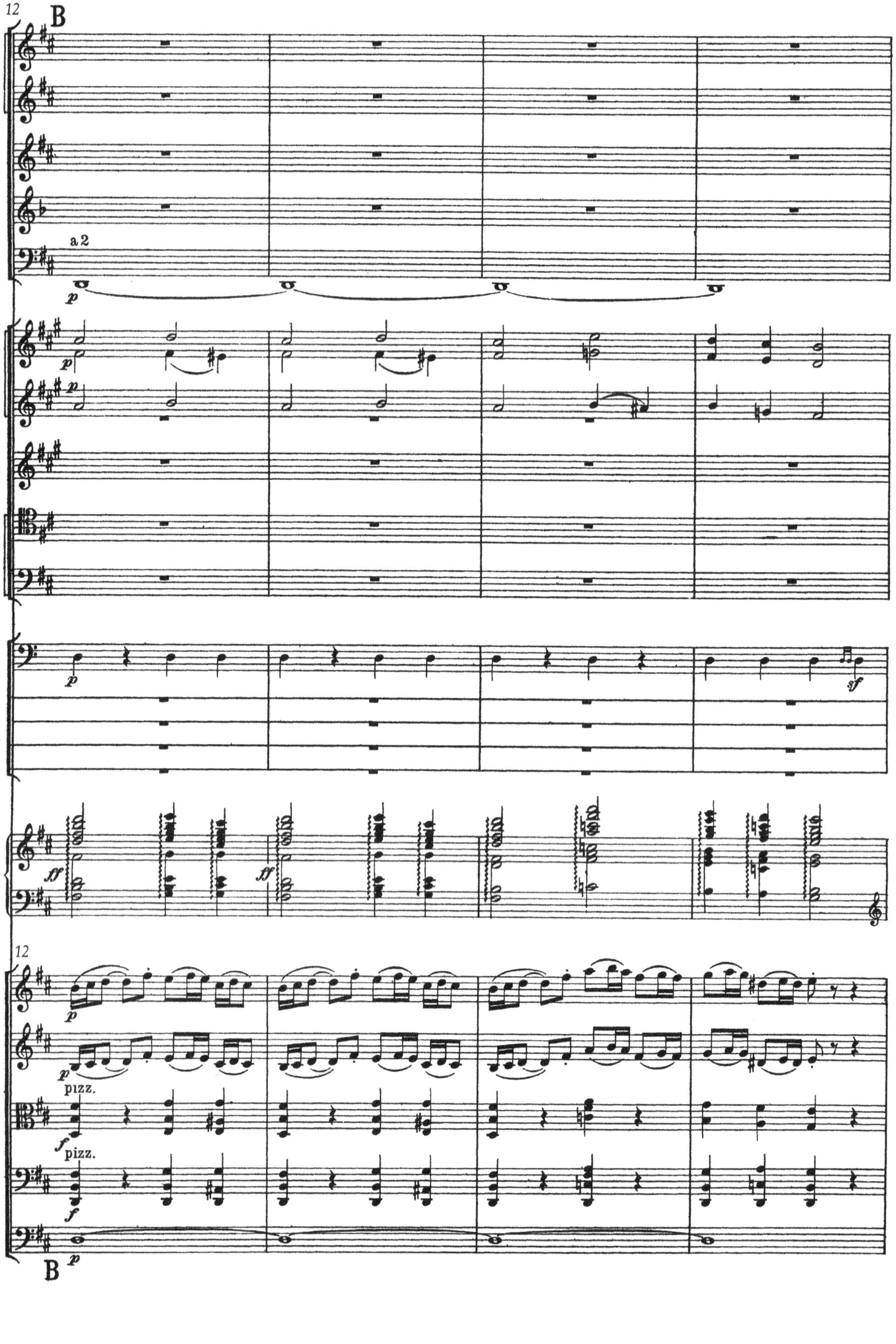
12
B
a 2
p
ff
sf
pizz.
f
pizz.
f
12
B

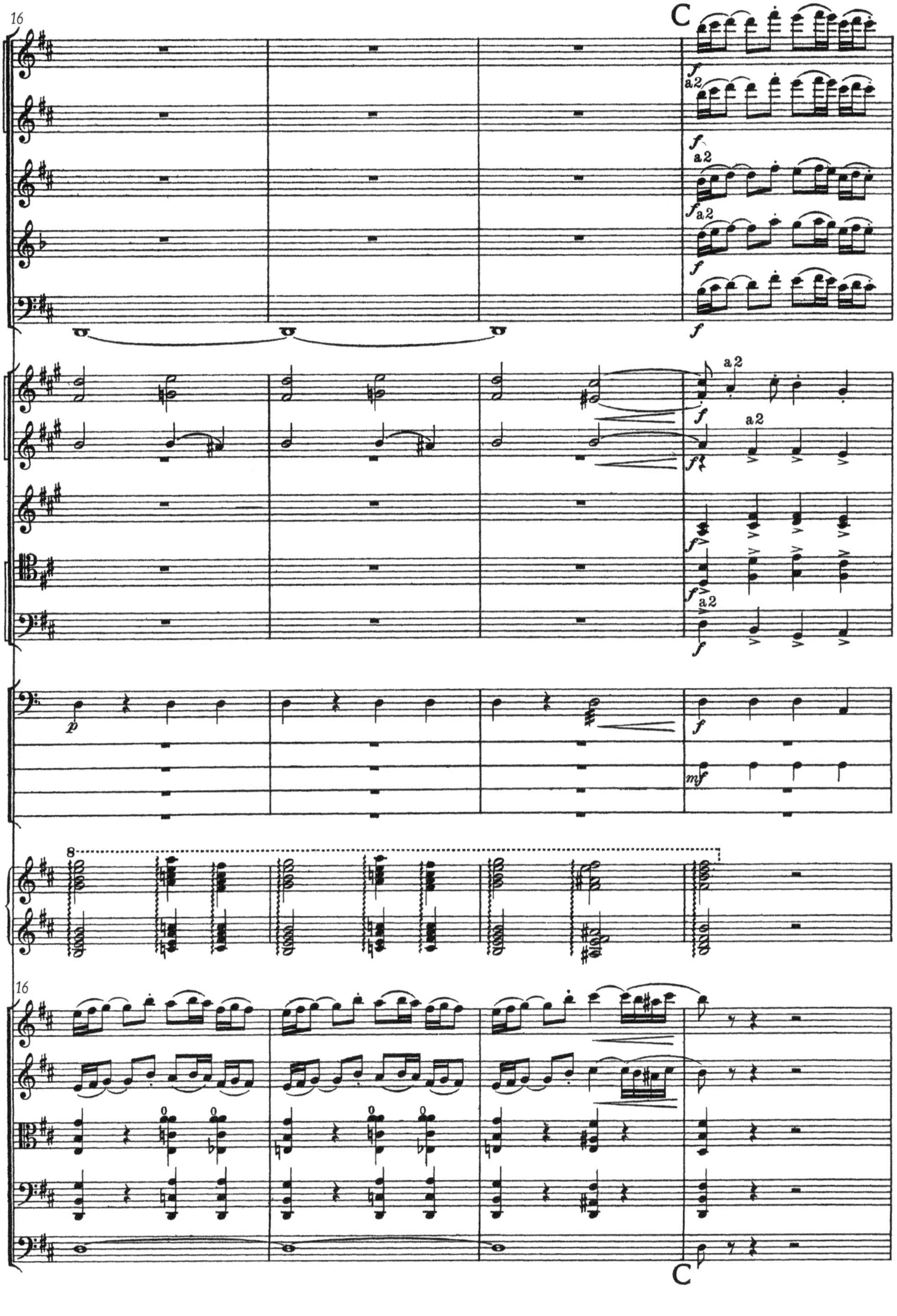
16
C
a2
f
mf
p
8
C

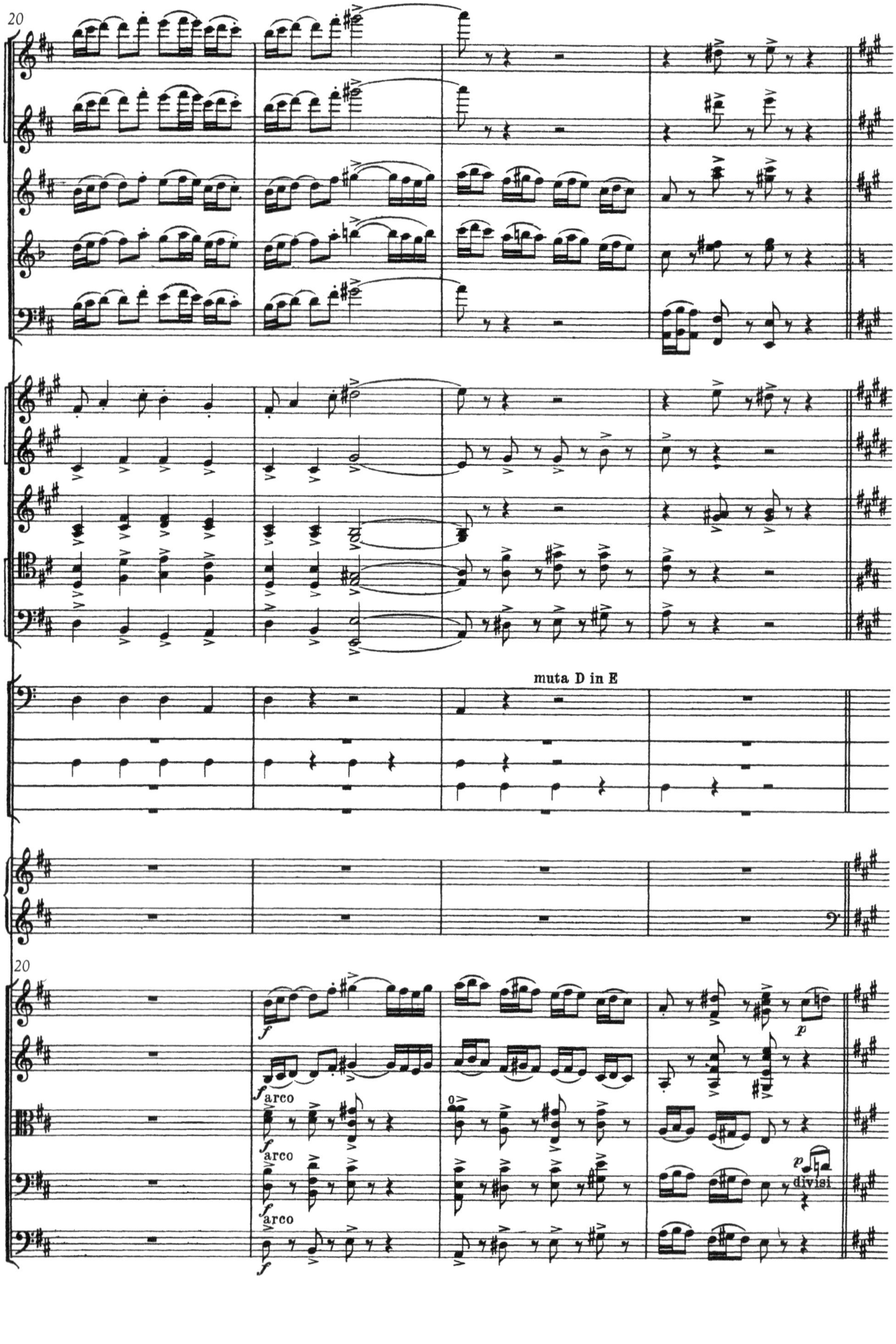
20
muta D in E
20
f
arco
f
arco
f
arco
f
p
p
divisi

D
Viol. I
Viol. II divisi
Vcell. div.
pizz.
Cb.
pizz.
D
Fl.
Clar. in A
a 2
Fag.
Cor. I II in F
Solo
Vle

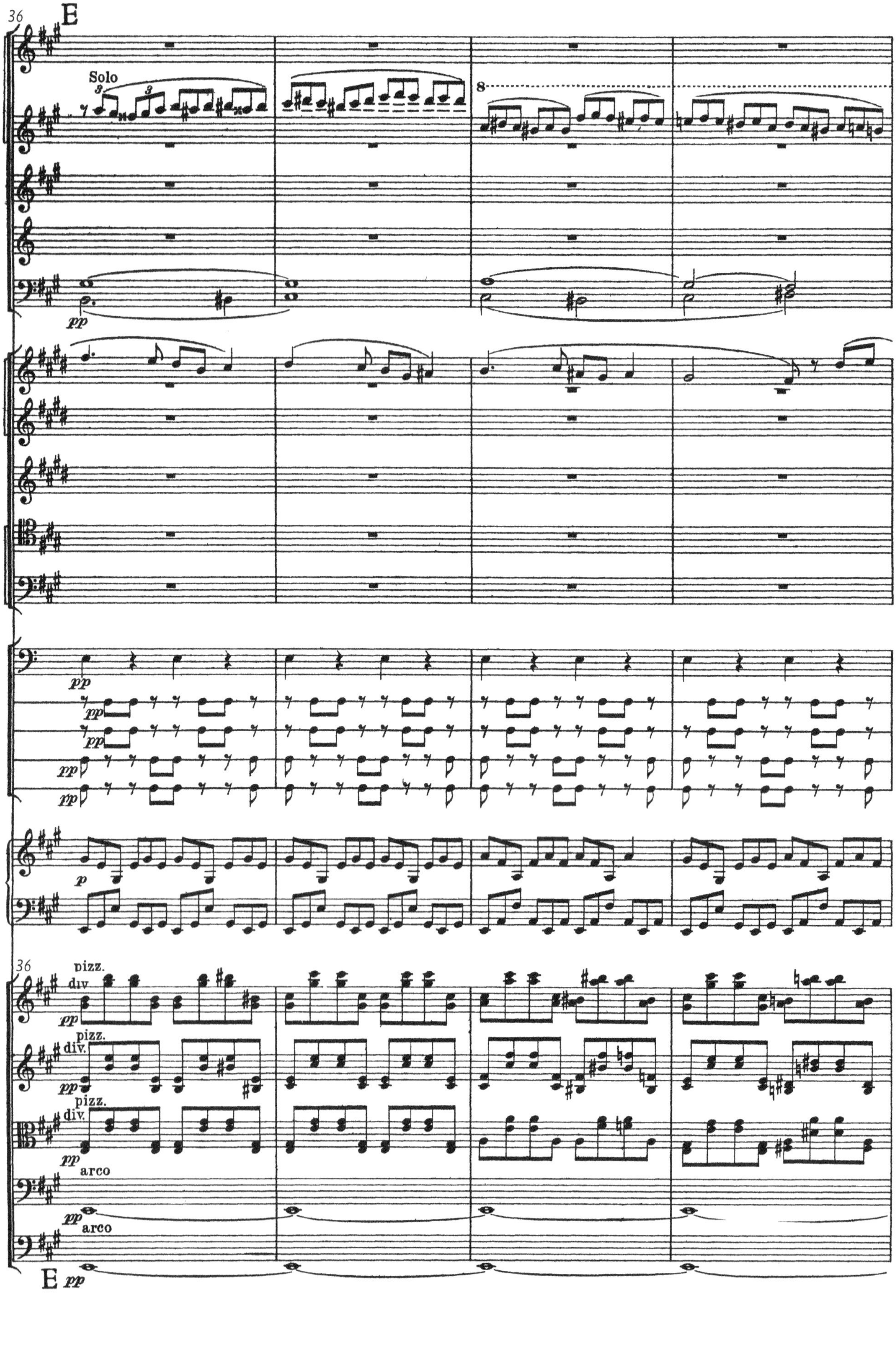
36
E
Solo
8
pp
p
pizz.
div.
arco
E

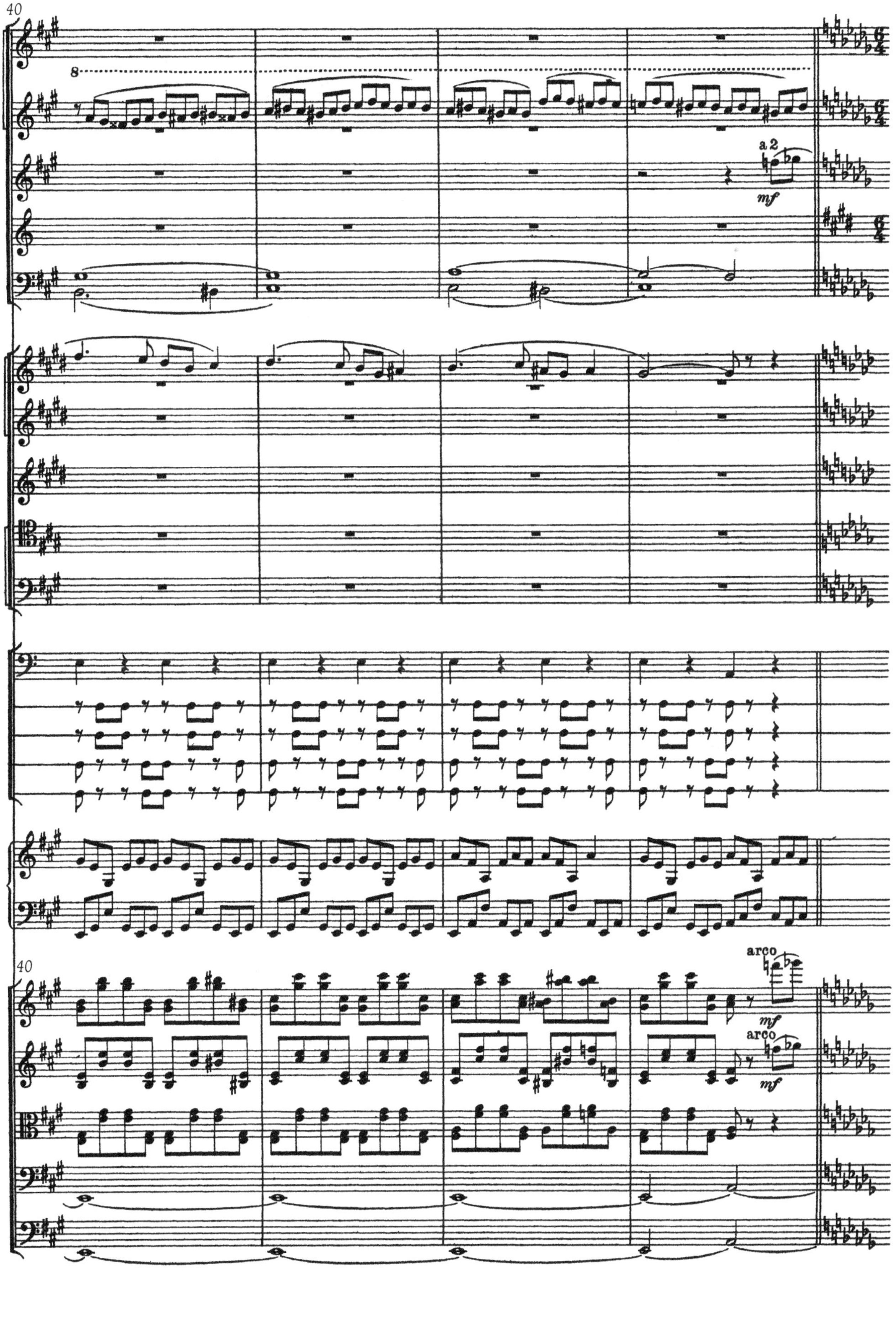
40
8
a 2
mf
40
arco
mf
arco
mf

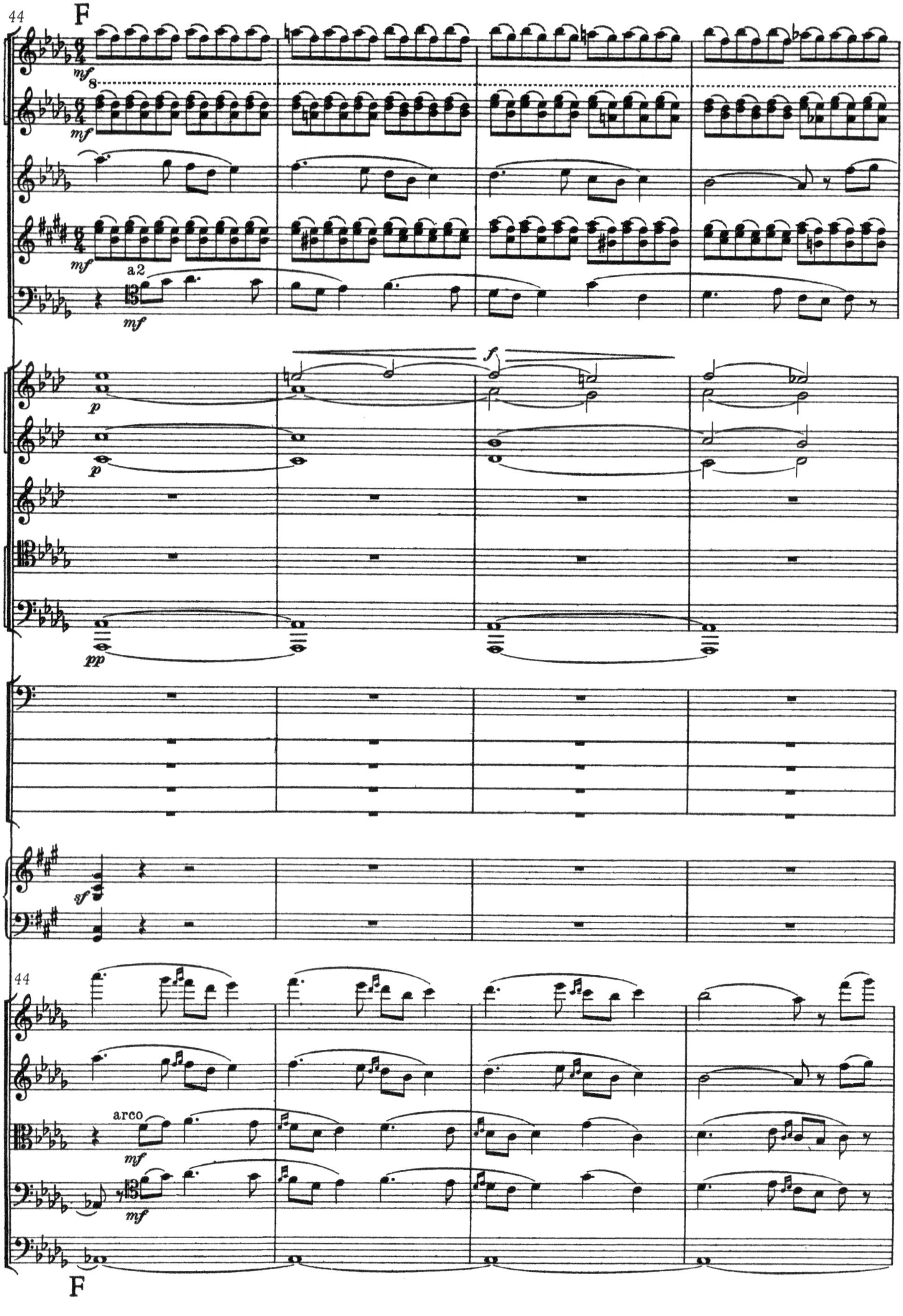
44
F
mf
a2
p
f
pp
sf
arco

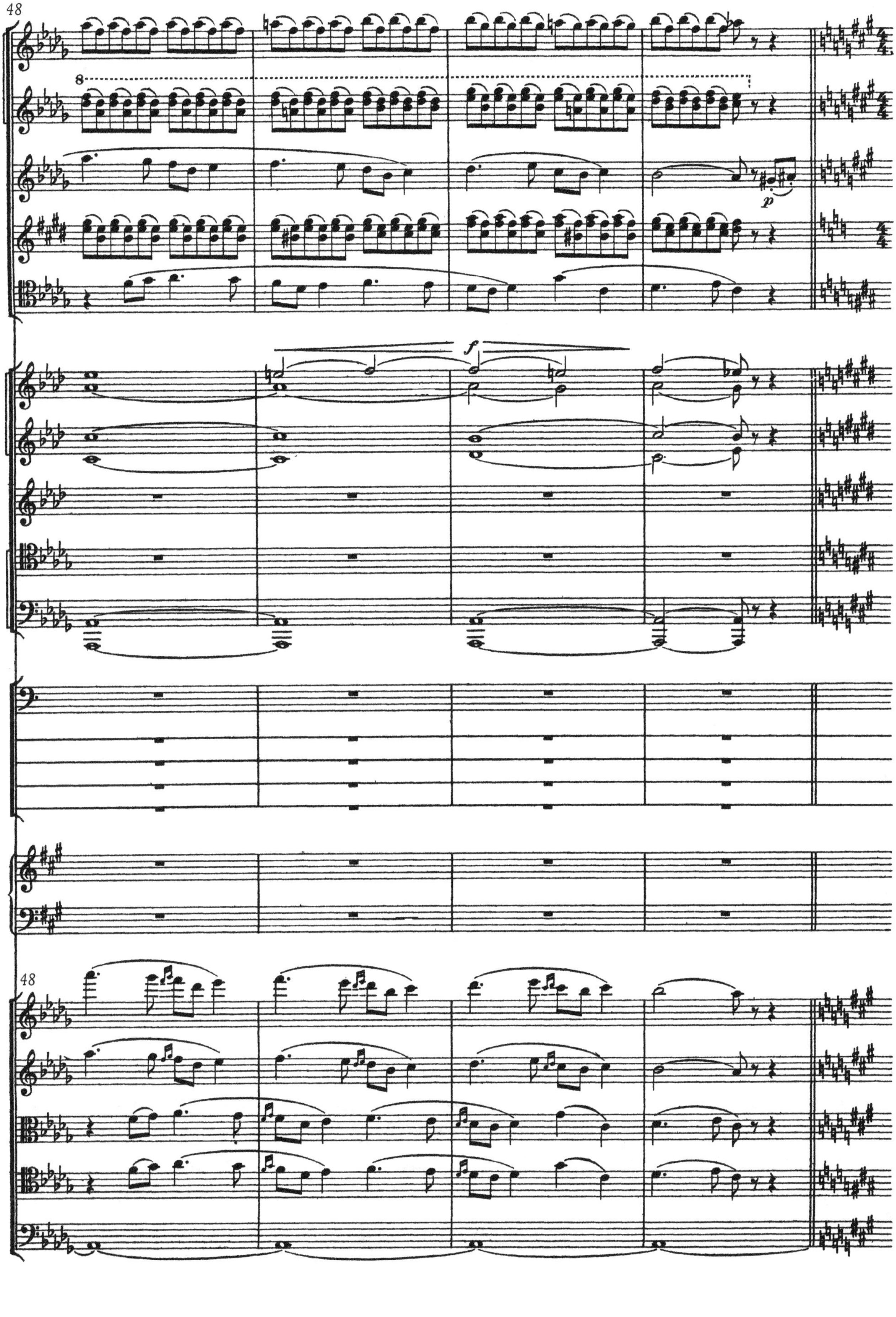
48
8
p
f
48

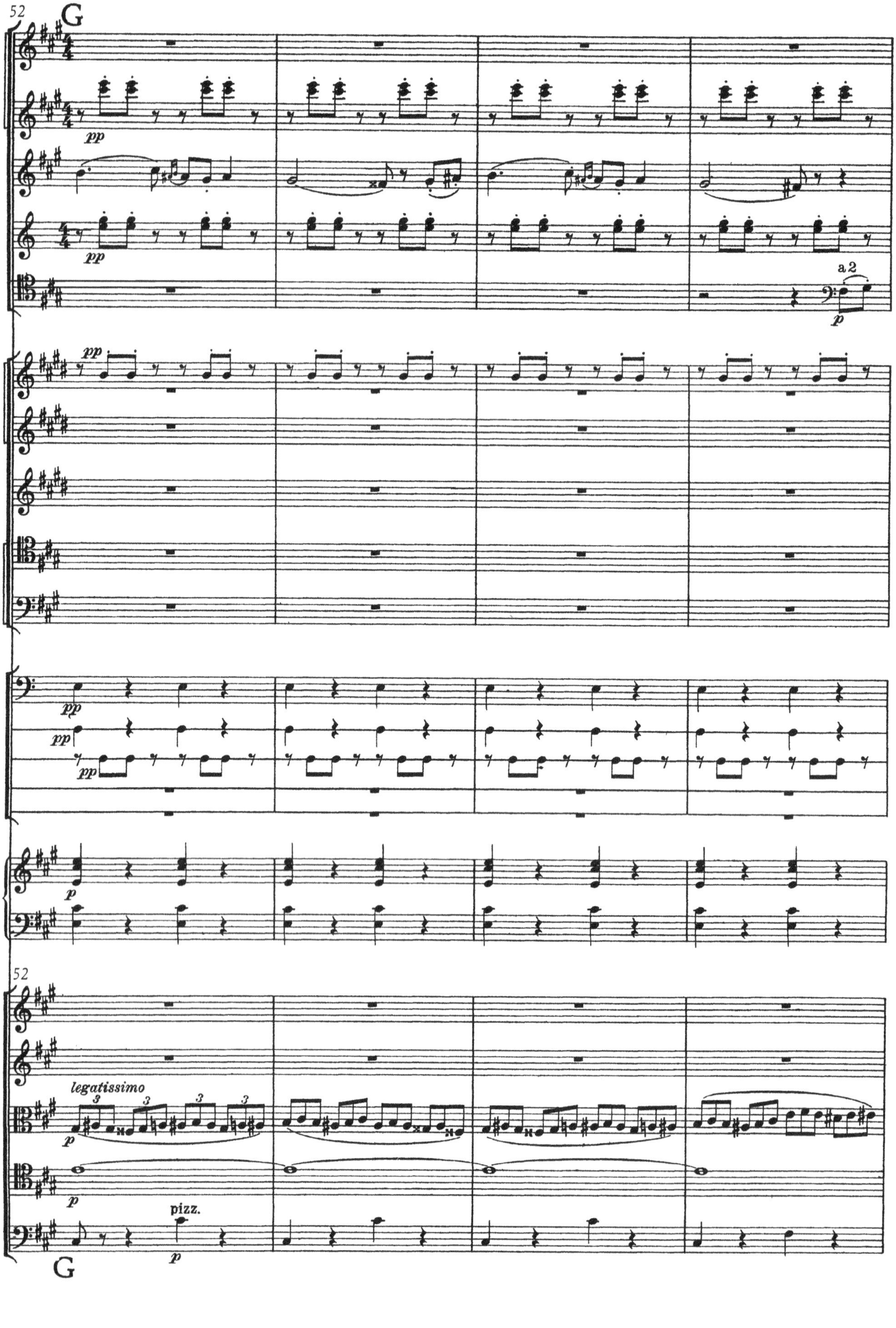
52
G
pp
pp
a 2
p
pp
pp
pp
pp
p
52
legatissimo
3
p
p
pizz.
p
G

56
H
poco cresc.
poco cresc.
poco cresc.
mf
poco cresc.
pp
56
p
poco cresc.
mf
p poco cresc.
mf
p
poco cresc.
poco cresc.
mf
poco cresc.
H

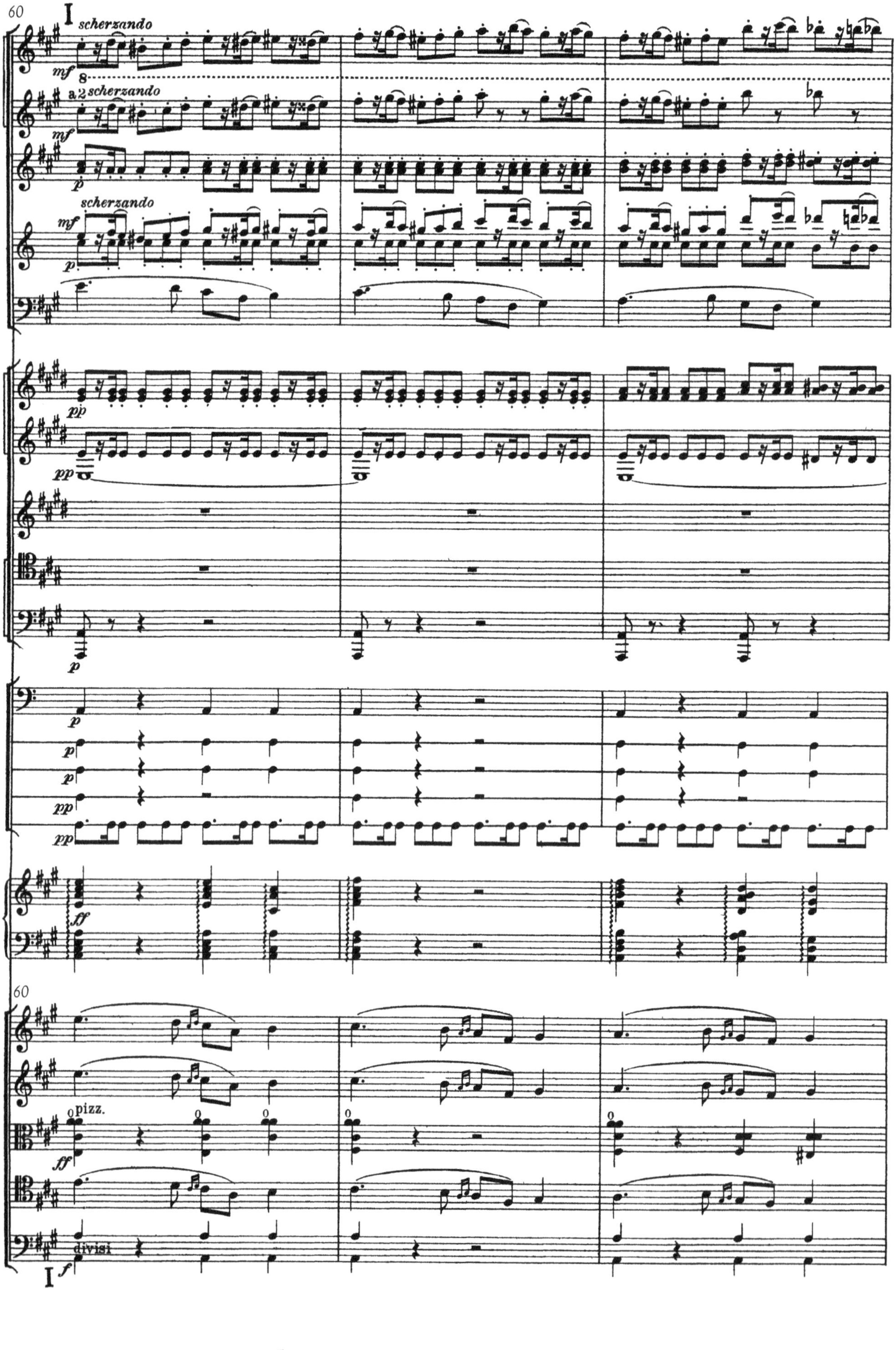
60
I
scherzando
a 2 scherzando
scherzando
60
pizz.
divisi
I

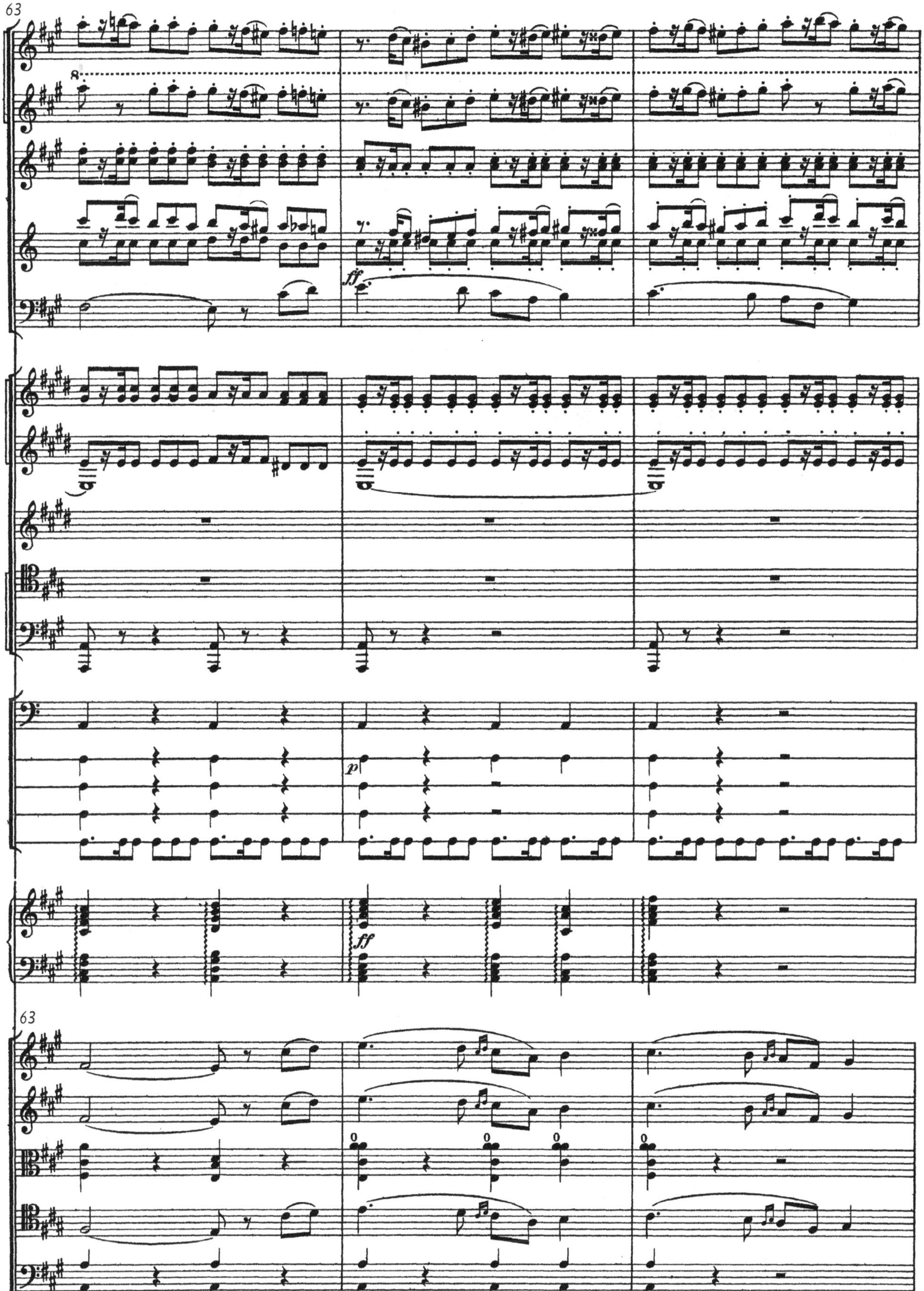
63
ff
p
ff
63

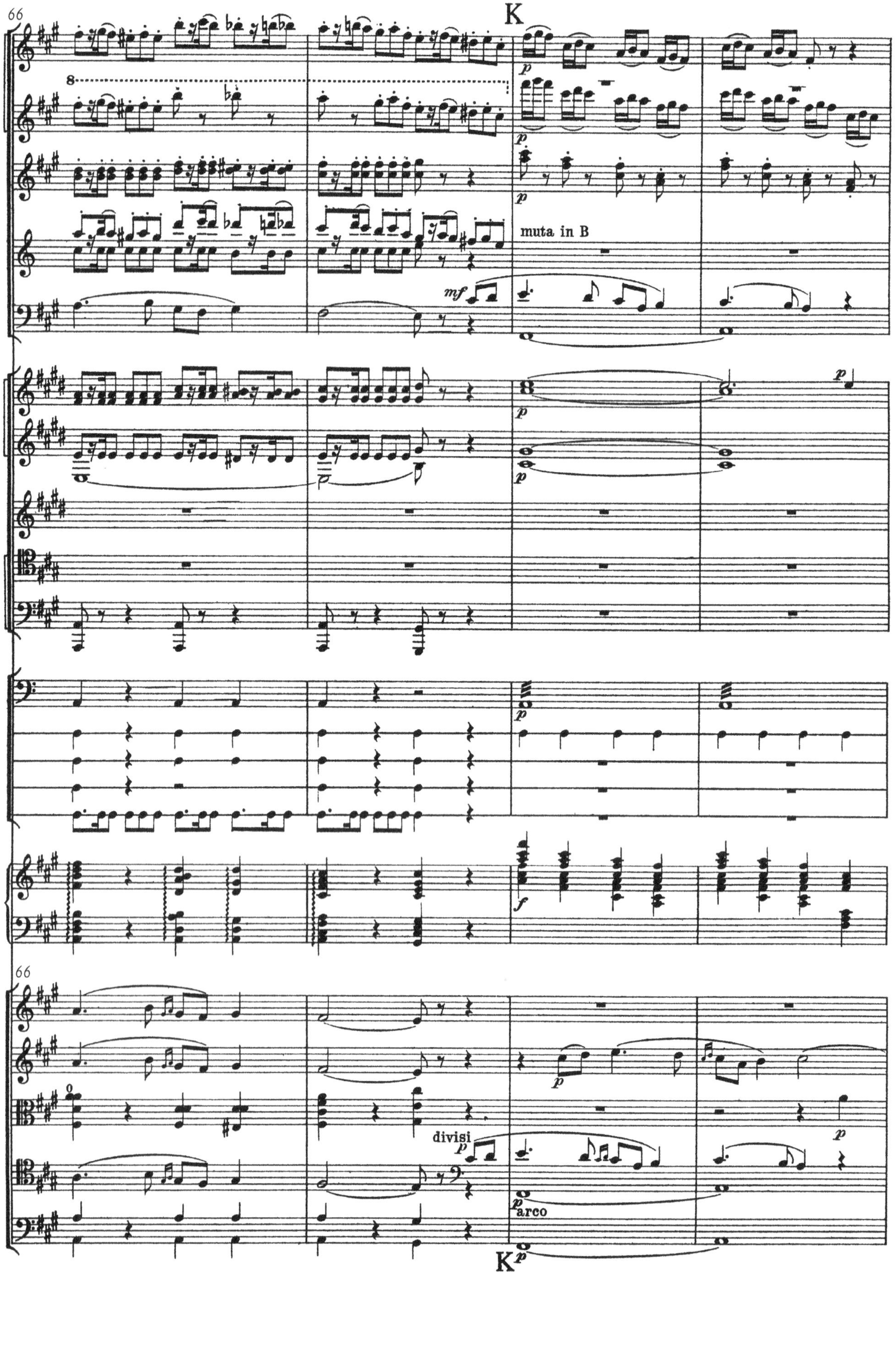
66
K
8
p
mf
muta in B
f
divisi
arco
66
K

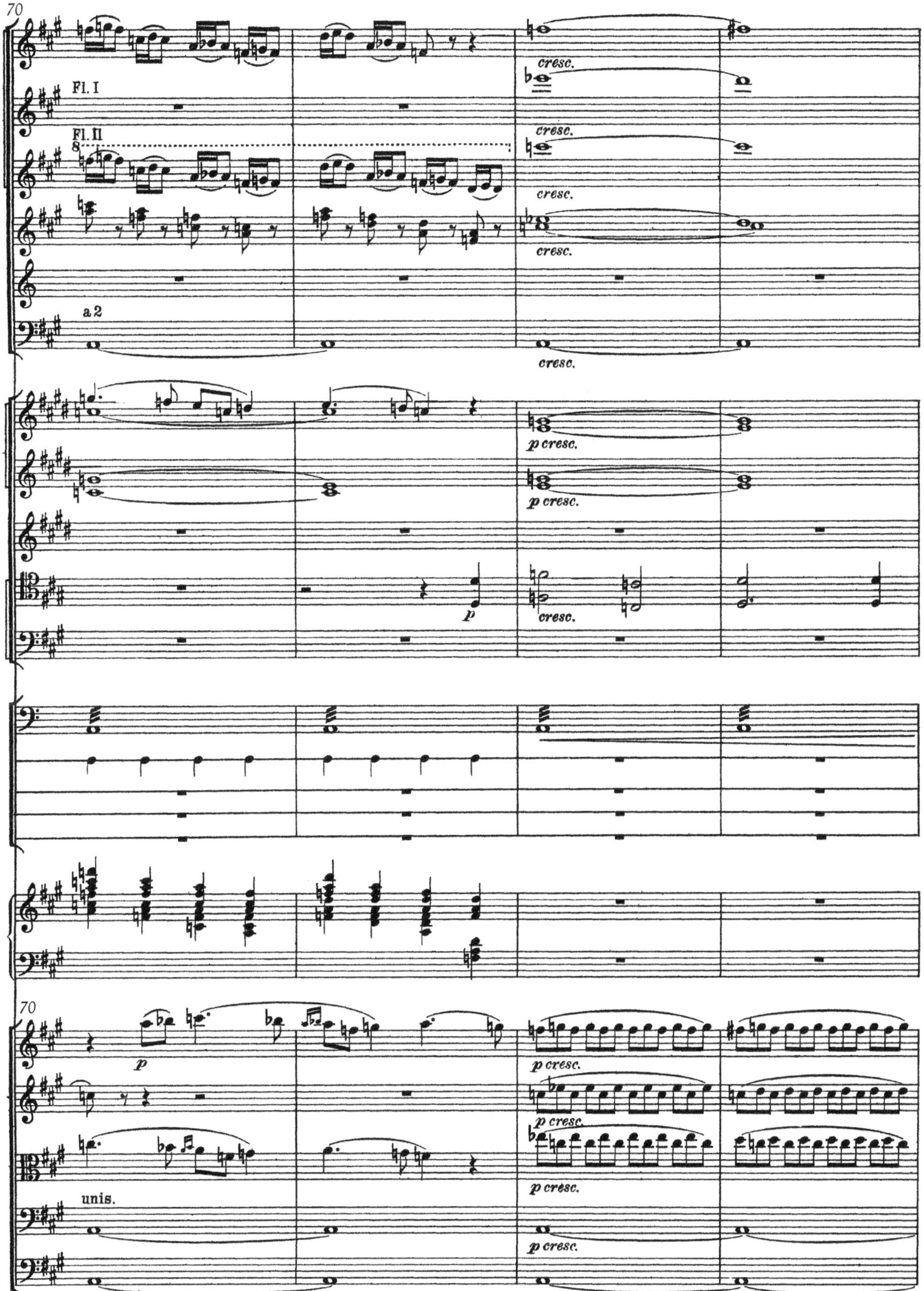
70
Fl. I
Fl. II
8
cresc.
a 2
p cresc.
p
unis.

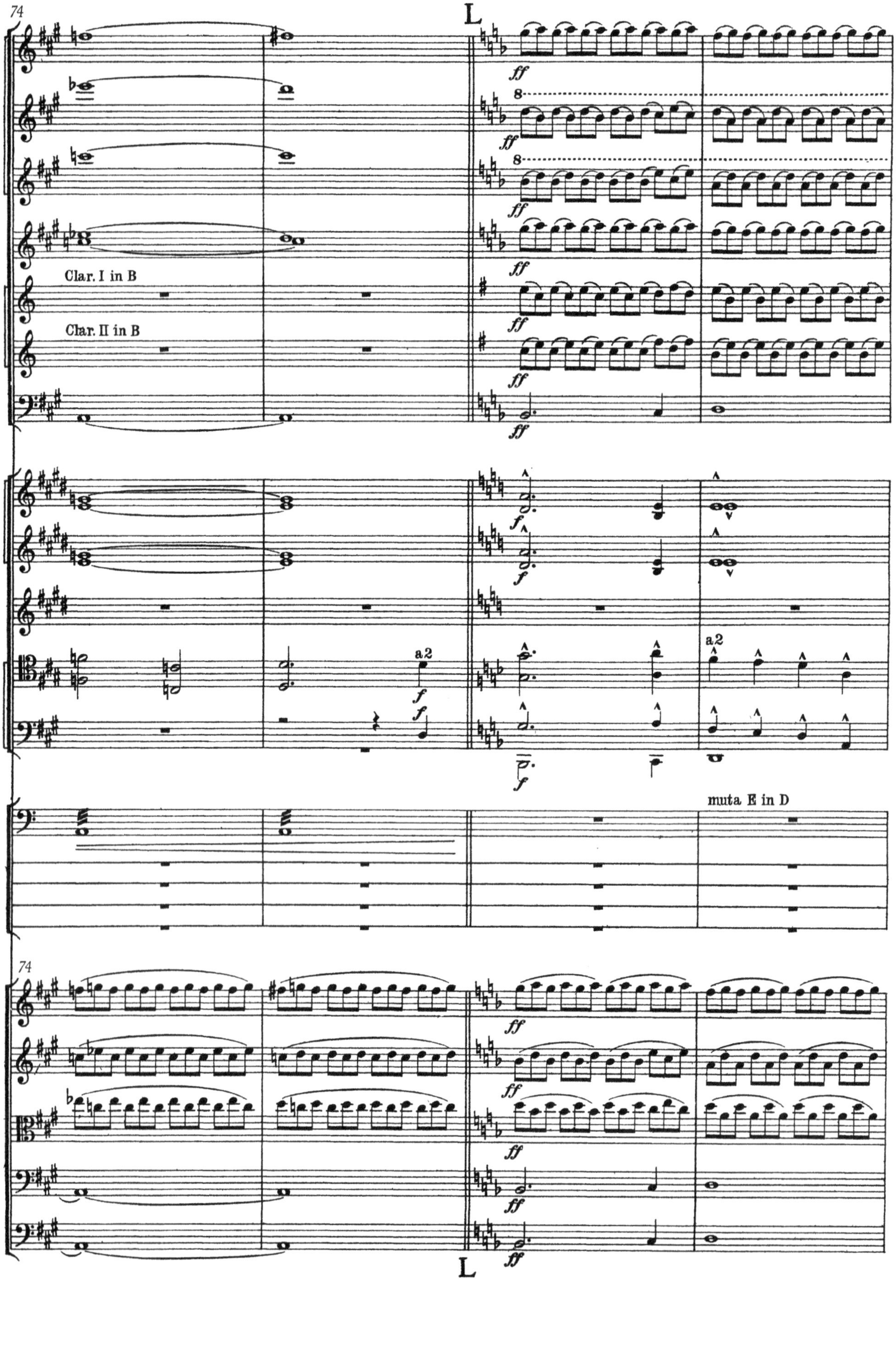
74
L
Clar. I in B
Clar. II in B
ff
8
f
a2
muta E in D
74
L

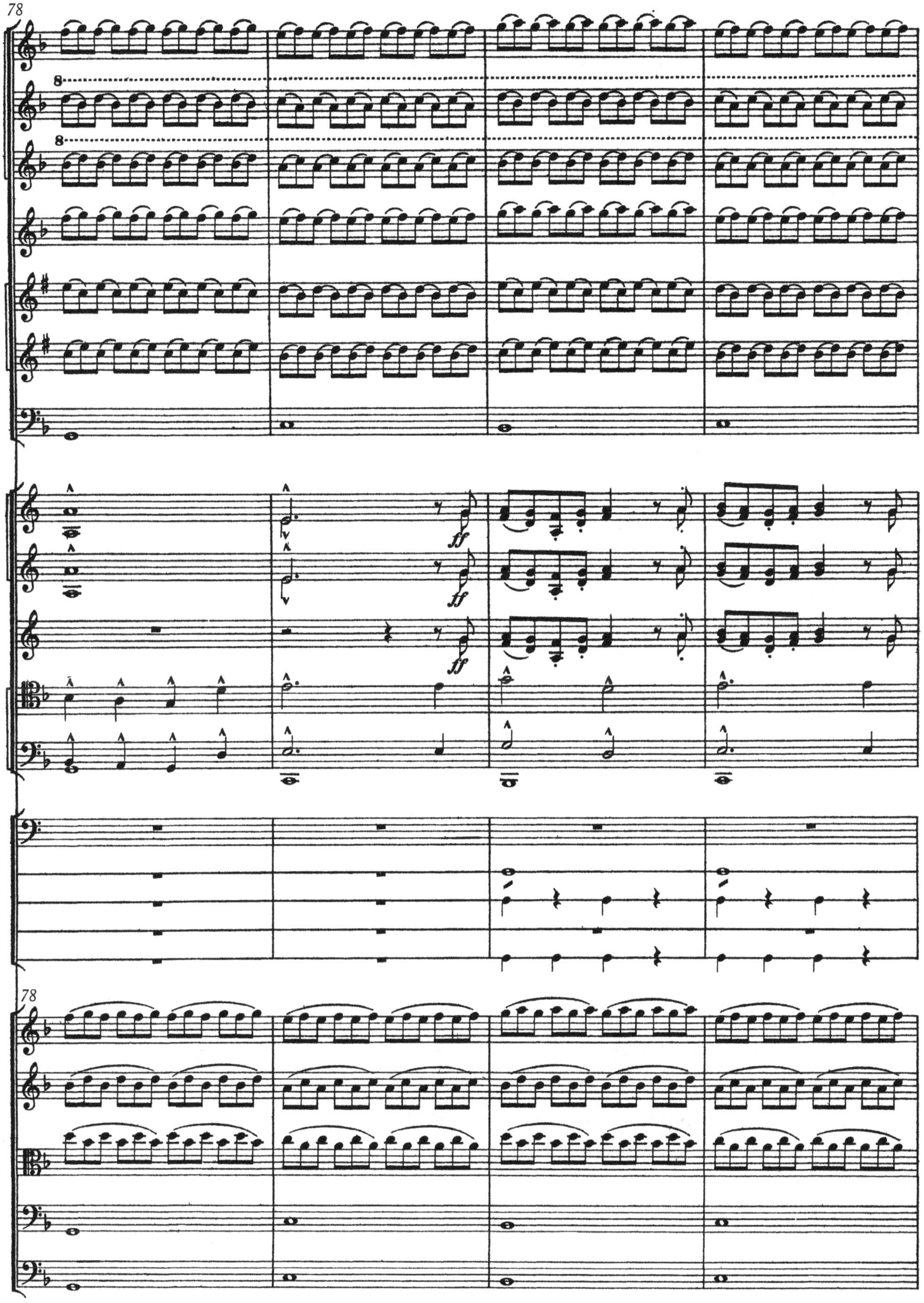
78
8
8
ff
ff
ff
78

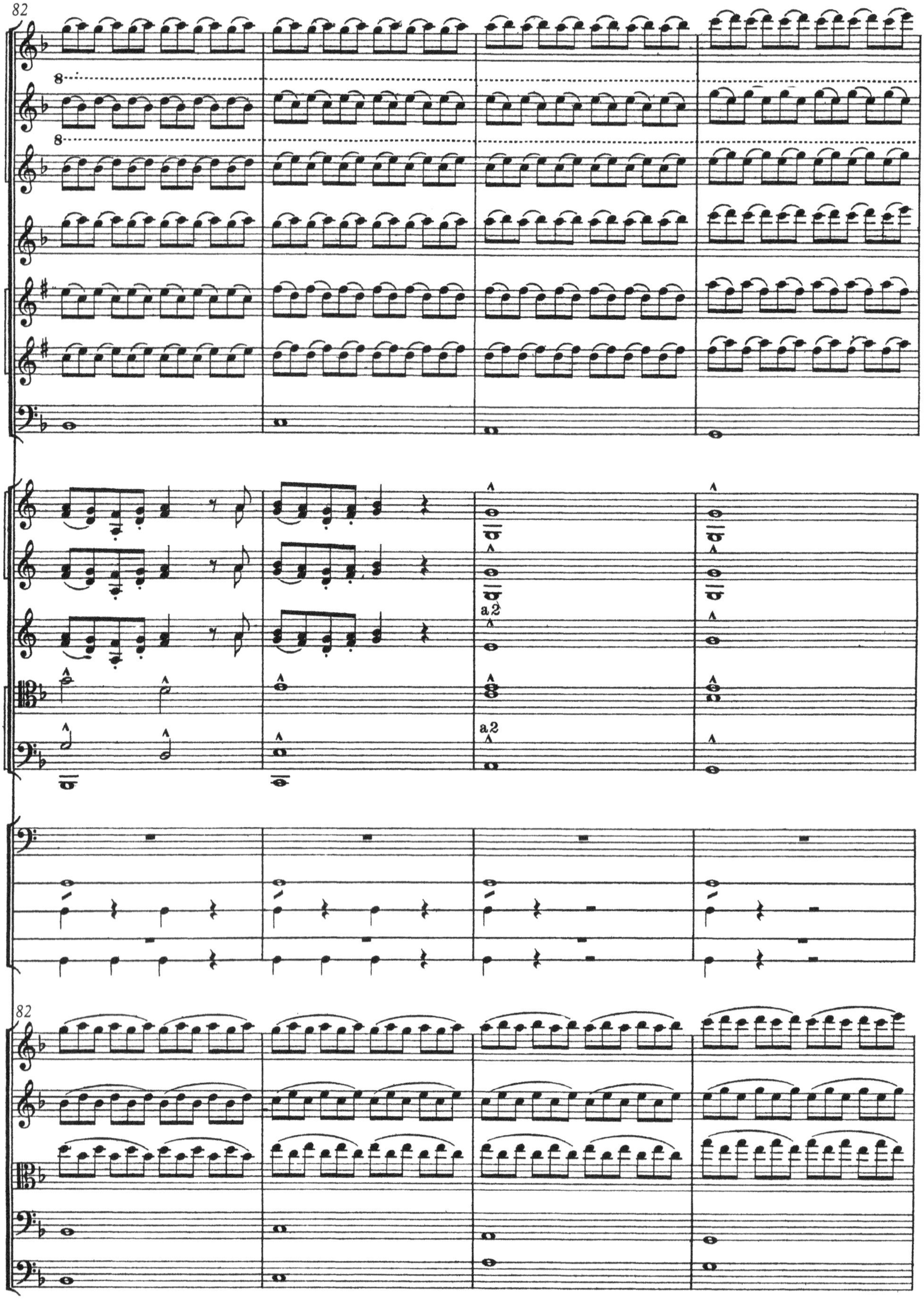
82
a 2
a 2
82

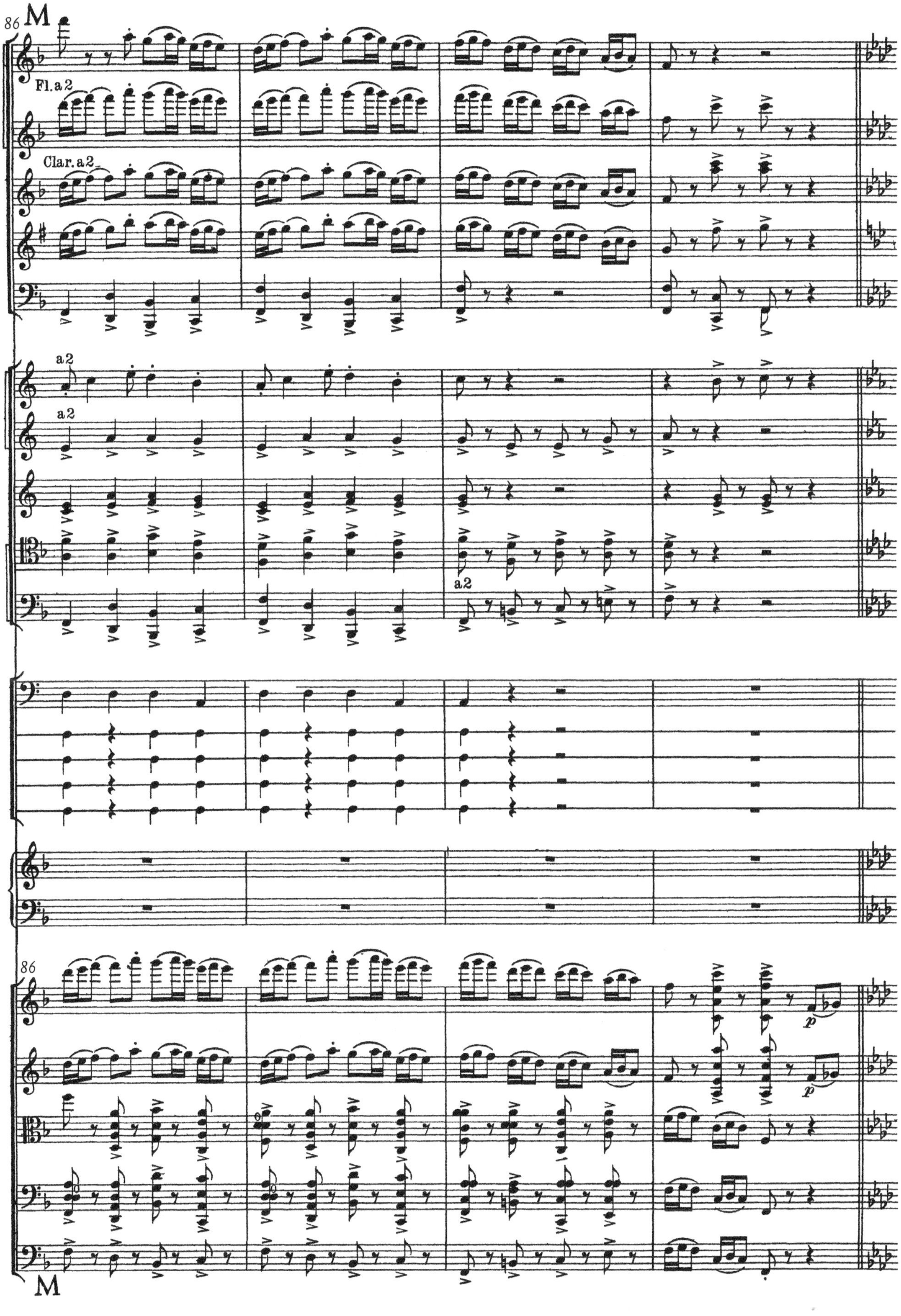
86
M
Fl. a 2
Clar. a 2
a2
a2
a2
86
p
p
M

90
N
Fl.
Clar. in B
90
Viol. I
sul G
Viol. II
sul G
Vle
divisi
pp
Vcell.
pizz.
pp
Cb.
pizz.
p
N
94
pp
pp
p
p
94

O
98
Ob.
pp
Fag.
pp
Cor. I II in F
pp
98
p
unis.
O
P
102
pp
a 2
p
pp
102
pizz.
p
pizz
p
pp
divisi
pp
arco
P
p

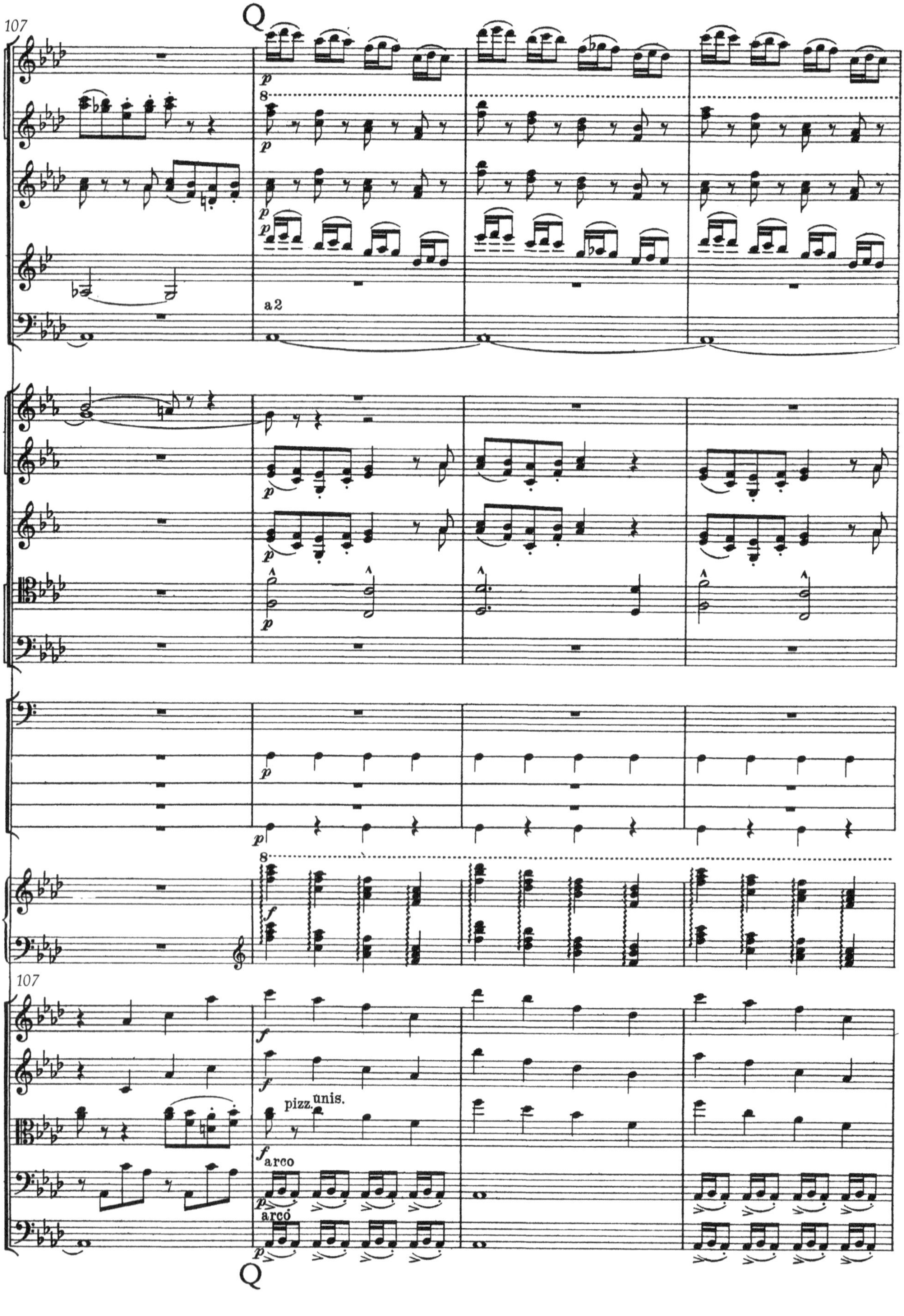
107
Q
p
8
a2
pizz.
unis.
arco
f
Q

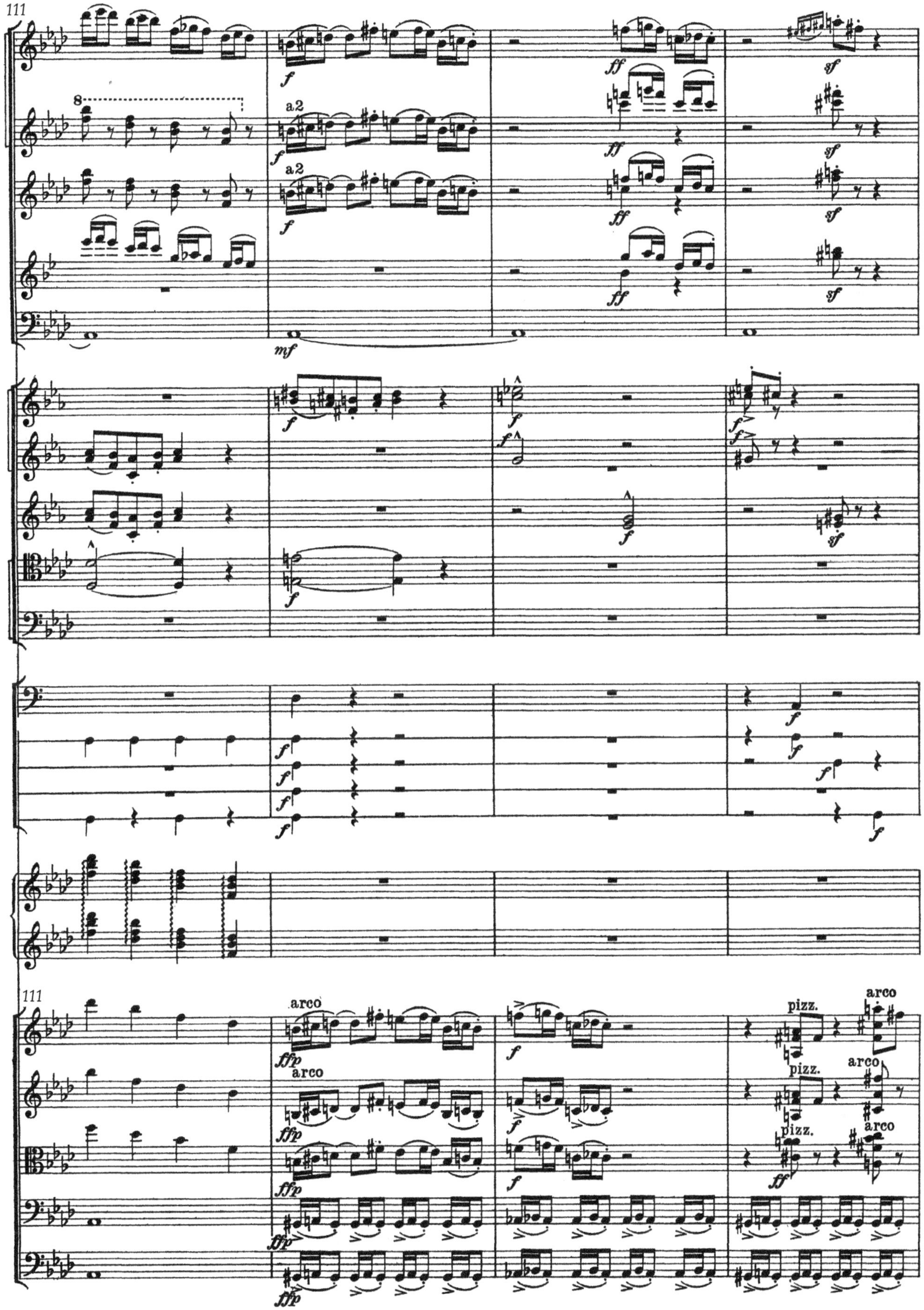
111
a2
a2
111
arco
arco
pizz.
arco
pizz.
arco
pizz.
arco

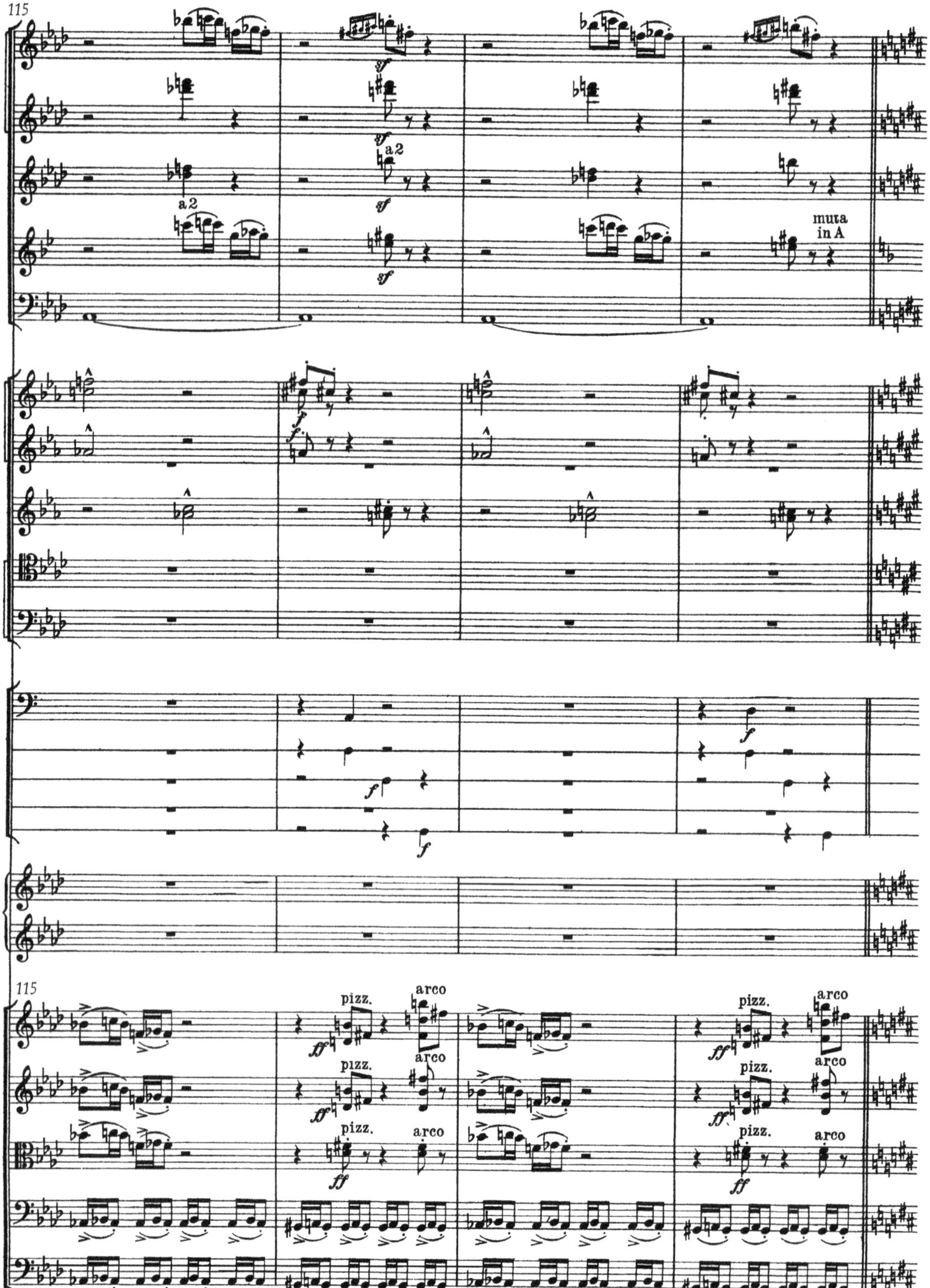
115
a2
a2
muta in A
115
pizz.
arco

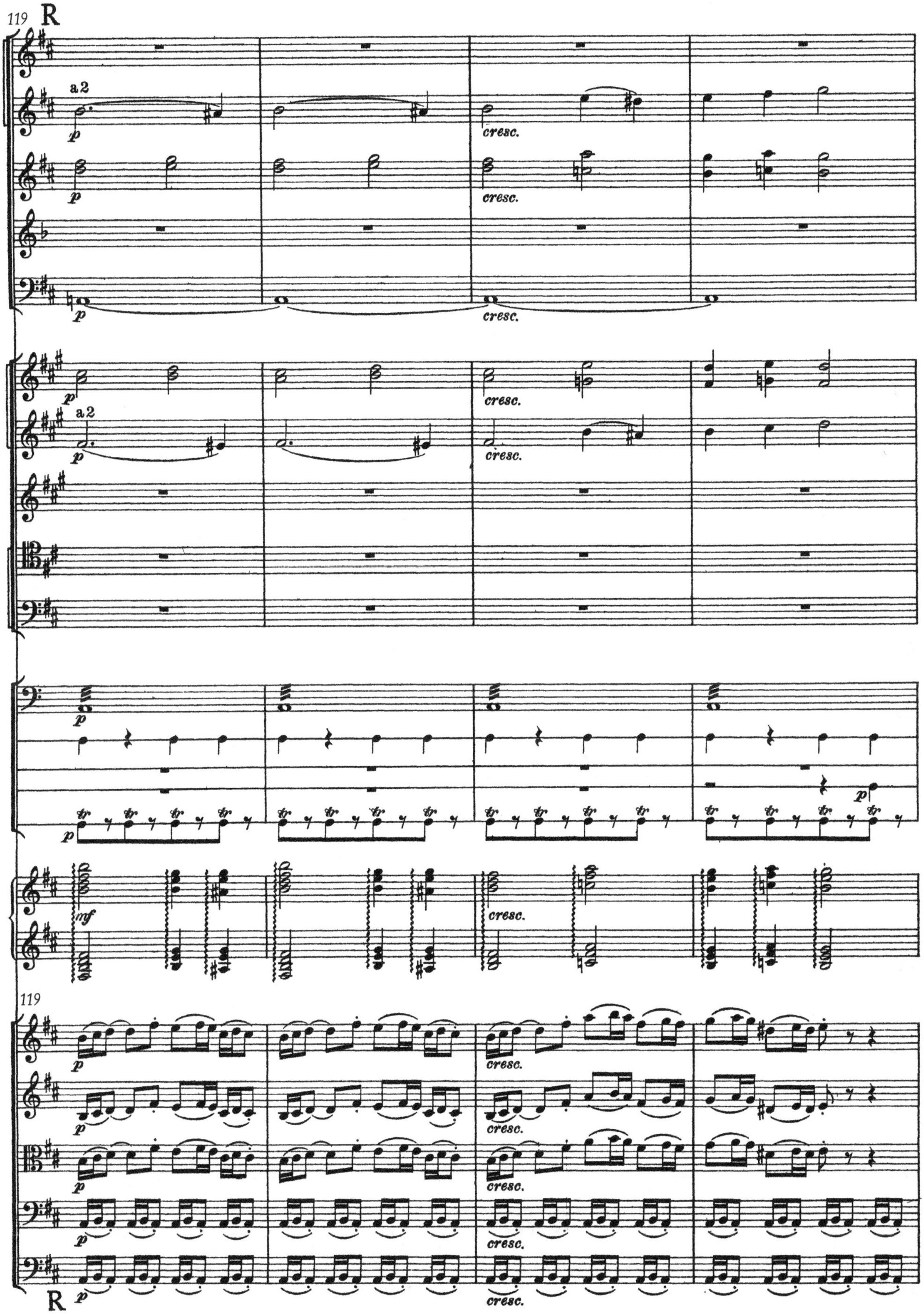
119
R
a 2
p
cresc.
mf
tr
R

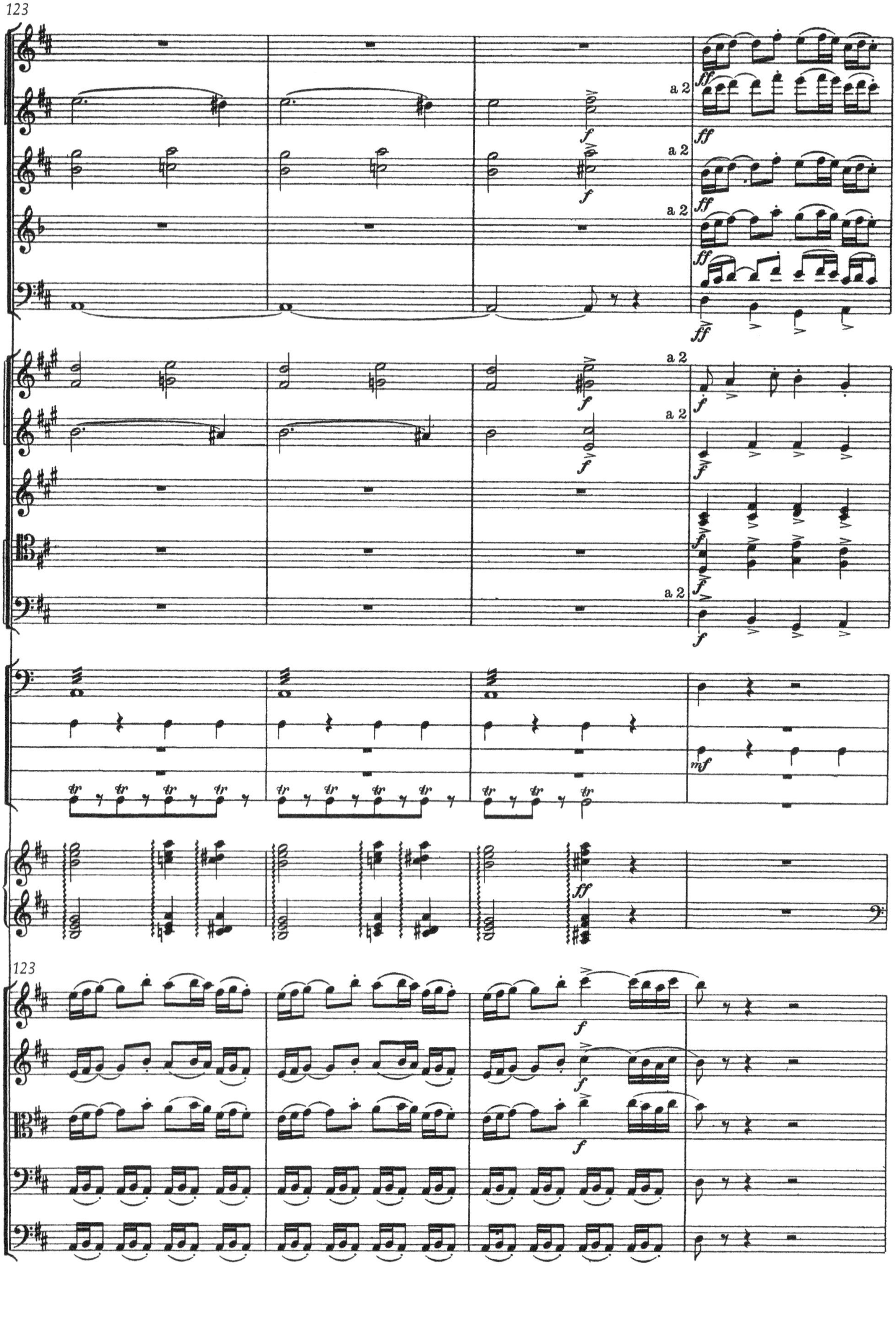
123
a 2
a 2
a 2
a 2
a 2
a 2
ff
f
mf
tr
123

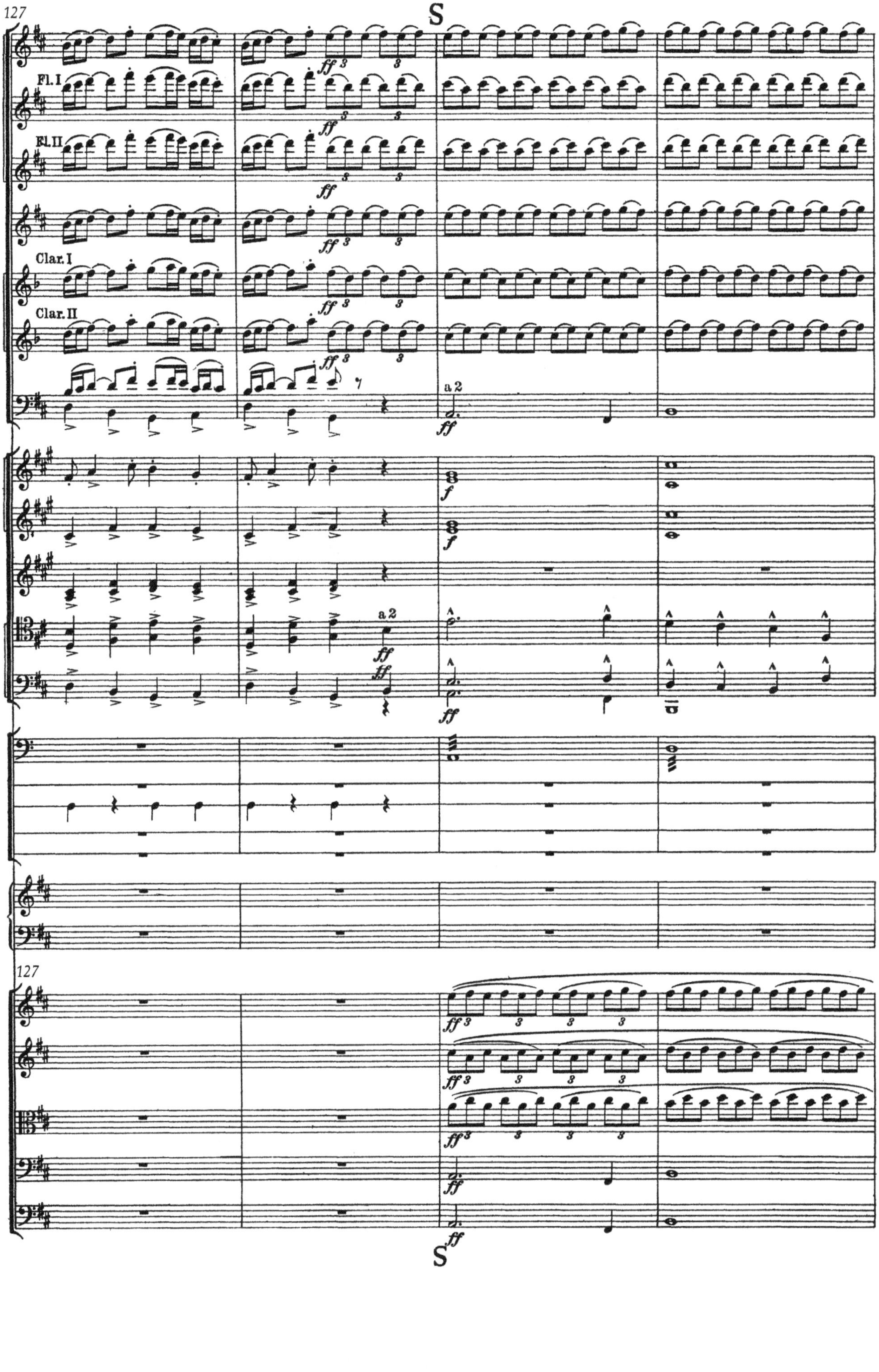
127
S
Fl. I
Fl. II
Clar. I
Clar. II
a 2
ff
f
127
S

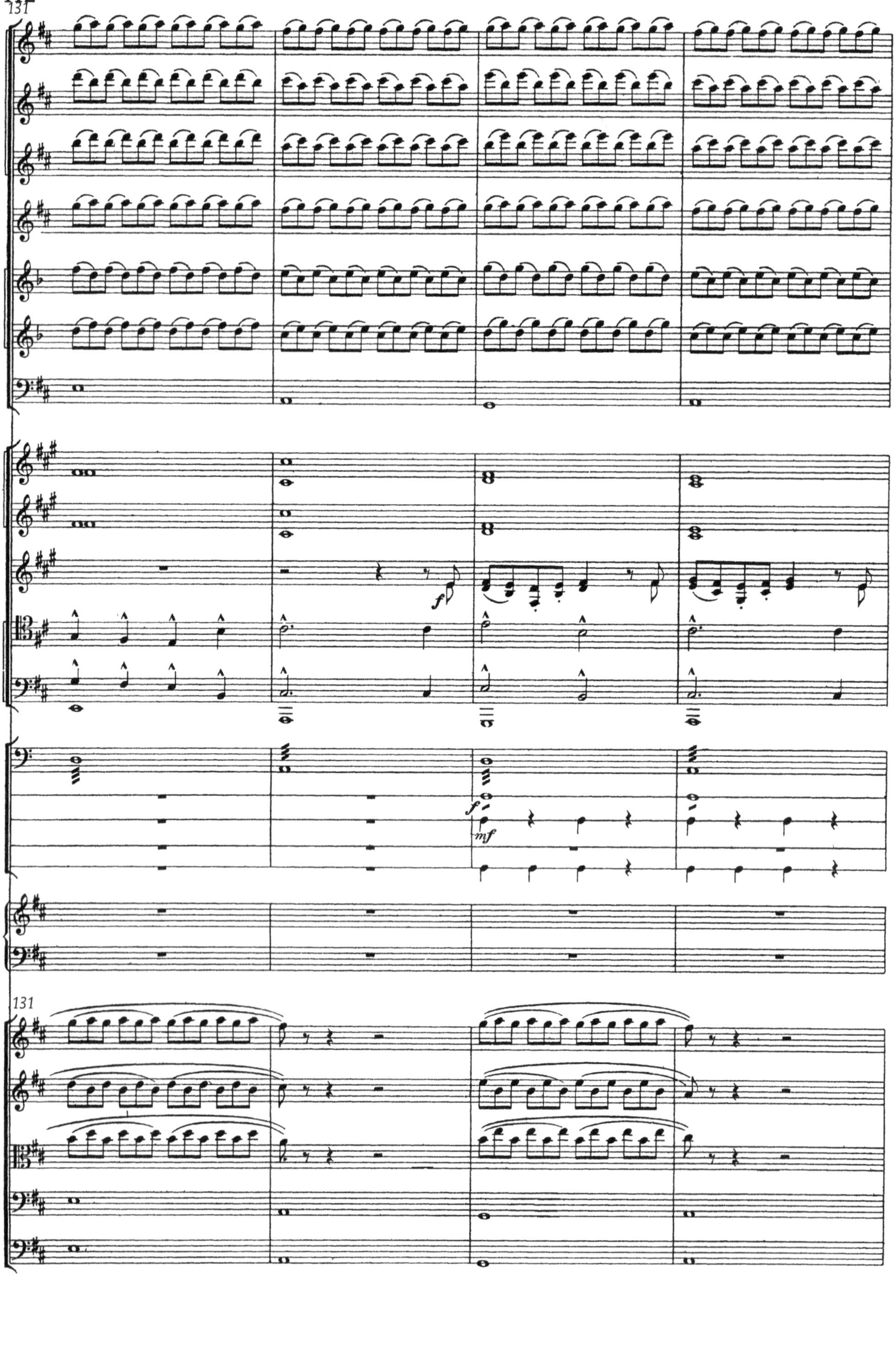
131
f
f
mf
131

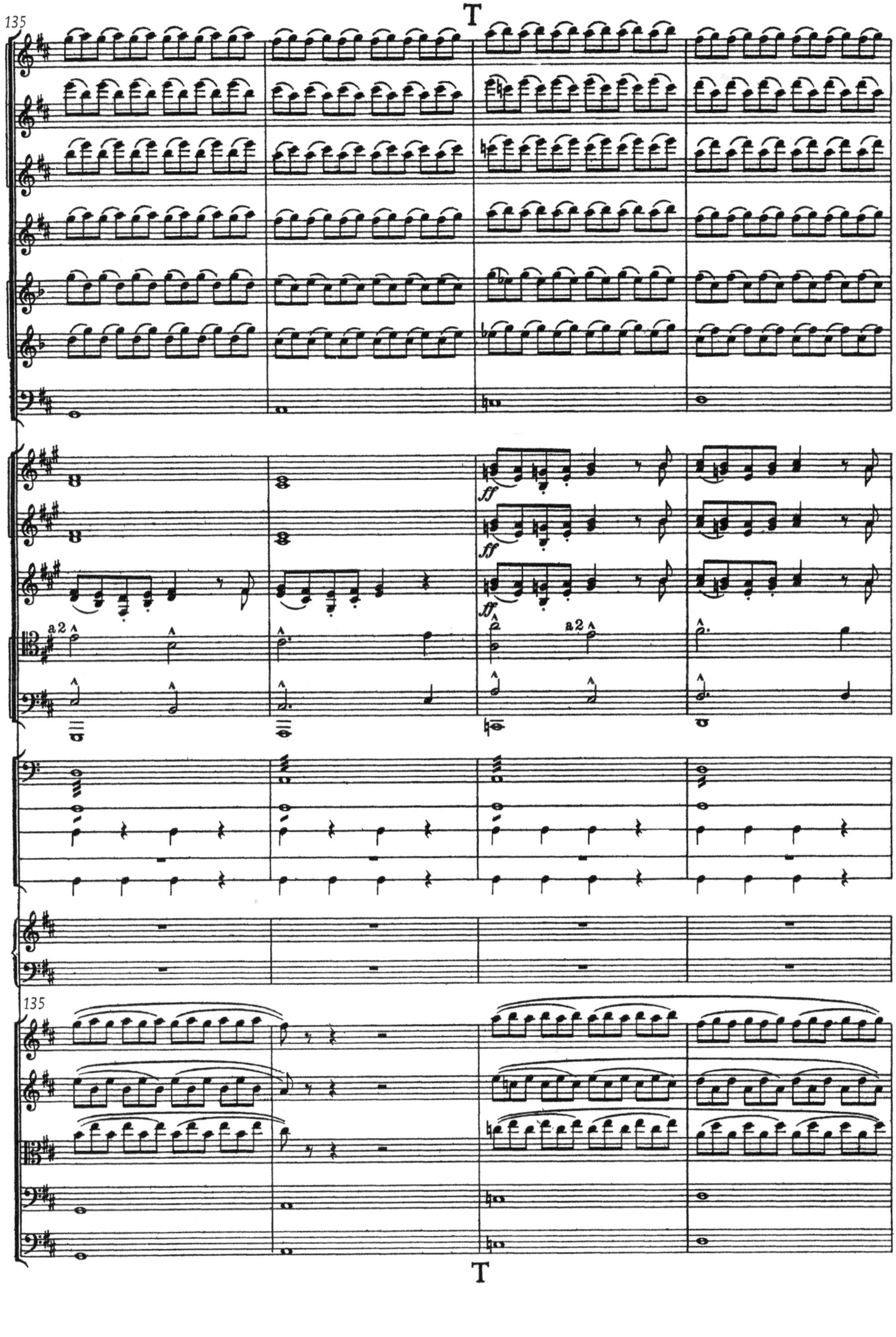
135
T
ff
a2
135
T

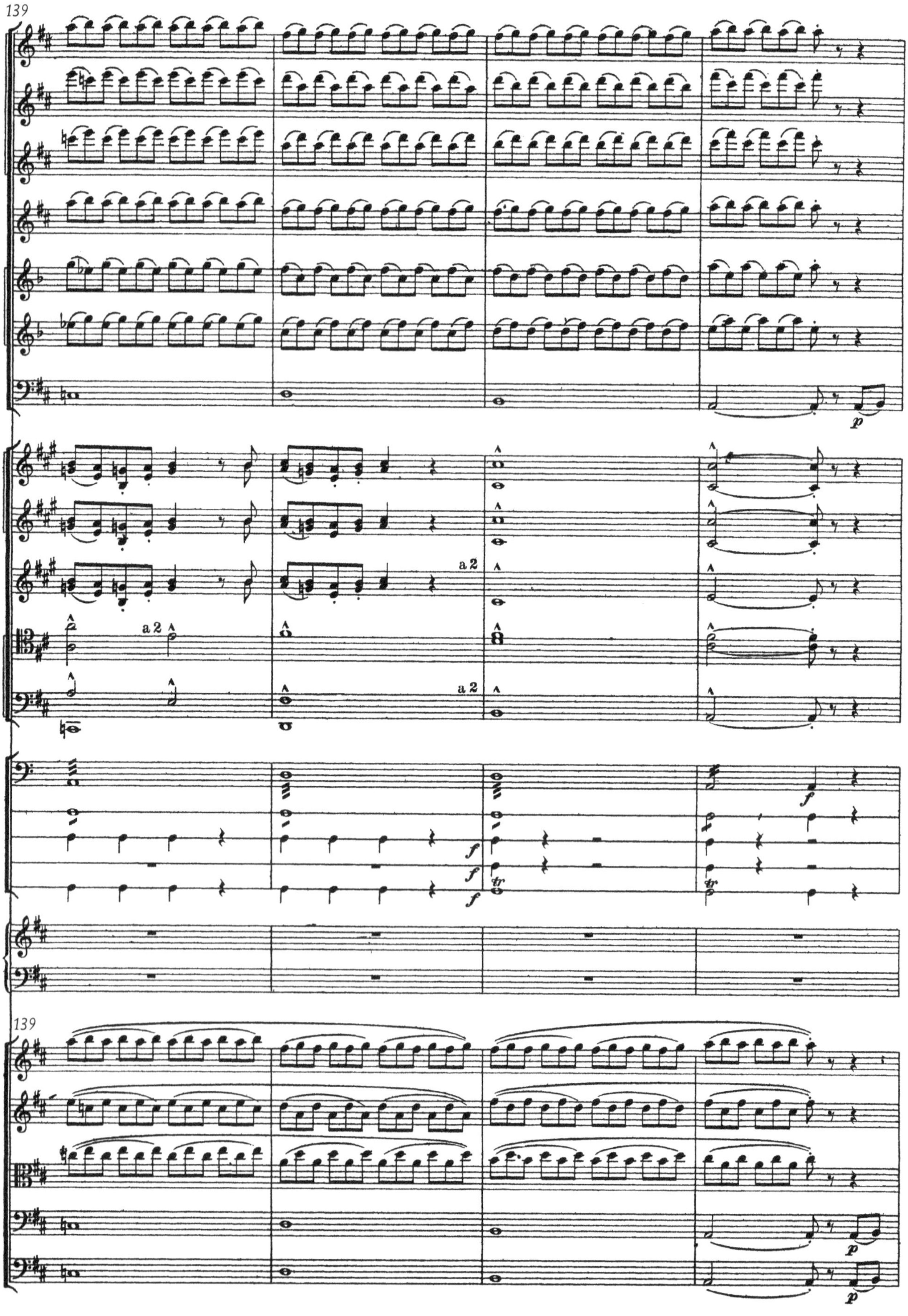
139
a 2
a 2
a 2
139

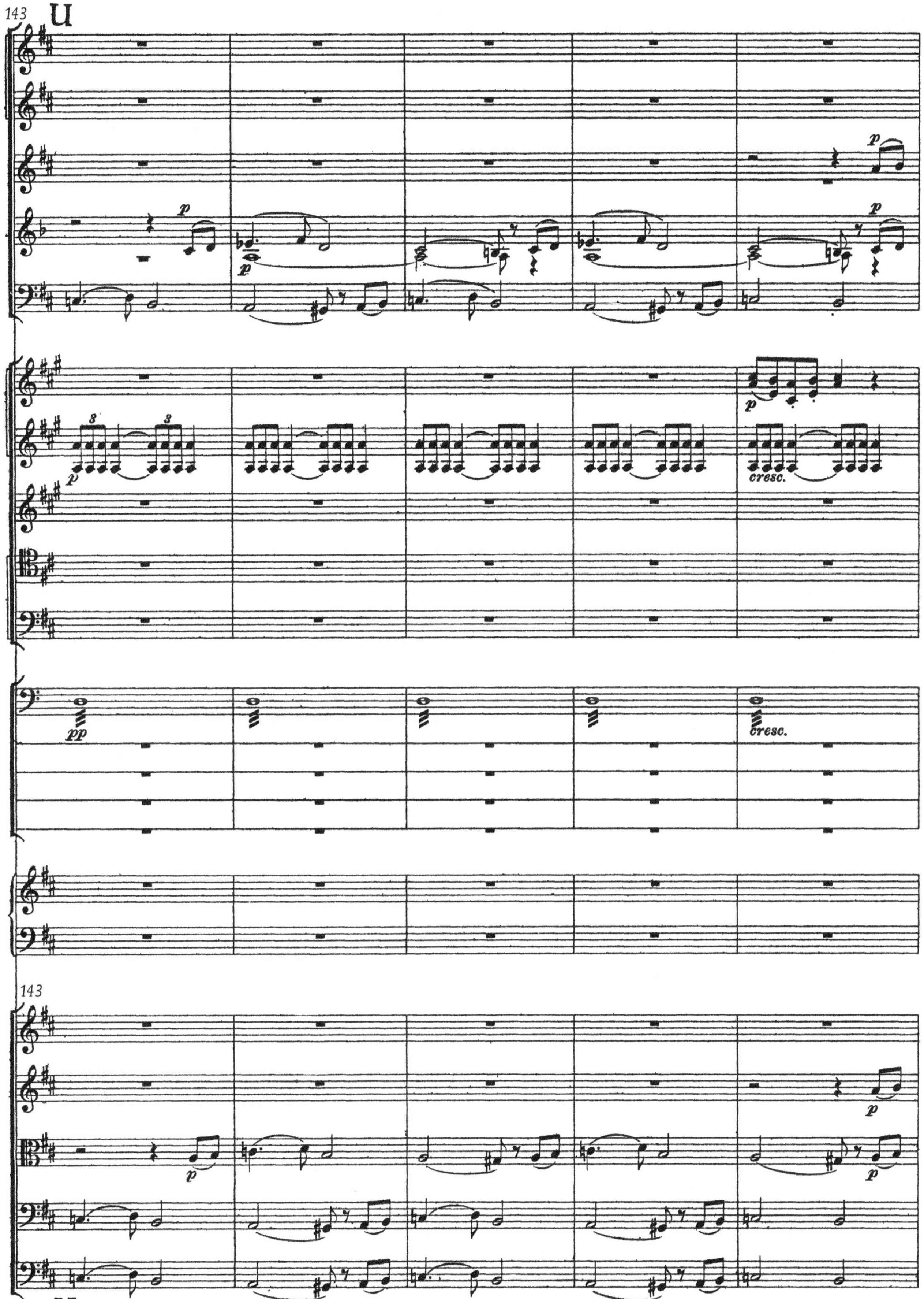
143
U
p
p
p
p
p
cresc.
pp
cresc.
143
p
p
p
U

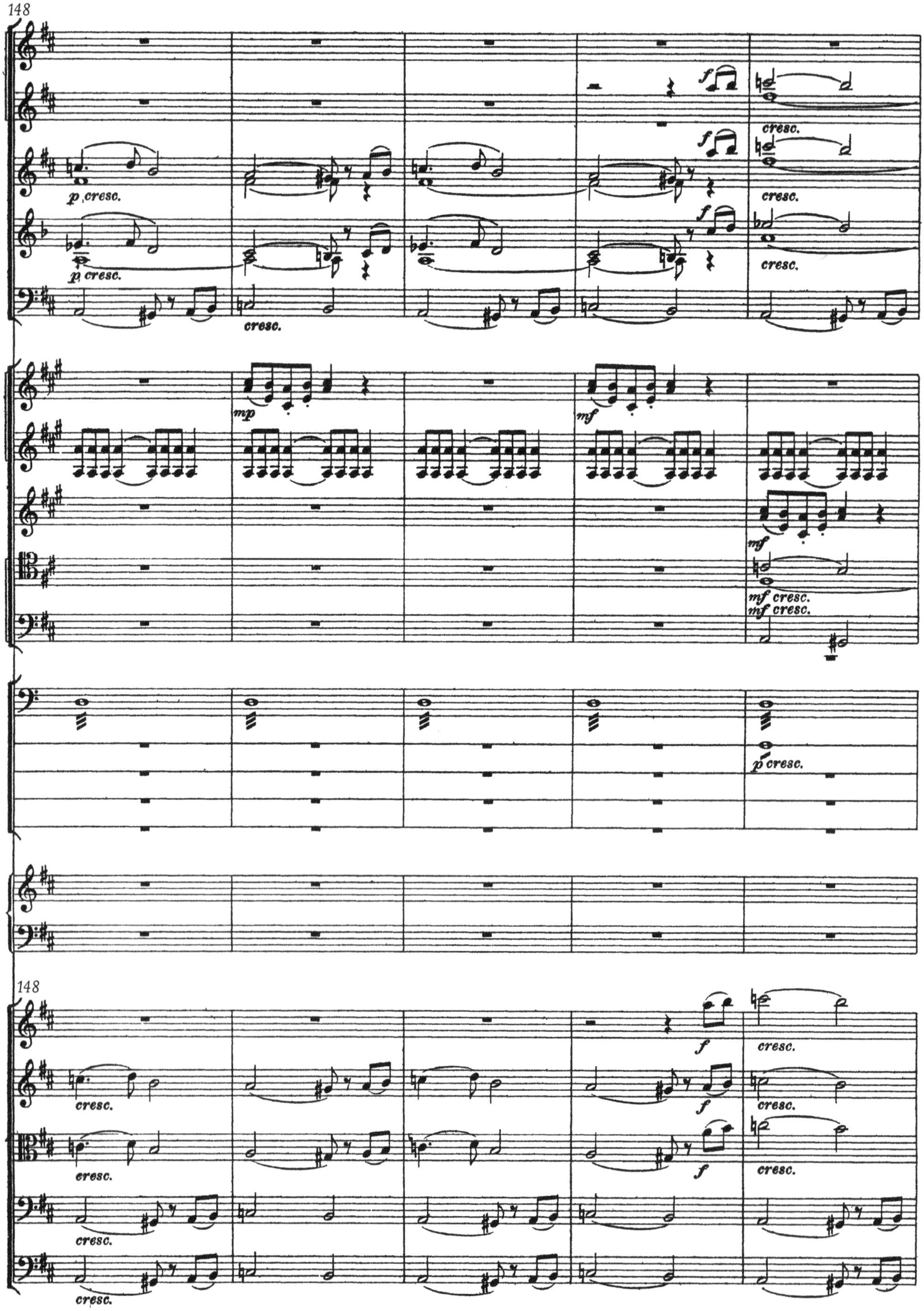
148
p cresc.
cresc.
mp
mf
mf cresc.
f
148

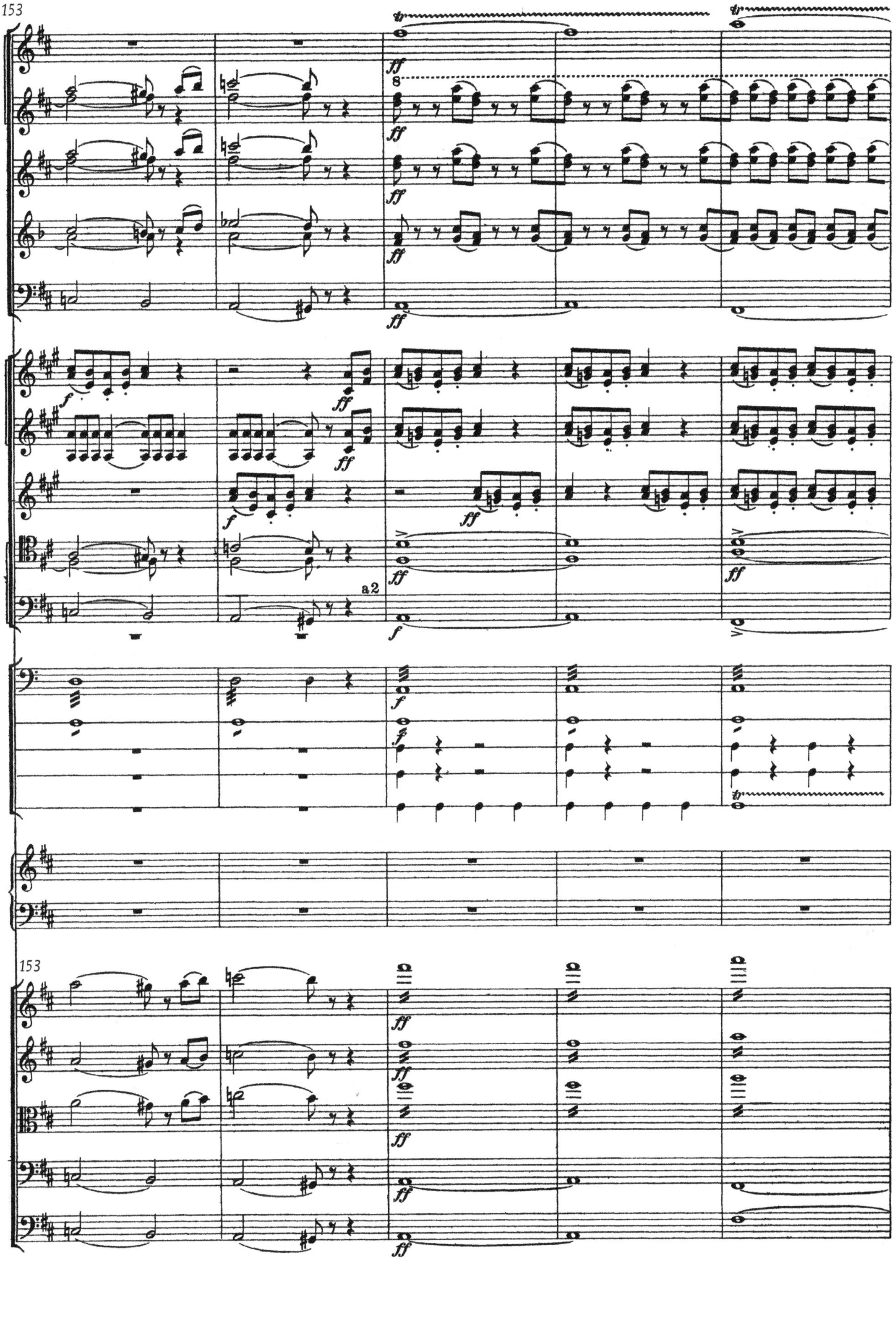
153
a2
153

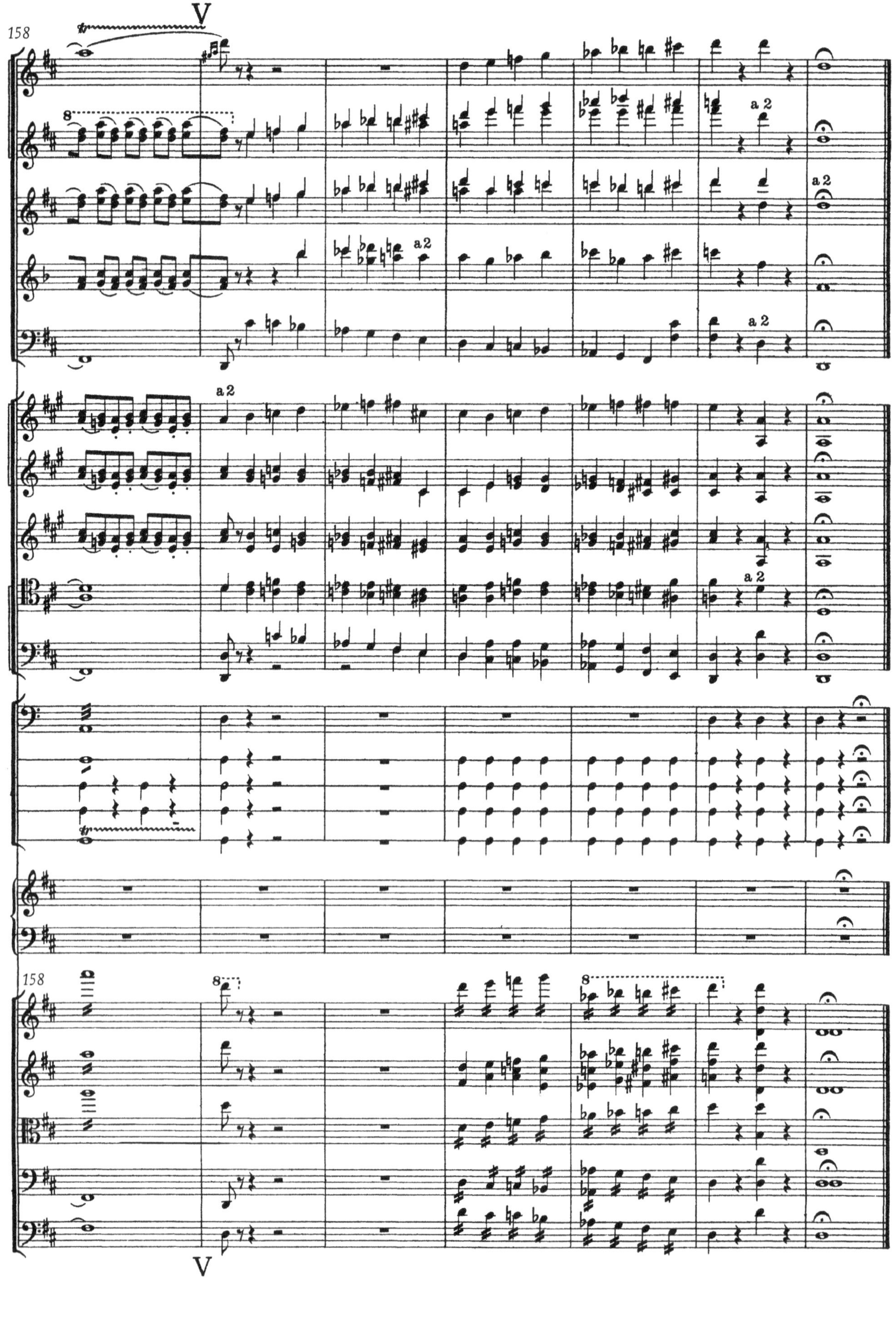
V
158
a 2
158
V

IV

Allegretto vivace
I
3 Flauti
II III
pp
pp
Oboe
Corno inglese
I in B
2 Clarinetti
II in A
2 Fagotti
4 Corni in F
pp
Timpani in F, As, F
Tam-Tam
Arpa
mf
div.
Violini I
pp
div.
Violini II
pp
Viole
Violoncelli
Contrabassi
Allegretto vivace

Andante amoroso

A Melodie arabe – Арабская мелодия

A Andante amoroso

21
Fl. I
p
Cor. I II
pp
30
Fl. II
p
p
p
38
B
pp
38
Viol. I
con sord.
ppp
Viol. II
con sord.
ppp
Vle
con sord.
ppp
B

44
pp leggieramente
pp leggieramente
p
Solo
mf
5
5
pp
pp
pp
muta in B, Cis, Des, Eis, F, Ges, Ais
glissando
simile
pp
44
2 Vcell.
Soli
pizz.
mf
pizz.
mf
div.
pizz.
mf

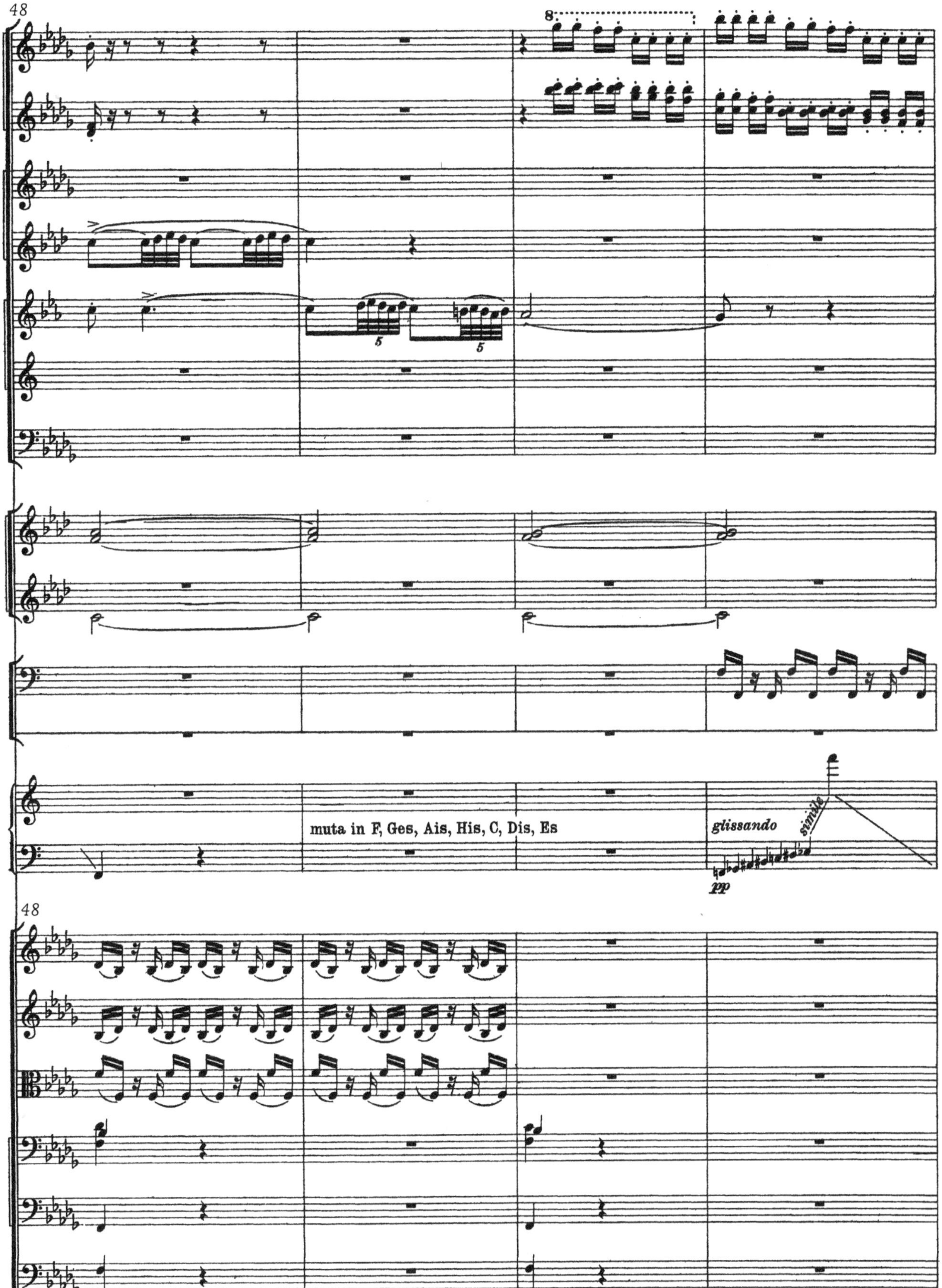
48
8
5
muta in F, Ges, Ais, His, C, Dis, Es
glissando
simile
pp
48

muta in Dis, Eis, F, Gis, As, H, Ces

glissando

simile

pp

muta in A dur

coi tutti Vcell.

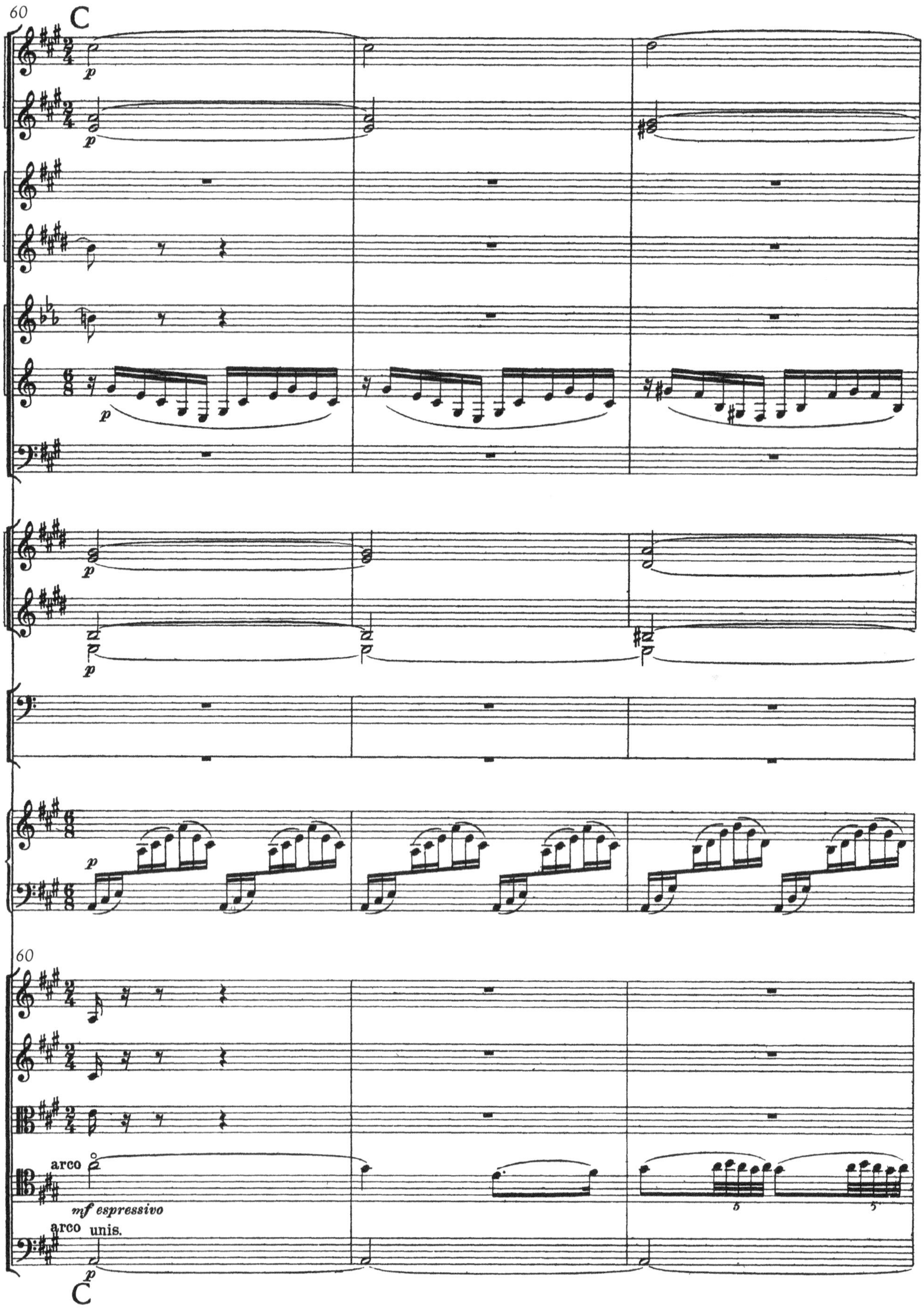

60
C
p
p
p
p
p
p
60
arco
mf espressivo
arco unis.
p
C

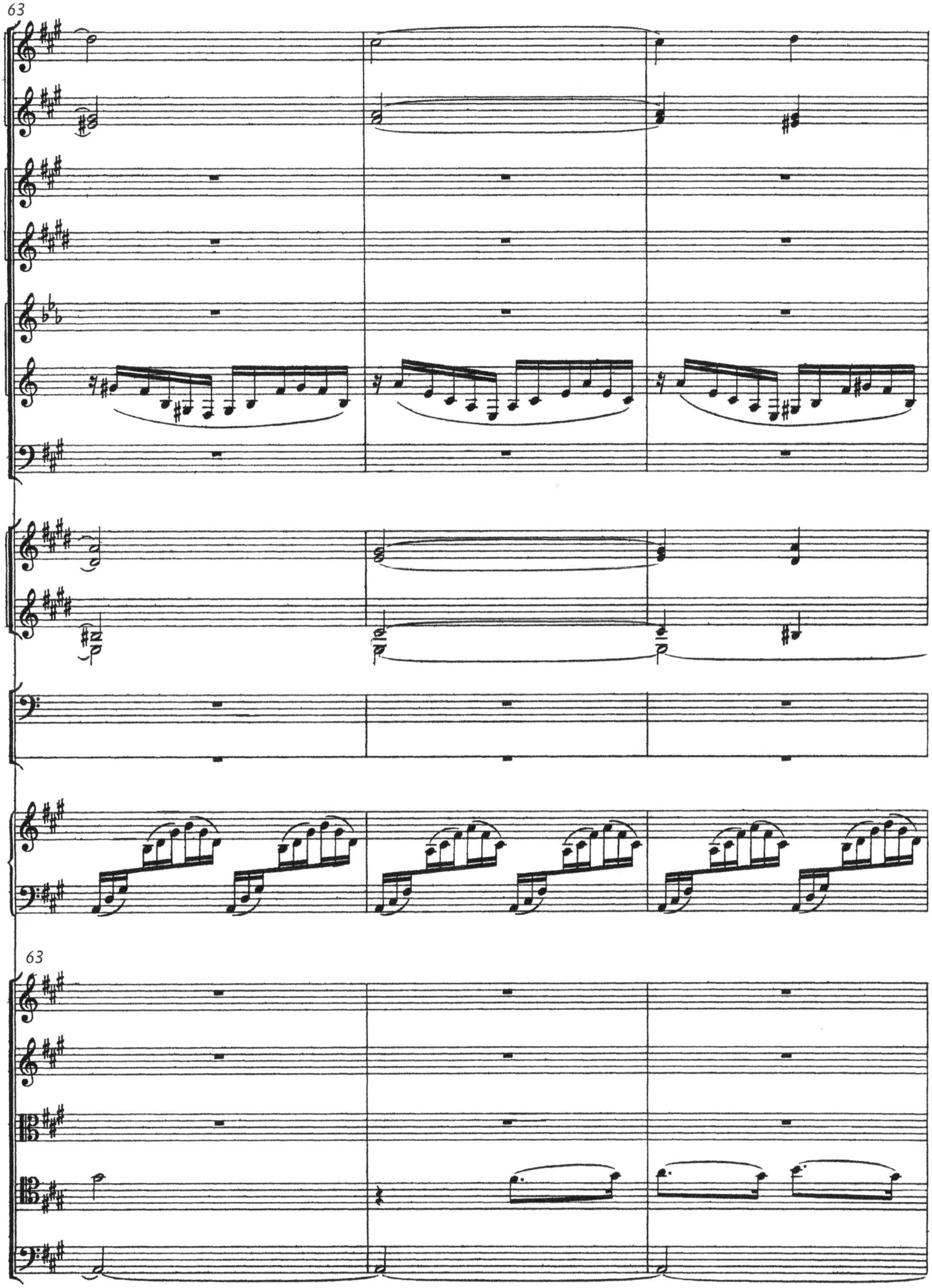
63
63

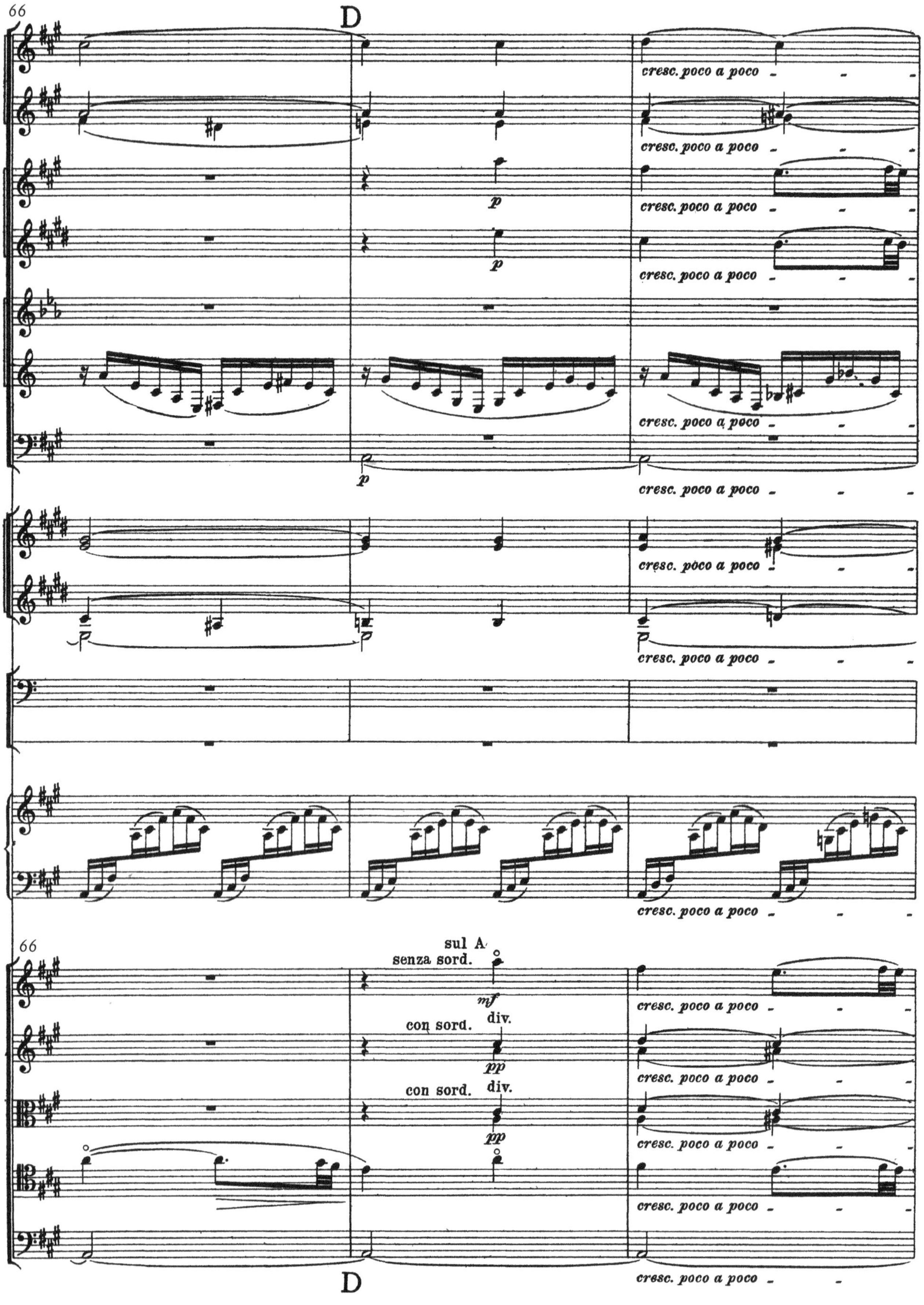
66
D
cresc. poco a poco
p
sul A
senza sord.
mf
con sord.
div.
pp

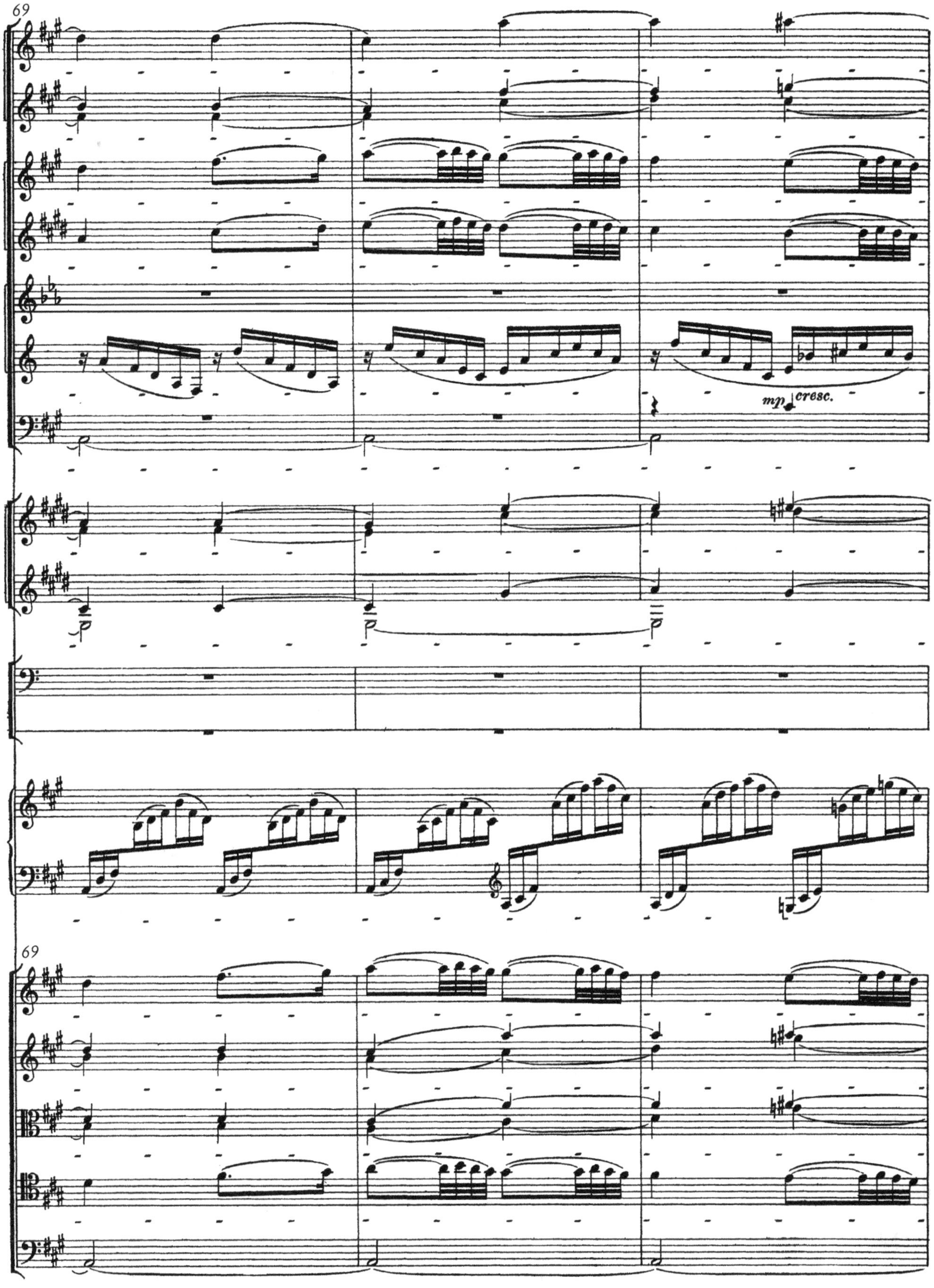
69
mp cresc.
69

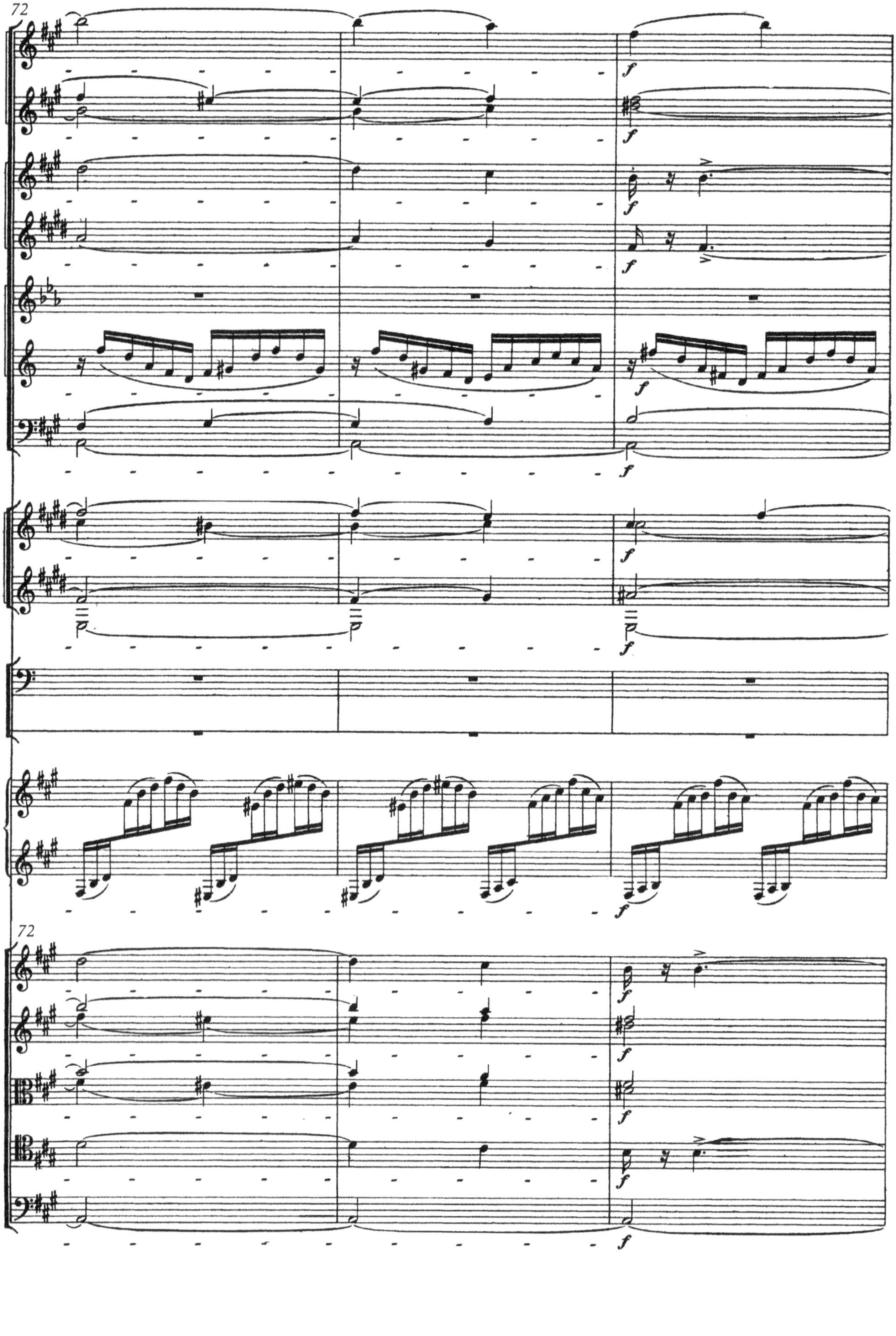

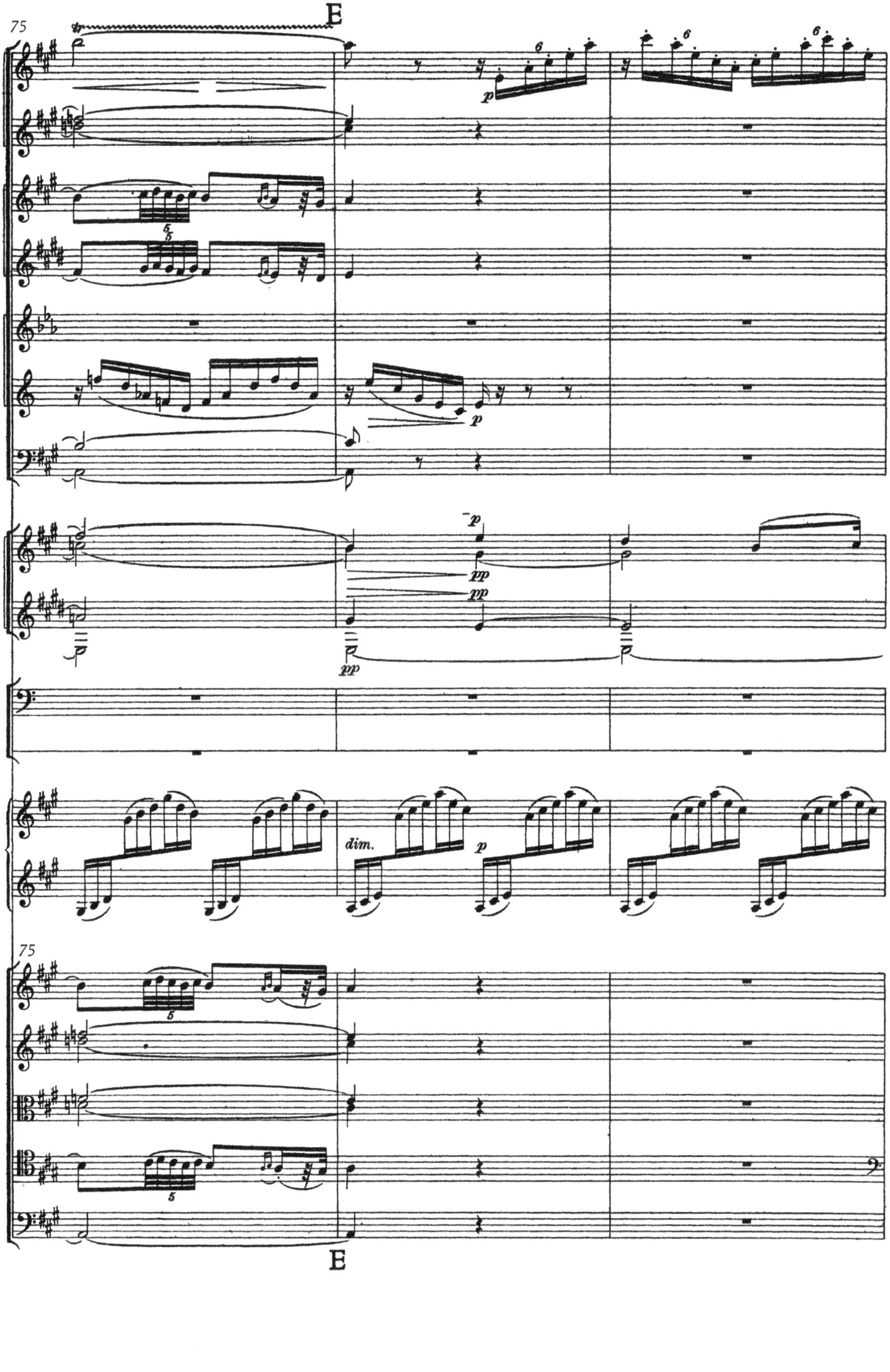
75
E
tr
6
p
5
pp
dim.
75
5
E

78
Fl. I
Clar. II
mf
muta in B
Cor. I II
Cor. III IV
Arpa
Vcell.
pizz.
p
Cb. pizz.
p
81
Fag.
F
p
Vle
senza sord.
f
pp
85
pp
Vcell.
arco
pp
Cb.
arco
pp

89
Fl. II III
G
f
Arpa
f
89
Viol. I
p
Viol. II senza sord.
p
arco
pizz.
arco
pizz.
G
93
pp
pp
93
p
arco
Vcell.
pp
97
Ob.
p
Fag.
p
97
Viol. I
con sord.
p
Vle

102
102
con sord.
p
unis.
con sord.
p
H
106
Fl. I
Ob.
p dolce
pp dolce
106
pp
pp
pp
H
111

118
I
Fag.
a 2
p
Cor. I II
Cor. III IV
mf
Timp.
118
Vcell.
I
122
Cor. ingl.
mf
122
Viol. I
p

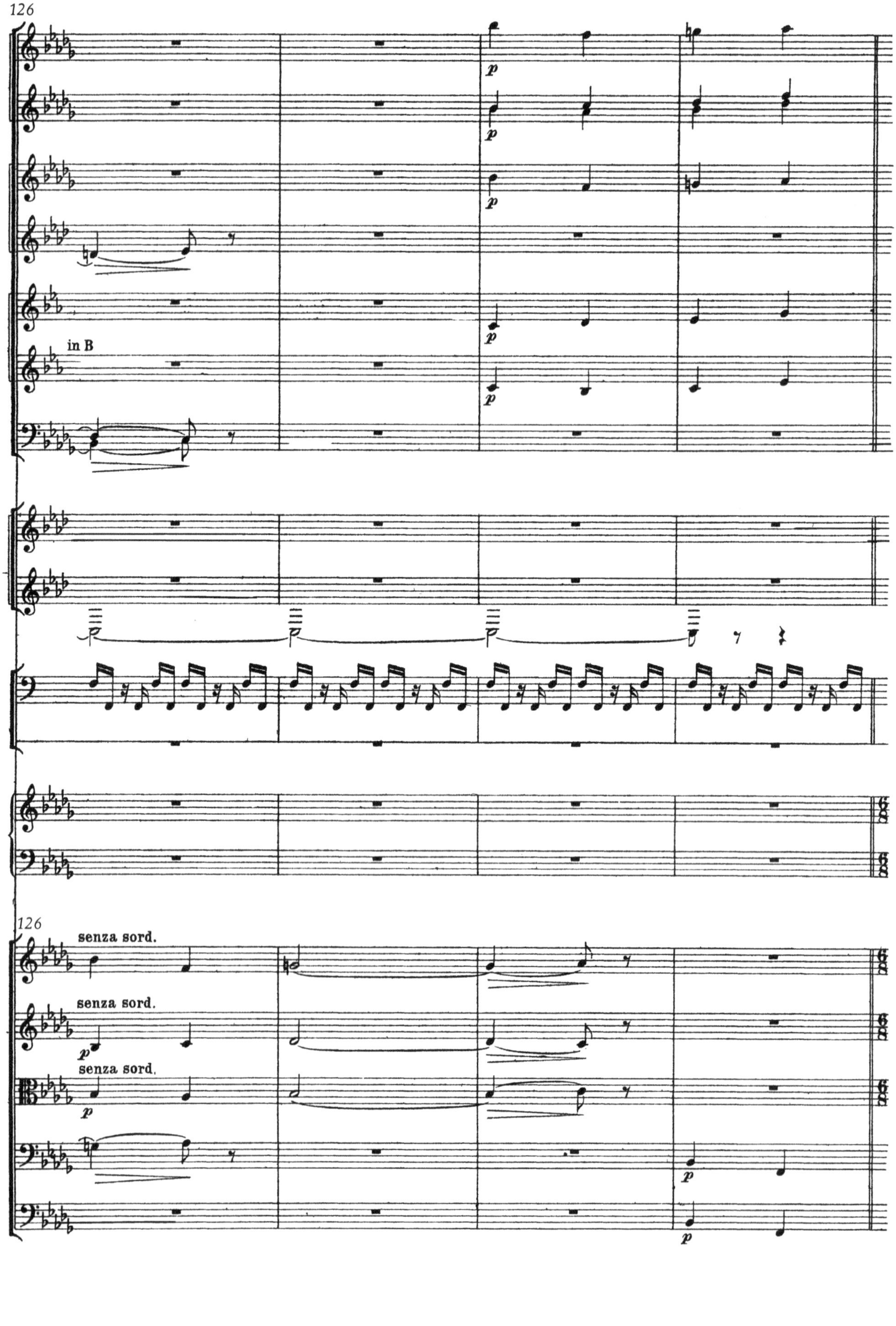
126
p
p
p
p
in B
p
126
senza sord.
senza sord.
p
senza sord.
p
p
p

K Animato assai
130
p
p
pp
pp
pp
pp
pp
f cantabile
K Animato assai

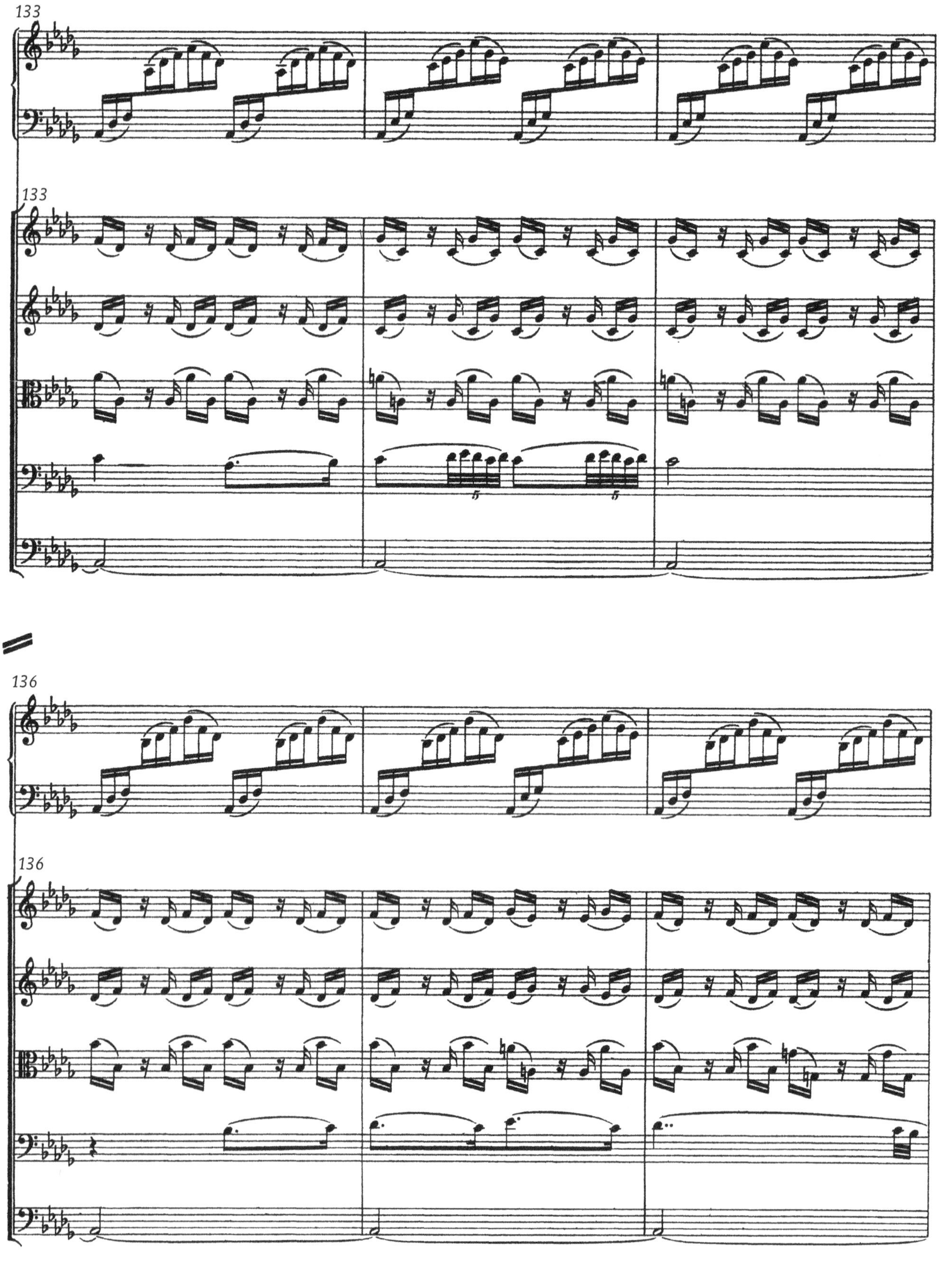
133
133
5
5
136
136

L Poco accelerando

L Poco accelerando

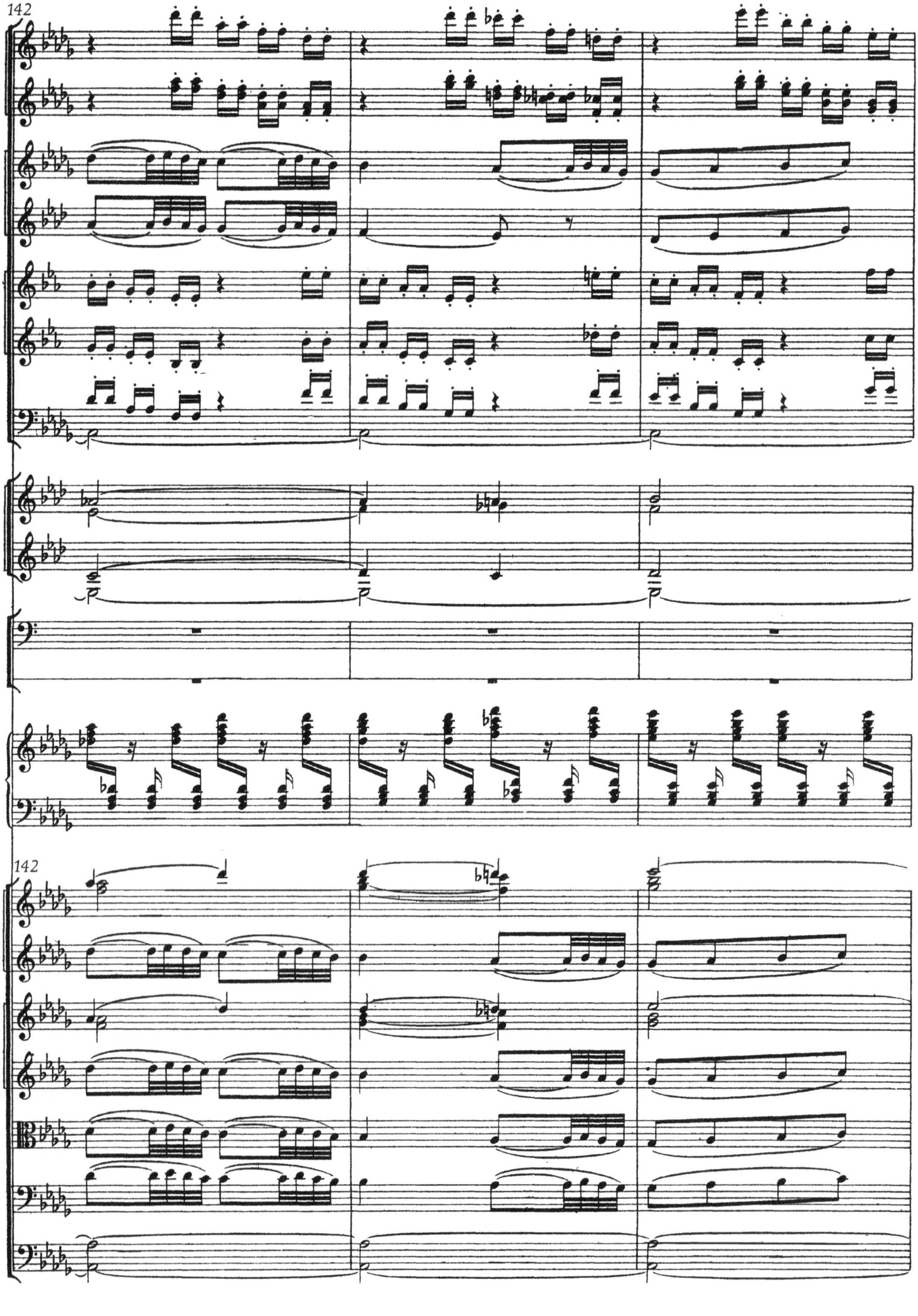
142
142

145
M
p
cresc. poco
cresc. poco·
Tutti Viol.I
Tutti Viol.II
p con passione

148
a poco
a poco
a poco
a poco
a poco
a poco
a poco
a poco
a poco
pp
a poco
148
cresc. poco a poco
cresc. poco a poco
cresc. poco a poco
cresc. poco a poco
cresc. poco a poco

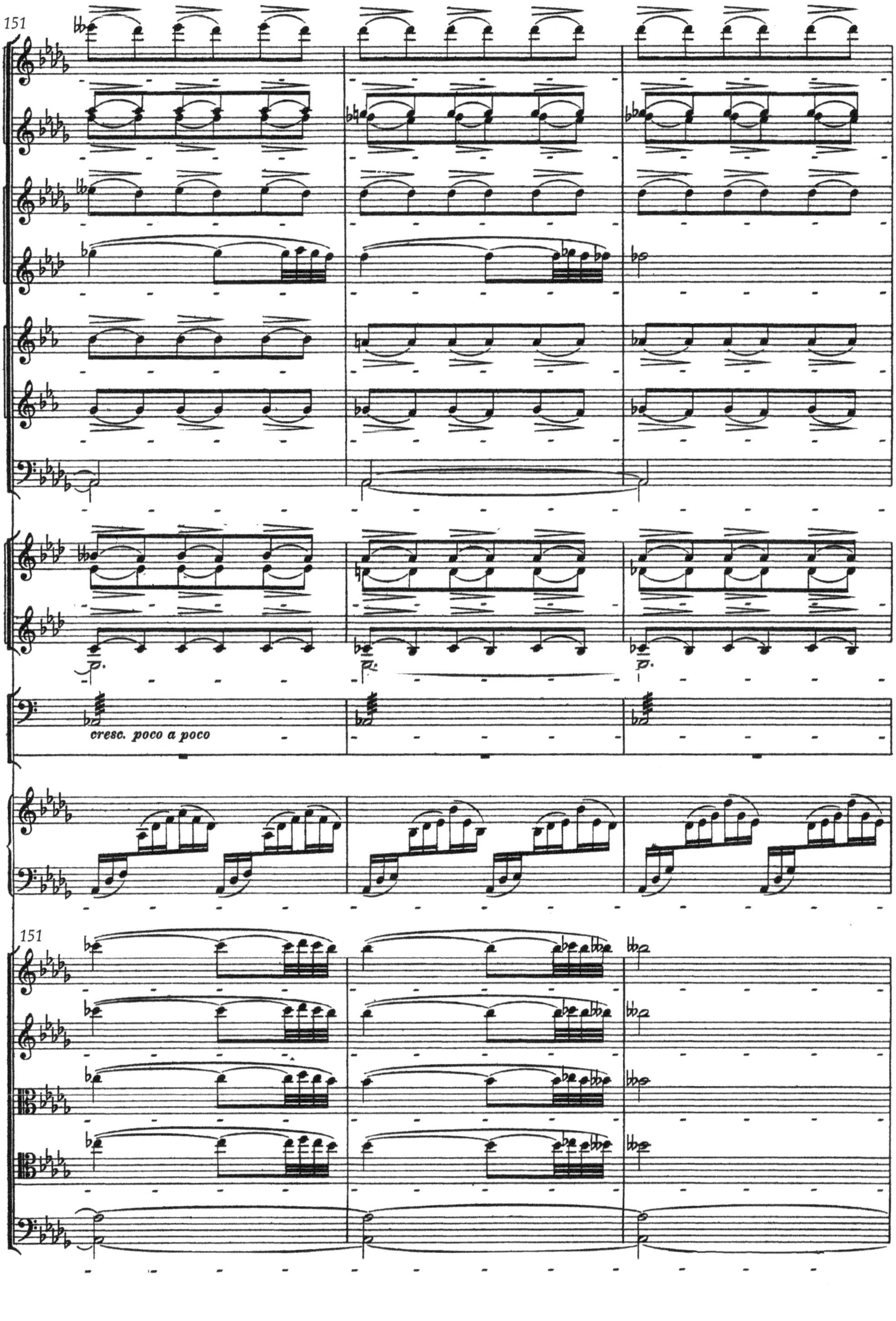
151
cresc. poco a poco
151

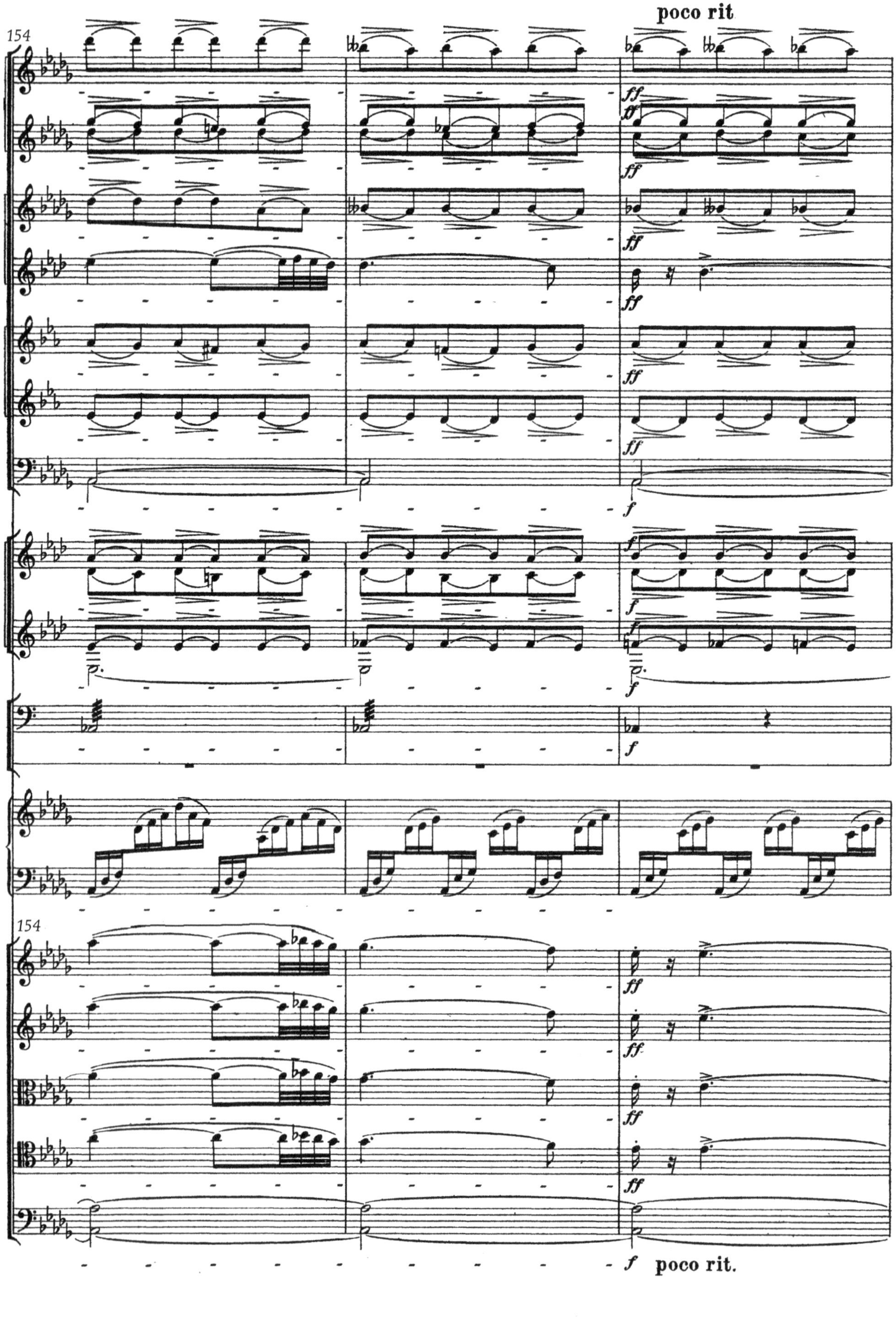
poco rit
154
ff
f
154
poco rit.

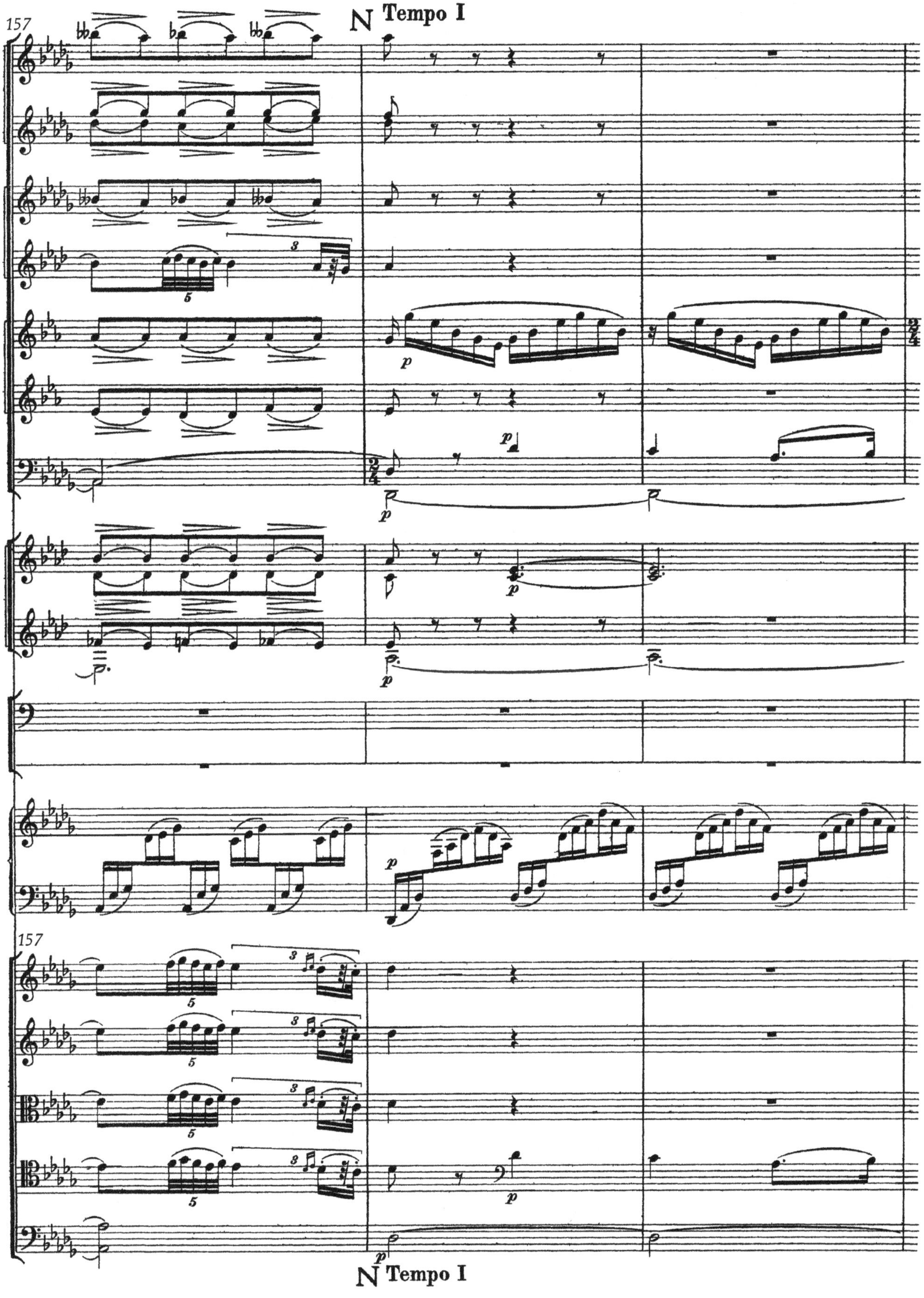
157
N Tempo I
p
3
5
2/4
157
N Tempo I

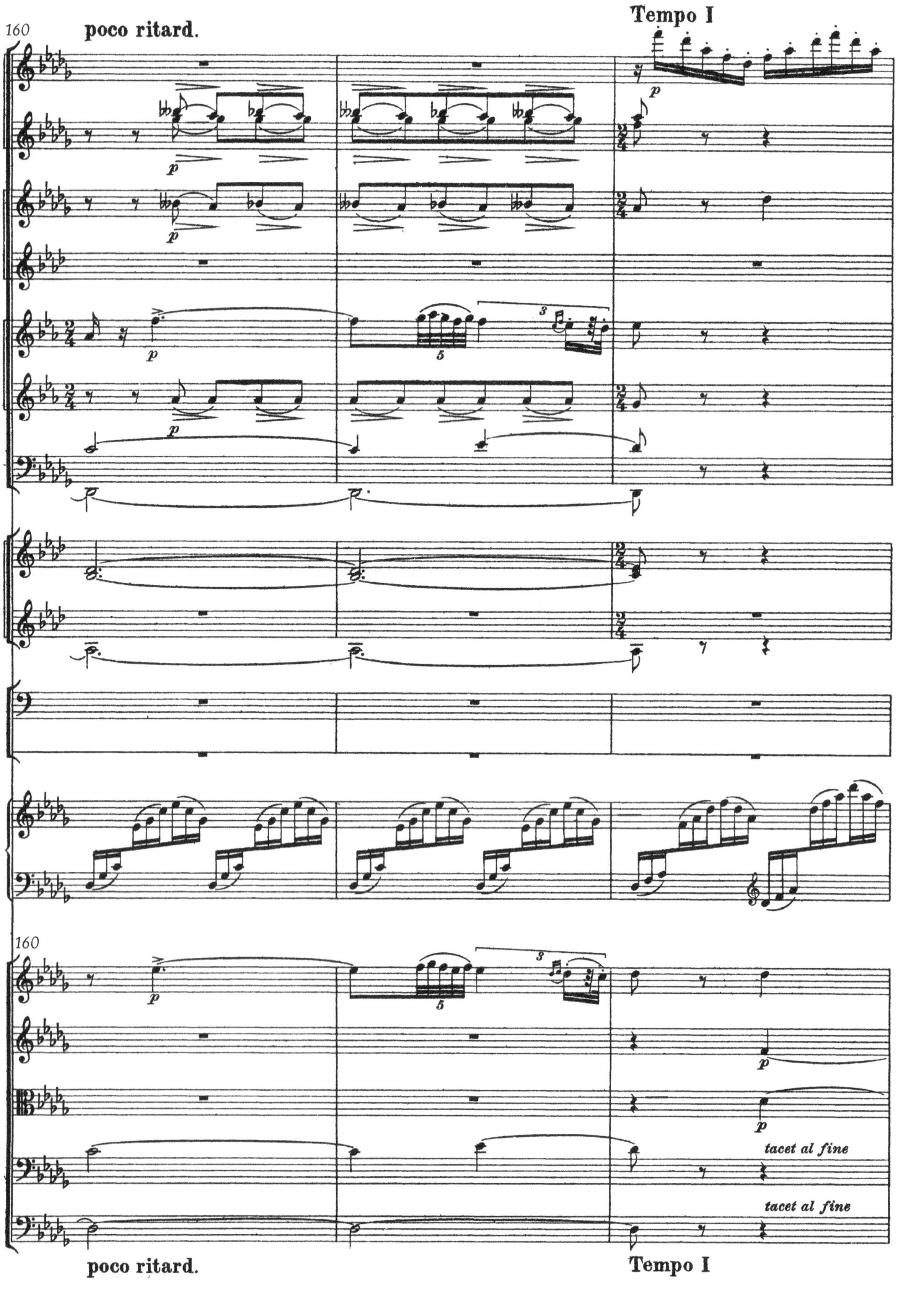

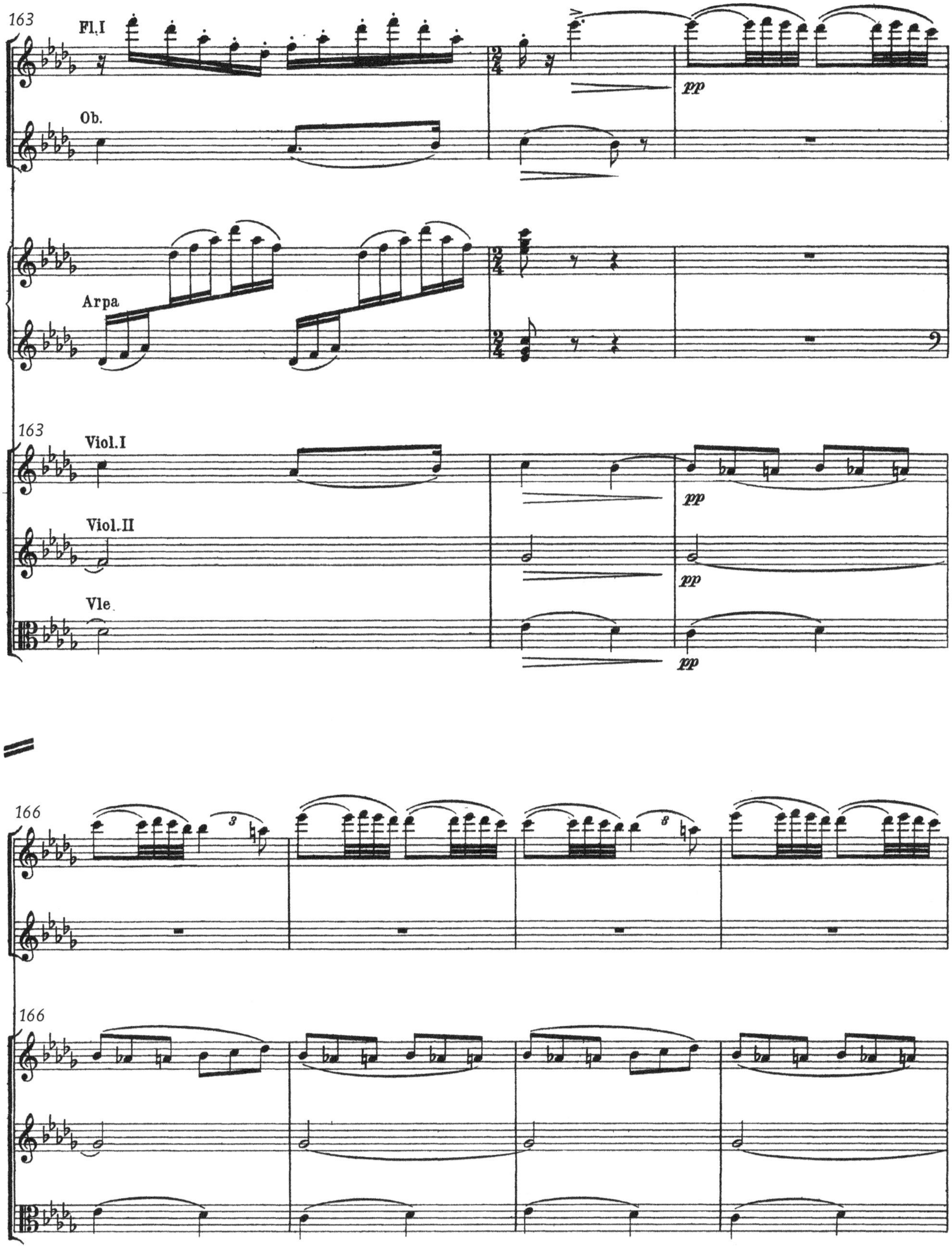
163
Fl.I
Ob.
Arpa
Viol.I
Viol.II
Vle
pp
166

O
170
Fl.I
pp
Fl.II III
pp
Ob.
p
Cor.I II
p
Timp.
p
170
Viol.I
p
Viol.II
Vle
175
pp
pp
Arpa
muta in F, Gis, As, H, Ces, D, Eis
175
O

180
Tam-Tam
glissando
180
Viol. II
Vle
185
glissando
muta in Cis dur
185
Viol. I
con sord.

192
p
a tempo
pp
Ob.
a piacere
dolce
a piacere
192
p
a tempo
201
a tempo
poco ritard.
p
pp
201
a tempo
poco ritard.
Fine

www.ingramcontent.com/pod-product-compliance
Lightning Source LLC
Chambersburg PA
CBHW081936110426
42742CB00040BA/3095